The Psychology of Consumer Profiling in a Digital Age

T0295731

"This excellent volume provides an up-to-date overview of the current state in consumer profiling. I highly recommend the book to students, teachers, and all those interested in current developments in consumer research and marketing."

—Dirk vom Lehn, King's College London, UK

Understanding how consumers choose between different products and services is a crucial part of professional marketing. Targeting brands at the consumers most likely to be interested in them is another critical aspect of business success. Marketers need to know what consumers think about brands, why they like them, and what purposes they serve. This means delving into the psychology of the consumer to find ways of differentiating between consumers and matching brands to consumer niches at the level of consumers' relationships with brands. Using psychology to segment consumers has been regarded as a valuable adjunct to standard geo-demographic definitions of market segments.

The Psychology and Consumer Profiling in a Digital Age examines how this field of 'psychographics' has evolved, the different approaches to the psychological segmentation of consumers, the different ways in which it has been applied in consumer marketing settings, and whether psychographics works. It draws upon research from around the world and incorporates its analysis of the use of psychographics with an examination of major shifts in marketing in a digital and global era.

Barrie Gunter is an Emeritus Professor at the University of Leicester, UK, where he was formerly Professor of Mass Communication and Head of the Department of Media and Communication. A psychologist by training who has also worked in broadcasting as an audience researcher, he has written nearly 60 books on media, marketing, and management.

Routledge Studies in Marketing

This series welcomes proposals for original research projects that are either single or multi-authored or an edited collection from both established and emerging scholars working on any aspect of marketing theory and practice, and provides an outlet for studies dealing with elements of marketing theory, thought, pedagogy, and practice.

It aims to reflect the evolving role of marketing and to bring together the most innovative work across all aspects of the marketing 'mix'—from product development, consumer behaviour, marketing analysis, branding, and customer relationships, to sustainability, ethics, and the new opportunities and challenges presented by digital and online marketing.

The Psychology of Consumer Profiling in a Digital Age

Barrie Gunter

Routledge
Taylor & Francis Group

NEW YORK AND LONDON

First published 2016
by Routledge
711 Third Avenue, New York, NY 10017

and by Routledge
2 Park Square, Milton Park, Abingdon, Oxon OX14 4RN

First issued in paperback 2018

Routledge is an imprint of the Taylor & Francis Group, an informa business

© 2016 Taylor & Francis

The right of Barrie Gunter to be identified as author of this work has been asserted by him in accordance with sections 77 and 78 of the Copyright, Designs and Patents Act 1988.

Library of Congress Cataloging-in-Publication Data
Names: Gunter, Barrie, author.
Title: The psychology of consumer profiling in a digital age / by Barrie Gunter.
Description: New York : Routledge, 2016. | Series: Routledge studies in
    marketing ; 2 | Includes bibliographical references and index.
Identifiers: LCCN 2016000870 | ISBN 9781138957961 (hardback : alk. paper) |
    ISBN 9781315661438 (ebook)
Subjects: LCSH: Consumer profiling. | Consumer behavior. | Marketing—
    Psychological aspects.
Classification: LCC HF5415.32 .G86 2016 | DDC 658.8/34—dc23
LC record available at http://lccn.loc.gov/2016000870

ISBN 13: 978-1-138-34074-9 (pbk)
ISBN 13: 978-1-138-95796-1 (hbk)

Typeset in Sabon
by Apex CoVantage, LLC

Contents

1 Types of Consumer Segmentation

The world of consumers and consumerism is a complex and multifaceted place. No two consumers are exactly the same, but some groups of consumers may share characteristics, needs, and interests which in turn influence their commodity tastes and brand choices. Consumers can be distinguished by their biological characteristics, their age, their ethnicity, their family background, the location and type of neighbourhood in which they live, their education, and their economic circumstances. Each of these distinguishing features can be linked to activity preferences and patterns of behaviour that people display, but they do not represent causal agents. Men and women might differ in their commodity needs because of their gender, but it tends to be socially conditioned roles in each case that tend to trigger these differences. This means that even though these characteristics can be used by marketing professionals to differentiate between consumers, to understand fully how they interplay with different patterns of consumer behaviour, we also need to understand the psychology of consumers themselves to explain thought processes that underpin decision-making about which products and services to buy and use.

In this vein, therefore, consumers can be differentiated in terms of their psychological makeup which can underpin and explain the consumer behaviour patterns they display, their motives for doing certain things and making certain choices, and the way they process information about the world around them. In this context, individuals can be differentiated and classified in terms of their 'personalities'. Human personality is defined by a range of factors that are determined by a combination of inherited biological attributes and environmental experiences and represent enduring aspects of a person that can determine how he or she will behave across a wide range of social settings.

All these different physical, social, and psychological characteristics have been used by professional marketers to define and distinguish between consumers and to understand the product and service choices they make. While demographic features can differentiate between patterns of consumer behaviour, they do not offer explanations for those behaviours. This chapter will provide an overview of the different types of consumer segmentation that draw upon different geographic, demographic, psychographic, and purchase attributes. In relation to consumer profiling based on psychological methods, there are two broad types that can be distinguished: first, those consumer classifications based on personality psychology and second, those based on custom-built consumer psychographic types.

Emergence of Market Segmentation

In contemporary marketing parlance, market segmentation features prominently. Modern marketing professionals are schooled in the idea that while there are 'mass' markets for some commodities, more often in competitive marketplaces, specific markets emerge not simply just for types of commodities, but more especially for 'variants' of the same types of products or services. These 'variants' tend to be identified by their brand names and images. Thus, although the concept of market segmentation has been in use for many generations, it has acquired greater significance as marketplaces have become increasingly crowded with large numbers of brands fighting for market ascendancy.

People have bought and sold commodities for millennia. Prior to the 19th century, however, most produce was made and sold locally. In most instances, people bought necessities such as food, clothing, household items, and treats or luxuries from single sources of supply that each specialised in selling a specific type of merchandise. There were exceptions, such as imported fabrics, valuable minerals fashioned into jewellery, beverages (such as tea), and indulgences (such as tobacco) being transported from afar, but these were generally only available to an elite few who could afford them. Most people, however, were either self-sufficient or relied upon their local suppliers for their day-to-day commodities.

With developments in systems of transportation and communication beginning in the 18th century and continuing apace into the next century, and with technology developments that created industrial infrastructures for mass production, a new world opened up in which non-local commodities could be more readily and speedily transported over greater distances, and the scale of production meant that costs to purchasers fell. Communications systems, such as the first large distribution media in the form of early newspapers and magazines, meant that commodities could also be promoted more widely.

The technological and economic changes that occurred with the Industrial Revolution in the 19th century and which then continued into the 20th century had important impacts upon the way societies were structured. Not only did the dominance of local production for local markets fall away in the face of competition from remote mass producers, but changes to the employment structures resulted in the migration of workers, the urbanisation of societies, and changes to the nature of communities (Kammen, 1991).

Social roles also altered. While men remained dominant in the workplace, new employment opportunities opened up for women, generating new forms of differentiation between gender roles. Women's roles were in some cases defined by employment, but in many more cases revolved around their domestic support functions in the home (Roberts, 1998). Whereas in rural communities, women might have helped with manual work, in the new urban communities, they more often stayed at home to nest build and take on primary responsibility for the management of domestic affairs (Demos, 1986; Mintz & Kellogg, 1988).

In addition, the emergence of diverse product markets resulted in new types of 'community' being created linked to brand choices. These 'consumption communities' were defined in terms of the commodities they bought that in turn signalled their social standing (Boorstin, 1974). The arrival of 'mass' media provided opportunities for competing manufacturers of branded variants in the same product fields to self-promote and differentiate themselves from their rivals. As these promotions grew increasingly sophisticated, they presented more than basic information about the product being promoted. They began to associate a 'branded' version of a product range with specific advantages to users that went beyond the core functionalities of the product. Brands were associated with certain styles of living and with social status (Plummer, 1974).

Local producers began to experience competition from non-local rivals and citizens as 'consumers' of commodities for the first time were presented with product choices. This was an era in which 'mass' production emerged. To assist consumers in making choices, 'mass' marketing practices were developed that were designed to provide people with information about variants of the same product type to assist them in making up their minds about which ones to purchase and use. During the early days of mass marketing, mass producers still specialised in the production of a single commodity, and they became known for it. Other mass producers might produce their own versions of that commodity type, and created the first competitive markets. In time, mass producers came to extend their product ranges and marketed a range of products under their generic corporate brand (McKendrick, Brewer & Plumb, 1982).

Such product extensions confronted people as consumers with additional choices whereby they were required not only to decide between the same type of product made by two or more manufacturers, but also between different variants of the same product from the same supplier. To help consumers with fresh challenge, a new form of marketing practice emerged—in the shape of product-differentiated marketing—which helped people differentiate between brands in more subtle ways than simply the name of the original manufacturer. In this context, early ideas about brand image appeared, with manufacturers and marketers identifying differences between product variants based on physical attributes, variances in functionality, and definitions of quality (McKendrick et al., 1982).

Following the differentiation of consumers according to the attributes of the product variants they used, marketing practices moved forward by differentiating consumers by their own characteristics and qualities. Thus, consumers came to be divided up into groups and sub-groups defined by their physical attributes and psychological qualities. This approach enabled marketers to identify the specific tastes and expectations, needs, and interests of consumers and how their psychological characteristics might position some consumers to be more available than average to purchase and use specific commodities or branded variants of product/service ranges. This approach came to be known as 'target marketing' (Gunter & Furnham, 1992).

Across the 20th century, products and services multiplied in type and in respect of the numbers of distinct choices offered to consumers. During the second half of that century, as the big developed economies and many developing economies grew, people in general acquired more wealth and a greater ability to consume. In many everyday consumer goods markets, brand choices evolved as more manufacturers and suppliers produced a greater range and variety of variants of products and services (O'Guinn, Allen & Semenik, 2009).

Consumers adopted the concept of 'shopping around' to find the best deal for them. The role of branding in defining and differentiating product and service variants grew in its significance to consumers. Consumers, in consequence, gradually became more 'brand conscious'. Many products and services were evaluated more extensively before choices were made, and these choices were driven by a range of factors. Those factors included actual price (and perceived value for money) and premium values as defined by brand image. Brand image in turn was determined in part by the actions of manufacturers/suppliers in partnership with their marketers in developing product variants with specific distinguishing qualities. Brand reputations also depended upon the judgements of consumers, which were increasingly shared with other consumers (O'Guinn et al., 2009).

If a new product came on the market, it would have to define itself not only in terms of the functional applications consumers usually associated with its type, but also according to its specific qualities that set it apart from other variants in the same product class. This was true whether the product in question comprised a relatively cheap, fast-moving consumer product, such as soap powder, or a more expensive, luxury item, such as a car. A new soap powder might lay claim to being more powerful as a cleaning agent than its competitors, therefore needing less of it to be used per wash, resulting in it being cheaper because each pack would last longer. A new model car might lay claim to being more economical in its use of petrol than its competitors. Or it might be more expensive to run, but sold on the basis that it has a more advanced design and therefore would convey greater social status. Hence, brand appeals for luxury items such as cars often moved from being reliant on functional claims to making references to the social status attributes a brand could convey about its user. In that sense, the market differentiation could centre on the nature of the product or the nature of the consumer.

Finding the Right Target Market

Target marketing defines much consumer marketing in modern, crowded, and competitive markets. The complexity of modern consumer markets means that it is essential for brand marketers to be clear about which consumers they most wish to reach. Even in the mass market era of the 20th century, when there were limited media platforms for advertisers to choose from, the concept of the segmentation of consumers into distinct groups was already established. Then, segmentation was largely defined by geographical and demographic classifiers of populations, although from the middle of that century, initial inroads were made with psychological classifiers, which focused on consumers' motivations to purchase specific products or services (Gunter & Furnham, 1992).

In this context, marketers identify which consumers are most likely to be interested in a specific type of product or service. The branded variant of the product/service type being promoted is further defined in terms of the type of image it might convey to consumers in terms of how it differs from competing brands in the same product/service range. The 'brand image' confirms the point of origin of the brand, which is generally defined by the name of the manufacturer or supplier and also by the location from which it (or the manufacturer/supplier) originates.

In ever more crowded marketplaces, however, the brand image also needs to convey a message to consumers about the type of person that might use it and what their association with the brand might say about them. In other words, there is a sense of consumer identity acknowledged by the brand that reflects the needs, aspirations, and character of people likely to make up most of its customer base. The latter awareness is usually obtained through market research.

Thus, in developing a target marketing strategy, the marketer must begin with a generic consumer segmentation map usually defined by standard geographic, demographic, economic, social, and cultural classifiers. Through relevant and appropriate market research, the marketer should then seek to narrow down whether the people most likely to be consumers of a specific product type are defined by a particular geo-demographic/economic/social/cultural profile. Going further, can these generic classifiers be used to narrow still further the most likely purchasers and users of a specific brand? If, at the brand market segmentation stage, the generic population classifiers emerge as blunt instruments that lack the sensitivity to pin down the most probable market for a brand, further research might be necessary to determine whether product or brand-specific classifiers of consumers are needed that focus more on the psychological drives that need to be articulated to identify who the most likely consumers could be.

A marketing strategy thus proceeds through these stages of: (1) Identifying the generic population segments, (2) Determining which specific generic segments can be used to narrow the focus for brand promotion, and then (3) Finally, deciding how the brand itself can be positioned within potential consumer markets to have relevant and sufficient appeal to potential customers (Gunter & Furnham, 1992).

This process is important because it helps marketers make further decisions about how to communicate promotional messages about a brand to consumers as well as determining what kinds of messages about a brand are likely to work best with the target market. A marketing campaign must be defined in terms of the promotional devices it will use. Most marketing campaigns will use various forms of advertising as their central features. The nature of the consumer target group will also help marketers decide which media to use as promotional platforms. Thus, should advertisements be rolled out on television, or radio, or in print media, or on outdoor media, at the cinema, or increasingly these days, on a digital platform available through the Internet?

Decisions about the media planning of a marketing campaign need to draw upon what is known about which media outlets the target consumers are most likely to use. Thus, if a brand's target consumers are known to watch a lot of peak-time commercial television, a televised advertising campaign could make a good promotional fit. If they are known also to be regular readers of specific magazines, those publications would likewise be chosen as advertising vehicles. Hence, consumer segmentation information is important to marketing professionals not simply in relation to a brand or to the product range of which it is a part, but also in connection with the media consumption habits of the target consumers they are trying to reach.

Such multilayered segmentation of consumer markets has grown still further in its complexity in the digital era, in which additional promotional platforms have been added to the old media (e.g., broadcast, print, cinema, and outdoor) mix. Moreover, the new digital platforms operating over the Internet offer marketers new formats for advertising that do not appear outwardly as advertisements. Instead, promotional brand messages are integrated with other (mainly entertainment-oriented) content in online settings, and can often become virtually indistinguishable from non-marketing content (Gunter, 2015). This phenomenon raises many other issues about the practice and regulation of marketing methods, which represent a whole other area of concern and we will not dwell upon them here (see Nairn & Hang, 2012; Brodmerkel & Carah, 2013).

Types of Market Segmentation

It will be helpful at this point to outline the main market segmentation bases that have traditionally been adopted by marketing professionals. The

Physical Attribute Segmentation		Psychological Attribute Segmentation	
Geographic segmentation	Demographic segmentation	Behavioural segmentation	Psychographic Segmentation

Figure 1.1 Types of Consumer Market Segmentation

main theme of this book is an analysis and review of the evidence concerning the use of psychological bases of consumer classification. These segmentation approaches, however, represent one type amongst a suite of variables marketers have adopted. These segmentation devices can be presented as a single classification matrix, but they also have a hierarchical aspect (See Figure 1.1).

One class of segmentation approaches utilises the physical attributes of consumer populations that have not been established exclusively for marketing purposes, but nonetheless have proved to have relevance for defining market segments in consumer contexts. Another class of approaches is more closely tied to marketing objectives and depends upon the measurement of consumer behaviours and the psychological variables that underpin those behaviours.

Physical Attribute Segmentation utilises generic population classifiers. Geographic segmentation divides consumer markets according to their physical locations. Thus, national geographic areas are sub-divided into units defined by different kinds of regional mapping systems that might be determined by political boundaries, economic boundaries, or by other physical characteristics (e.g., urban versus rural). Demographic segmentation is determined by people classifiers such as age, gender, ethnicity, marital status, family status, education level, income level, and type of occupation. Sometimes, these factors can be combined. Thus, age, marital status, and family status could be combined to define 'life cycle' classifiers of consumers.

Psychological Attribute Segmentation is defined more by consumer and product/service-related factors. Behavioural segmentation divides up consumer populations in terms of the behavioural patterns they display as consumers. These patterns might be defined by the propensity to use certain product/service types or to use specific brands with product/service ranges. Psychographic segmentation either confines itself to generic psychological characteristics of consumers, such as their values and personality attributes, which are in turn linked to product/service/brand usage patterns, or is based upon newly researched sets of attitudes and beliefs about products/services/brands and/or the intentions and motives linked to those entities.

Physical Classifications

In the beginning, the segmentation of consumers was based primarily on their physical characteristics and social circumstances. The most obvious distinguishing attributes that we can use to categorise people include which gender they are, their age, and their ethnic origin. While these classifiers have social, cultural, and psychological aspects, they are most readily apparent in terms of the physical appearance of a consumer. Men and women as human beings share some physical features (e.g., they both have a head, two eyes, two ears, one mouth, two arms and two legs, and the same number of most internal organs); they are also different in some aspects of their external appearance and their internal physiology. Children likewise are not simply smaller (to begin with) than adults; they also are less knowing and experienced in regard to many aspects of life. Older people differ from young people in that they may have more wrinkles, less hair (in the case of some men), and often poorer physiques. People of different ethnic origins often differ in their outer appearance, having different skin tones and facial characteristics.

Socially, people can be differentiated in terms of the nature of their family background, their level of education, the kind of job they have, the sort of house in which they live, their marital status, and whether they have children of their own. These differences are also linked to economic circumstances and can sometimes be determined by them. People who have greater wealth are able to live different lifestyles.

There are further geographic factors that can be used to group people differently. These tend to comprise whether a person lives in an urban, suburban, or rural setting, and the kind of neighbourhood they reside in. Neighbourhood classification is also closely tied to the type of dwelling in which a person lives, and as we saw above, that is also associated with an individual's social circumstances. The social-economic classifier is also a measure of wealth in that it tends to focus on the value of a home as well as its physical type. Physically, dwellings can be differentiated into houses (which might be detached, semi-detached, or terraced), apartments (which might be purpose-built or converted from houses), mobile homes (which might be on land or water), and so on. A further factor is whether the individual, regardless of the type of dwelling in which they live, owns or rents their home.

These attributes represent important marketing devices if they provide valid and reliable signs of how people are likely to behave as consumers. There does not have to be any inherent reason why these characteristics should serve as predictor variables relevant to consumers' purchases, but if through empirical research, they can be demonstrated to signal the product or service choices consumers might make, they can be used to help define the potential or actual markets for specific commodities and brands (Darden & Reynolds, 1971; Darden & Perreault, 1976).

Of course, there may be many instances when it is clear that a product is directed to a specific geo-demographic group. Women and men might share similar preferences for food products and similar needs for toothpaste and other oral hygiene products, but, in general, have different dress styles and use different kinds of products designed to enhance their appearance. Some of their distinctive consumer purchases are determined by their biological differences (e.g., men do not wear bras and have no need for sanitary protection products).

At a social and economic level, there are further consumer behaviour differences that reflect the individual circumstances of people. People from more affluent families can develop tastes for more expensive brands even though they may share the same product needs. Thus, two consumers, one from a well-to-do background and the other from a poor background, might both need to own their own car, but will buy different models with different price tags.

Similarly, a person who owns a house with a garden might have the need for a lawn mower and other garden tools, whereas one who lives in a flat above the ground floor may have no garden and hence no need for such products. But then, a person with a large detached house that externally displays signs of wealth might also install an advanced household security system with alarms and cameras, whereas one who lives in small, terraced property might feel no need to do this.

During the 21st century, the marketing environment has changed dramatically with the spread of digital communications systems, most notably the Internet and mobile technologies. More businesses now operate online, where the ways they engage with their customers have evolved. Big and small corporate, product, and service brands have a presence on the World Wide Web. Early, relatively static websites still exist, but have been supplemented and in some instances virtually supplanted by more interactive online interfaces, particularly within social media environments, in which consumers can become actively involved with brands and their providers and assume a stronger sense of ownership creatively and functionally over how they are developed and promoted.

Thus, geographic and demographic attributes or consumers can provide a system for mapping consumers' needs, preferences, and behaviours and predicting whether a consumer might potentially be in the market for a specific type of product or service, or a specific version (or brand) of it. Sometimes, demographic characteristics provide unequivocal indicators of consumer-product matches because a product is tied to a specific demographic type (e.g., bras to women). On other occasions, demographically linked brand preferences are known through empirical demonstrations that entail consumer research to ascertain whether specific demographic groups purchase or use specific products more than anybody else.

The important point here is that the recognition and understanding of these kinds of differences between people can yield valuable data for businesses seeking to sell their products or services. It can help businesses design relevant marketing strategies that concentrate on promoting what they are trying to sell to those consumers most likely to be interested in buying. Marketers who try to reach everybody and promote commodities in ways designed to appeal to everyone are likely to fail. This is because consumers do not comprise a single homogeneous community or population. As people, they can be divided up into many different groups defined by geography, demography, and socio-economic circumstances. These groups have different product/service needs, interests, tastes and preferences, and consumption-related behaviours.

Geographical and demographic variables are often combined in professional market research to yielded classification systems that draw upon the physical locations of consumers, the types of dwellings in which they live, their income levels, and life cycle factors such as age, marital, and family status. In the United Kingdom, for instance, a number of population classification systems of this kind have been developed, including ACORN (A Classification of Residential Neighbourhoods), CCN's MOSAIC, Pinpoint's PIN, and McIntyre's Superprofiles. ACORN devised 11 different neighbourhood types with 38 further defining factors or sub-types. MOSAIC produced a similar residence-type system with personal financial data integrated into the mix. PIN produced a further system similar to ACORN. These population classification systems have frequently been applied to consumer marketing research and can differentiate between some consumption patterns. There have been reliable differences found between neighbourhood types as defined by, for example, ACORN and media consumption patterns (Gunter & Furnham, 1992).

In the United States, a system known as PRIZM was developed by Claritas Inc and subsequently acquired by Nielsen, the leading market research corporation. This consumer classification system divided American consumers into 14 superordinate groups and 66 further types defined in terms of demographic attributes and behavioural characteristics. This segmentation model was designed to help marketers seeking to classify and target consumers according to the kinds of homes in which they lived, their commodity preferences, shopping habits, and media-related behaviours[1]) Nielsen also developed P$YCLE to understand consumers' financial and investment-related behaviour and household wealth, and ConneXions, which classified consumers according to ownership and use of technology. Such information can be useful for media planners who determine the media strategy for brand marketing campaigns. The PRIZM system was based on geo-demographic data and utilised zip code information about consumers as the basic building block. Further data were then compiled and integrated with location data to flesh out consumer types in terms of their household type, occupation, and selected behavioural habits and interests.

Geo-demographic segmentation systems have the advantage that most of their defining variables (e.g., age, gender, type of household, neighbourhood type, etc.) can be readily and consistently applied. These variables cannot explain differences in consumer behaviour, but they can help marketers to know whether there are certain population sub-groups that are likely to be most interested in the brands they are seeking to sell. Women may display different consumer tastes and patterns from men, but their behavior can also evolve as they pass through different life stages and events such as getting a job or getting married (Douglas, 1975).

These physical attribute classifiers can also help marketers to determine the potential size of the market for their brands in particular locations. If one geographic area contains few of the types of people (as defined demographically) known to be the principal target market for a brand, there may be little point in running a special regional campaign there. An example of this type of insight might be a brand that is targeted at married couples with young children. If population classifier statistics show that there are relatively few of these in a specific area of England, this area might be excluded from a promotional campaign with different sub-national (i.e., regional) activities.

As was noted earlier, demographic classifiers can be combined to yield richer insights into consumer activity patterns. Age is an important population segmentation variable in its own right, but there are people of the same age that might have reached different 'life stages' where those stages are defined in terms of finding a partner, getting married, and having children. A 40-year-old man who is single and has no children may have different consumption patterns from a 40-year-old man who is married with three children of school age. It is possible that each of these men will live in different types of dwellings and inevitable that they will have different consumption needs. Even if they have similar incomes, the married man with children will probably have less disposable income if he is the sole breadwinner. Hence, there will be differences in the type of products they need to buy and even where they are both in the market for similar products (e.g., men's clothing), the single man may be financially better able to purchase more expensive brands.

Bearing these points in mind, some marketing researchers have championed and developed systems of population classification based on the concept of 'life cycle' or 'life stage'. While demographics such as age and income can often provide useful classifiers, in consumer contexts they could be blunt instruments for understanding differences in consumer behaviour patterns when their impact upon consumption can be modified by other factors such as marital and family status (Lansing & Morgan, 1955; Wells & Gubar, 1966; Arndt, 1967).

Composite classification measurements that combine distinct geo-demographic variables can provide more sensitive predictions of target consumers. One reason for this is that they paint a richer picture of the consumer and the way he or she lives that can in turn provide clearer and more logical links to behaviour patterns. Young adult consumers who live alone will have different product consumption patterns than same-age consumers who are married with young children. The latter in turn may display different consumer behaviours from young adults who are single parents. There could be differences between these consumer types in their everyday needs for food and household products. There may be disposable income differences that influence the variants of products they can afford to buy.

In the 1950s, Lansing & Morgan (1955) developed a seven-stage life cycle model of consumers that drew principally on the age and marital status of the head of household and the age of the youngest child. In the 1960s, Wells & Gubar (1966) extended the earlier model to include the employment status of the head of household, including whether they were retired. They found that this system of classification could reliably distinguish between consumers in terms of their consumption of food, household items, and holiday types and destinations.

Such life cycle classifications of consumers have needed to be periodically updated as society evolves and changes occur in the ways people live their lives. The early life cycle models were based significantly on the traditional concept of the nuclear family comprising two parents and up to several children. Over time, as social values and traditions evolved, they often reflected developments in opportunities for women and the effects of immigration on the ethnic and cultural composition of populations, and so too did the nature of family life change. Increased divorce rates created more divided nuclear families with solus parents or newly formed extended 'step' families as divorcees found new partners who might also have children.

By the end of the 1970s, new family structures meant that new life cycle and life stage classification systems were necessary to provide a more comprehensive representation of the true status of population 'types'. In this vein, Murphy & Staples (1979) developed a family life cycle model with 13 stages. Yet, even this model was outmoded within a few years, with omitted types such as cohabiting (unmarried couples) with and without children, married couples who were separated (but not yet divorced), and young widows/widowers becoming more prevalent.

There has been debate about the value of life cycle classifications in describing and predicting consumer behaviour differences. Some critics have claimed that income is a key variable and that when it is controlled, the other classifiers prove to be less sensitive as predictors of consumer behaviour variances (Ferber, 1979). It has also been observed that separating out the distinctive predictive significance of life cycle and family composition variables can be difficult (Frost, 1969; Murphy & Staples, 1979). The bottom line here is that societal changes over the last few decades of the 20th century produced a volatile set of circumstances that resulted in the emergence and general social acceptance of new forms of family structures. The early family structure-based life stage models therefore needed to be continuously updated and extended to reflect the consequences of this social volatility.

Tests of the predictive value of life cycle and life stage models using food consumption and household energy utilities expenditures found that early models of family structures lacked much sensitivity largely because they failed to include many new family types. The inclusion of certain new types managed to improve the performance of these types of consumer classifiers in predicting specific patterns of consumer expenditure (Derrick & Lehfield, 1980; Fritzsche, 1981).

Other investigators in this field have found that extensions to family life cycle classifications systems can further enhance their predictive value in relation to household consumer expenditure patterns. Key extensions included single-parent families (and not just ones caused by divorce and death) and childless married couples (through a matter of choice as well as biological circumstances) (Stampfl, 1978; Murphy & Staples, 1979; Gilly & Enis, 1982; Wagner & Hanna, 1983). These extensions reflected not simply changes to structural configurations, but also to social mores and traditions relating to family life. This meant that some family structures were entered into by the family members as a conscious decision rather than as a consequence of circumstances (e.g., family breakdown). As such, family structures could also serve as signifiers of life*style* choices and hence linked in turn to changes to social values concerning family life and how it ought to be configured.

Changes in life cycle or life stage, whether they follow traditional or non-traditional pathways, can represent new challenges for people in their lives. Such challenges might be welcomed or they could trigger stressful reactions. Changed life circumstances can in turn introduce changes in people's daily needs and such changes might then be reflected in consumption patterns. When under stress, people can be more ready to accept the advice of others if it eases decision-making for them. That is, for a stressed person, having to make decisions in their lives only adds to the stress they are already experiencing. If marketers can present consumers with choices that make decisions easier in terms of which products to purchase, stressed consumers could be rendered more malleable and receptive to persuasion (Warren, Stevens & McConkey, 1990).

Some indicative empirical evidence emerged in the 1980s to show that when consumers experienced a number of critical 'life events', such as job change, getting married, getting divorced, moving home, change to financial status, and so on, they could experience stress as a result. Such stressors, especially if they produce a radical change in lifestyle or life stage, can affect consumer behaviour. Consumers might feel pressured to change their habits and switch to new brands under these circumstances. They were also found to feel less satisfaction with their brand choices, which might in turn reflect a wider uncertainty about the right things to do or decisions to make in their lives (Andreason, 1984).

Behavioural Classifications

The use of behavioural features to segment consumer markets is a long-established practice. As we have seen already, the use of consumer behaviour data is relevant in the context of validating the predictive potential of physical attribute classifiers. In other words, knowing that a specific category of consumer defined by the type of home in which they live can differentiate consumers in relation to the kinds of furniture they purchase is not something that magically emerges from simply knowing about a consumer's dwelling alone. It is knowledge based upon analyses of the purchase patterns of people who live in different dwelling types.

Behavioural data can be utilised without reference to physical attribute factors. This activity has generally taken the form of examining the purchase patterns of samples of consumers across product types or across variants of specific product types. Initial data runs can indicate whether consumers can be organised into different groups purely on the basis of their level of use, where they go to make purchases, and whether those who purchase one product also display distinctive patterns of other product purchases.

More than one basis of 'behavioural' segmentation has been used, and not all the measures used here can strictly be defined as measures of behaviour. The measurement of product use, which includes purchase patterns, is central to this type of classification. In addition, purely behavioural measures can be embellished by measures of perceived product benefits. This type of measure usually involves asking consumers what makes a particular product/service good or bad, reliable or unreliable, and so on. Finally, under the broad heading of behavioural segmentation has been included the psychological classification of consumers. Such classification embraces measures designed to assess consumers' perceptions of products beyond simple evaluations, including their attitudes and beliefs about products/services or specific variants or brands within a product/service range. It often also entails consumers' perceptions or themselves as individuals in terms of the reasons underpinning their product/service tastes and preferences; their expectations, motives, and objectives in making purchases; and their value systems governing the lifestyles they lead and their personality attributes, which determine how they usually behave or respond to different social experiences and circumstances (Wansink, 1997).

Benefits Segmentation

Beyond purchase and usage behaviour as segmentation variables, consumers exhibit relationships with products and services based on their judgements about these experiences. Consumers develop opinions about products and services and different variants of them based on personal experience as well as from the promotional messages that marketing professionals publish about brands. Commodities can be differentiated by consumers in terms of the benefits they bring. These perceived outcomes may not be the same for all consumers of a specific product or service. Some consumers may be very satisfied with a product, whereas others are less so.

The benefits perceived to be attached to specific products and services therefore came to represent another dimension for consumer segmentation (Haley, 1968). This meant that consumers could be distinguished in terms of the specific benefits they attached to products and according to how satisfied they were with a product's or service's performance in relation to specific benefits. The concept of benefit segmentation introduced the idea that there was an internal psychological component to consumers' involvement with products and services that went beyond the extent to which they used it. Closer analysis of the perceived benefits of a product or service revealed that they were not simply verbal descriptions of consumers' experiences with commodities, but also indicated the reasons why they were using them. 'Reasons' for use essentially equal motivations, and motivations are psychological constructs believed to drive behavioural dispositions. These dispositions can derive from intrinsic and enduring psychological characteristics or personality traits determine by genetics as well as early life experiences, or they might be enduring values systems that represent cultural codes and social aspirations that are acquired through experience.

In considering how these dispositions are linked to consumer behaviour, some theorists have surmised that consumers reflect on their own character and examine product variants for the best fit, or begin by looking at product variant characteristics and then work backwards to discover whether a particular commodity matches their character and their needs. There are also occasions when these two processes can occur virtually simultaneously, with reflections about the self being invoked at the point at which a product is being examined (Raaij & Verhallen, 1994).

One study found that product benefits were multidimensional in nature and determined by a combination of demographic, psychological/behavioural, and economic variables. Consumers judged brands of beer in terms of their functional, social, and emotional benefits and their overall value for money. Emotional benefits could be either positive or negative in nature. These benefits were then matched up to different brands as well as to lifestyle factors, demographics, and patterns of use. Consumers can engage in active profiling and matching strategies when choosing the right brand for them (Orth, McDaniel, Shellhammer & Lopetcharat, 2004).

Psychographics Segmentation

The use of psychographics to generate consumer types originated in the 1930s. Psychographics research continued to develop across the remainder of the 20th century. It was particularly influenced by a growing interest in media and marketing research circles in understanding consumers' motivations for engaging in different activities. These measures were acknowledged to give marketers a different perspective from demographics in trying to understand consumer behaviour. Demographics could be used to structure differences in patterns of activity between recognised population sub-groups, but they did not provide explanations for those behavioural differences. By examining the reasons consumers gave for their use of specific products and services and for preferring one brand over another, it was possible to look beneath the overt and visible behaviours to understand more about what consumers were thinking.

Product Use and Attitudes

Some psychological measures focus on the product or service or even on specific brands. Consumer segments derive from the behaviours of consumers towards specific commodities or from their attitudes or beliefs about them. A basic form of classification is built upon data concerning whether consumers are users and buyers of specific products/services or brands. Do they ever use a particular product range or type of service? Which brands within that product range or service type do they use? If they are users, are they regular or periodic or occasional users? Thus, data are collected about consumption patterns defined by product or service type or brand variant.

Consumers can also display psychological orientations towards products that are signalled in ways other than their use or purchase patterns. Products and services are evaluated by consumers in terms of the benefits they might bring. Consumers might have benefit expectations and can judge, after use, whether a product or service delivered as expected. Such judgements might, in particular, be applied to brands to determine whether a specific product variant represents a good product of its type. Knowing what consumers expect from a product or service can assist brand marketers in designing promotional campaigns by revealing the types of message appeals likely to work best among consumers.

Marketing research has been used to develop comprehensive product orientation or 'benefit' segmentation profiles of large numbers of brands across a wide range of product and service categories. In the United Kingdom, one such widely used system of segmentation is the Target Group Index (TGI). Data are collected from large national samples each year to measure self-reported usage of specific branded products and services and the use of different media. It enables brand use to be related to media use, and such data can be useful for media planners tasked with devising a media strategy for promotional and marketing campaigns. TGI collects demographic information from its respondents and is then able also to indicate the demographic profiles of heavy versus light users of specific brands. This database can thus be used to define consumers segments demographically and behaviourally for different brands and to add a further layer of media use profiles over this.

Marketing researchers have been particularly interested in the segmentation of consumers according to their thoughts and feelings about products and services and the brands available in specific commodity fields. Questions often address the value consumers place on specific products and services, quite independently of how often they actually use them. Consumer samples are recruited to provide evaluations of lists of brands in terms of their idiosyncratic qualities as well as the generic qualities of their product or service types. These evaluations are recorded along linear numerical scales that generate data that can be entered into clustering analyses as well as correlated with demographic variables. It is then possible to determine the degrees of similarity and difference between specific brands in terms of their idiosyncratic attributes as well as between product and service classes in terms of the functions they serve and benefits they bring to consumers (Haley, 1984a, 1984b).

This approach to consumer segmentation can yield elegant solutions that might provide some guidance to marketing professionals in deciding how to position their brands when designing promotional campaigns and media strategies. Such findings, however, can be volatile and might change from one year to the next. This means there is a need constantly to update these segmentation profiles (Calantone & Sawyer, 1978; Yuspeh & Fein, 1982). Some researchers have focused even more tightly on the perceptions of consumers concerning product/service benefits that are statistically broken down into bundles. The extent of support for each bundle is then measured (Moorthy, 1984). A slightly different approach is to examine which advertising themes linked to brand promotions in specific commodity fields receive the greatest endorsement from consumers (Haley, 1971).

A further approach called BUNDOS (Benefit Bundle Optimization and Segmentation) has used the endorsement of sets of product benefits to provide data that is then used to segment consumers and seeks to find a statistical solution of bundle identification that manages to include the biggest proportion of consumers (Green, Kreiger & Schaff, 1985).

With any of these systems of benefit segmentation of consumers, it is essential to check the stability of their segmentation solutions. The degrees to which different benefits are endorsed for specific products and services can shift from time to time. If the benefits segments are found to remain stable over time, this means it is feasible for marketing professionals to adhere to the same advertising appeals and media promotions locations. If the nature of these consumer segments changes, however, other aspects of marketing strategies may also need to be altered. A product range for which specific old benefits are no longer perceived as relevant, for instance, would need to use different appeals in the advertising campaigns associated with it.

If the bundle configuration of any benefit segmentation scheme changes, this would likewise signal the need to change the marketing strategy. Let us suppose that the amount of consumer endorsement of one benefit category for a product type grew larger, whereas that for another benefit category became much smaller. A new marketing message might be needed that placed more emphasis on the first benefit bundle and less on the second.

An example might be that if one of the key original functional features of a motor vehicle that motivated consumers was its cost to run and that later this was less important as a decision-making criterion, whereas self-parking became endorsed by more consumers as a critical factor. Future marketing campaigns should give greater emphasis to self-parking and less emphasis to miles per litre.

With products for which there are fast-moving developments, consumers will be responsive to new features and these should take the pole position in marketing campaigns. For these products, market monitoring must be much more acutely tuned to fashion developments and how consumers are responding to them. For some product/service sectors, there might be considerable stability over time in the benefits most valued by consumers. However, new benefits may emerge and old benefits might disappear in their visibility to consumers, or the distribution of consumers' relative levels of endorsement of different benefits (or benefits bundles) may change over time. Marketers must be sensitive to such fluctuations and change their promotional appeals and marketing strategies accordingly (Calantone & Sawyer, 1978).

Digital Segmentation

In the contemporary consumer era of the 21st century, behavioural attribute segmentation has been extended further by the Internet, which has become an established business platform on which huge numbers of consumer transactions are conducted. This new consumer setting generates massive quantities of consumer-related data every day. Some of these data are quantitative and numerical in form, but much of the new data created online is unstructured and linguistic. As we will see later in this book, academic and commercial researchers have developed a range of computer software tools that can process massive quantities of unstructured data to convert them into structured and numerical formats suitable for statistical modelling. Some of these methods have enabled researchers to detect the psychographic characteristics of consumers in an unobtrusive fashion, extending the market segmentation tools available for marketers.

With the emergence of the online world, another major change has taken place in marketing practices. This change concerns the way consumers themselves can be monitored in terms of their behaviours, thoughts, and feelings. Consumers increasingly go online to engage in brand information searching and exploratory shopping trips, to make price comparisons, to find customer recommendations, and to make purchase orders. Their behaviour can be measured automatically and massive amounts of consumer data can be accumulated on an ongoing basis, enabling brand providers to track their business performance and to profile their customers in terms of their online behaviour patterns.

By tracking chatter on the social media sites where consumers interact and exchange views about brands, new computer software packages have been developed to extract consumers' opinions about brands from their online conversations with each other. Thus, marketers have access to huge amounts of consumer data on a continuous basis, enabling them to develop up-to-the-minute consumer profiles often more directly linked to their brand-related experiences.

There are many factors that have drawn marketers to online data analytics. Because huge amounts of consumer data are generated by consumers every day, it would be a pity not to take advantage of the value they might have. There is no direct data collection cost involved, as there is with offline consumer research using surveys, focus groups, or other methods. The online consumer data are generated naturally and do not involve an intervention in consumers' lives as do standard forms of market research. Conducting a face-to-face interview with a consumer means that the researcher and consumer must interact and the consumer must give up his/her time to help out with the research. There are always concerns that consumers will not behave naturally or report their naturally occurring behaviour accurately or honestly.

The sheer scale of online data collection—a feature that has led to the emergence of its fashionable description as 'big data'—cannot usually be matched by offline research because it would be far too costly to contemplate. Yet as we will see later in this book, big data does not represent a kind of Holy Grail or 'Gold Standard' of marketing research or understanding. It has its own distinctive limitations and weaknesses. Despite the need to understand more about online, passively acquired data, they do provide marketers and market researchers with sources of information about consumers' behaviours and attitudes concerning products/services that can in turn be related to other big-scale data about commodity markets. Such massive-scale activity can be statistically modelled to reveal patterns that can in turn help marketers to identify consumer behaviour trends and to predict future market movements. Alternatively, such analyses can raise hypotheses for further investigation that would not otherwise have become visible.

Psychological Measures of Consumer Classification

We have examined psychological measures based on consumers' behavioural and attitudinal orientations towards products and services that can be used as market segmentation tools. We now turn our attention to psychological measures applied directly to consumers themselves to classify them into different types. The key shift in perspective here is that we are now focusing on consumers rather than on products or services and how they are evaluated by consumers.

This section will provide a broad overview of the field. Later chapters will examine in more detail specific aspects of psychological classifications of consumers. To simplify matters, there are psychological approaches that have tried to develop generic classifications of consumers and others that have concentrated on the psychological segmentation of consumers within specific product or service ranges. Among the generic approaches, two broad types can be differentiated: (1) Lifestyles and values models, and (2) Personality profiles. Among the product- or service-specific approaches, again two types can be differentiated: (1) Custom-built psychographic measures, and (2) Personality tests originally used for non-consumer market segmentation purposes.

Lifestyles and Values Models

Lifestyles describe the way people live their lives. They can be defined by the nature of the home a person lives in, the possessions they own, the interests and activities they pursue, where they go to socialise, for leisure, and for entertainment. Values comprises sets of codes by which they live and are believed to underpin the attitudes and beliefs that people hold about the world around them, and expectations about how people ought to behave in different settings (Kahle, 1980, 1983; Homer & Kahle, 1988). These cognitive-level variables comprise internal representations of rules relating to people's social and cultural environments and the behavioural practices to which they are expected to adhere (Kahle, Kulka & Klingel, 1980; Piner & Kahle, 1984; Homer & Kahle, 1988)

Lifestyles and values are interconnected in that the way people live their lives is also shaped by their expectations about how one should behave in different situations. Lifestyles are also linked to the economic circumstances of the individual as determined by the kind of occupation and income they have. Along with values, lifestyle also has a socio-cultural dimension in that the way people live and the codes that shape their behaviour can vary from one culture to another regardless of their personal economic circumstances.

The significance of lifestyles and values in a consumer context stems from their potential influence over the way people live and whether their consumerism—that is, the value they attach to commodities and possessions—is in keeping with the cultural values that people embrace within their society. As we will see later, cultural value typologies have made a broad distinction between the collectivistic value systems of the Eastern world in Asia and the individualistic value systems of the Western world. The latter place much emphasis on individual achievement and the expression of that through the conspicuous consumption of branded items. The former systems, in contrast, place emphasis on the importance of the community and the individual's role within it, and this is expected to take priority over the needs and aspirations of the individual.

Although consumer societies exist that are governed by both values systems, marketing professionals need to be aware of the subtle differences between the two systems and design brand promotions that make appeals that are acceptable to collectivistic principles in societies that adhere to those values and appeals that place individual achievement centre stage in markets where that is important.

As we will see later, generic typologies based on values and lifestyles measures have been investigated. These typologies are often grounded in old models of human needs. They have demonstrated mixed success as predictors of consumers' product/service habits and preferences. These classification systems have not been developed around the use of specific product or service types. Instead, they represent attempts to produce generic profiling measures that can be used to classify entire consumer populations. The emergent 'consumer types' are statistical entities that emerged out of clustering analysis techniques applied to large batteries of items that describe attitudes, beliefs, opinions, interests, and expectations, to which respondents provide numerical scores.

The first major exercise of this sort was the Values and Lifestyles programme, which was launched in the early 1980s in the United States and evolved through further iterations in the following decades. Other values-based systems subsequently emerged, with the List of Values being among the most prominent. The growth of global markets triggered an interest in understanding cultural values systems and their universality. This work can be conceived as an extension of the marketing values and lifestyles research, but was influenced mostly by independent social psychological research into cross-cultural values measurement.

Although their protagonists were able to develop instruments to measure values-based consumer types, these segmentation systems were not always found to be powerful predictors of consumer behaviour. Chapter 3 will critically examine the evidence for this type of consumer segmentation measurement and its usefulness for understanding consumer markets. Lifestyle traits have been tested for their explanatory and predictive capabilities in relation to generic consumer behaviour (e.g., shopping), to broad categories of consumption activity (e.g., drinking alcohol), and to specific product types.

As well as custom-built normative typologies grounded in psychology, another approach to outlining the psychological nature of consumers has been to draw upon personality psychology in an effort to produce normative profiles of entire populations. Such approaches have been applied rarely, and the most significant empirical and theoretical developments of this sort have occurred in the 21st century. As Chapter 2 will show, there have been many attempts to link psychological profiles derived from tests developed and validated via clinical and empirical work outside marketing to consumer behaviour connected to specific products and services or differently branded variants of certain product and service ranges.

Personality Models

Personality models comprise sets of explanations of cognitive, affective, and behavioural dispositions. Specific models are usually grounded in a specific type of psychological theory that attempts to explain the building blocks of all human character. Personality comprises sets of attributes, each of which is linked to specific attitudes, beliefs, intentions, and behavioural patterns, and identifies reasons or motives that might underpin them. These traits were conceived by psychology theorists as stable characteristics of people that could explain why they behaved in the ways they did in different social settings (Smith, Bruner & White, 1956; Plummer, 1985). As such, personality models try to provide normative explanations of human behaviour that are distinct from demographic-style classifiers of populations. Thus, two people may differ in gender or age, but if they possess similar personality profiles, they might display similarities in their behavioural reactions to specific situations.

Personality traits are internalised components of an individual's psyche. As such, they cannot be directly observed, but must instead be inferred from the external responses research participants give to verbal questions designed to probe the situation-specific thought styles and emotional responses they describe for themselves. These models were generally developed and validated in clinical or empirical scientific contexts. In clinical settings, for example, personality measures were usually developed to assess and explain behaviour deemed to be either 'normal' or 'abnormal'. Such measures are then used to provide guidance concerning the necessity for clinical interventions and the nature of those interventions to effect changes to abnormal behavioural tendencies. In scientific analytical settings, the main objective is simply to understand and explain comprehensively the causes of human behaviour.

There is extensive literature on the measurement of human personality that has been established within psychology over a period spanning at least 100 years. Many personality researchers focused on the measurement and validation of just one or two psychological dimensions that actually assess only specific aspects of personality, whereas some theorists have attempted to develop more comprehensive models that try to account for all the major defining dimensions of human character. Over the years, a consensus has been reached among many psychologists working in this field that there are five superordinate dimensions of personality. These dimensions have been identified by different personality psychologists, although not usually within a single, all-encompassing model of personality (Digman, 1990). The consensus model has popularly become known as the "Big Five" personality factors. These are: Openness to experience, Conscientiousness, Extraversion, Agreeableness, and Neuroticism. The acronym OCEAN has been used as a short-form reference description of this model (Costa & McCrae, 1992a; Matthews, Deary & Whiteman, 2003). This model has been adopted for consumer segmentation purposes.

Personality measures have been tested for their explanatory power in relation to consumer behaviour, although most were developed in other fields first. Researchers have surmised that these traits might provide insights into how consumers might respond to marketing campaigns, the different values they attach to commodities for the benefits they bring, and other reasons why they might prefer one brand over another. The expectation has been that these generalised consumer population typologies might be yielded by personality measures (e.g., Kinnear, Taylor & Sadrudin, 1972). In addition, it was hoped that personality data might also provide a richer source of data about potential product/service purchase patterns than demographics alone (Koponen, 1960). The evidence that personality traits established outside consumer settings might be usefully applied to establish a better understanding of consumer behaviour was not always consistent (Kassarjian & Sheffet, 1991).

Some writers nonetheless adopted the view that personality traits were deep-seated aspects of the human psyche that governed standardised response patterns across different social situations, whereas lifestyle traits were less fundamental to the core of the human psyche and represented secondary consumer classifiers that were tied closely to response patterns of specific situations (Lastovicka, 1982). This observation was important because it questioned the efficacy of lifestyle traits to predict consumer behaviour with any degree of precision. Instead, they often needed to be combined with other variables, both physical attributes and psychographic attributes linked to orientations towards particular products/ services, to be effective (Lastovicka, Murry, Joachimsthaler, Bhalla & Scheurich, 1987; Murry, Lastovicka & Austin, 1997). The importance of more integrated models of consumer classification is examined further later in this chapter.

Personality Tests

Just as personality models have been applied to the general classification of consumer populations, specific tests have been drawn upon to understand the motives underpinning purchase decisions or the thought processes linked to beliefs and attitudes about specific product ranges, service types, and brands. Psychologists have developed many different tests to measure human personality. Most of these have not had the grandiose ambitions of the 'Big Five' modelling, which has been applied to classify entire populations. Instead, they have been applied in studies of consumers' behaviours, thoughts, and feelings in relation to specific types of commodities and brand marketing campaigns.

There are risks associated with using off-the-shelf personality tests in this way. These tests were not usually developed for the purpose of understanding consumer markets. If instruments provide only fairly generalised measures of specific dispositions, they may lack the sensitivity of relevance to predict the way consumers develop affinities to specific products or services (Kinnear, Taylor & Sadrudin, 1972). It can be hit or miss as to whether such tests can classify consumers in ways that are useful in predicting their purchase behaviour (Koponen, 1960).

Combined Models

Physical attribute and psychological attribute classifiers have been combined by some marketing researchers. Physical attribute classifiers often have the advantage that normative data are available on them covering entire consumer populations, whereas such census or establishment data are not so readily available for psychological classifiers. Large-scale behavioural databases can be found for product and service category purchases, but such data tend to be proprietary and owned either by manufacturing or supplier corporations or commercial market research agencies. It is feasible, however, to merge data from different sources to create aggregate databases that through data-matching procedures can produce composite consumer classifications.

Despite the movement towards psychographics as an independent system of consumer classification from demographics, arguments were made by some theorists that personality and lifestyle trait models should not be conceived as alternatives to physical attribute or geo-demographic systems of consumer classification. Instead, all these perspectives might prove more useful to marketing professionals and academic social researchers if they were combined as components of a more general framework for understanding consumers (Lutz, 1979).

The PRIZM lifestyle clusters introduced earlier in this chapter represent an example of this type of combined system (Weiss, 1988). Some marketing researchers have taken this model one step further by adding in further lifestyle trait classifications. Drawing upon the Values and Lifestyles (VALS) system, aspirational versus avoidance orientations have been mapped onto PRIZM categories to provide more detailed analyses of high and low users of specific product ranges (Englis & Solomon, 1995, 1997). In this enhanced consumer classification, structural classifiers based on geo-demographic variables were combined with product use frequencies and standardised measures of consumers' subjective judgements about the goodness of fit between specific products and specific lifestyles (Englis & Solomon, 1995, 1997).

For example, the "Upper Crust" category, classed as the wealthiest group, was usually associated with over-55s whose children have left home that have high incomes and significant assets, enabling them to live affluent lifestyles. At a slightly lower level in terms of affluence were the "Movers and Shakers" who were up-and-coming, suburban living couples who were often highly educated, younger at 35 to 45, with children still living at home. Yet, the dual incomes meant that despite their outgoings, they had sufficient disposable income to enjoy life. Another category called the "Young Influentials" was formerly the Yuppies—that is young, middle-class, well-educated and aspirational people in their 20s, not yet married, but career-oriented and still to acquire a lifestyle and the possessions associated with it of their better-off elders.

These vignettes illustrate how consumer types could emerge from a combination of distinct attributes that could be combined in different permutations to give rise to different lifestyle circumstances, motivations, and behaviour patterns. The importance of painting these multifaceted portraits of consumers was further endorsed by a psychological analysis of consumerism in that the ways consumers responded to the activities of marketers and in their orientations towards brands were controlled by key psychological dispositions that derived in part from the genetic makeup of individuals, but also importantly from their life experiences and prevailing circumstances (Day, 1990). The social experiences of consumers fuelled their beliefs about the world and these beliefs in turn could shape their behaviours, especially in terms of their responses to attempts to mould behaviour patterns (Ajzen & Fishbein, 1980).

Thus, beliefs about commodities that articulated their functionalities and also any culturally symbolic meanings they conveyed represented building blocks of brand images among consumers. Such psychographic variables interacted with physical circumstances of consumers' lives, as defined by geo-demographic variables, to yield a more integrated model of consumer classification and behaviour prediction (Murry et al., 1997).

Concluding Remarks

Marketers have been interested into the nature and composition of consumer markets for a long time. The use of standard descriptive population classifiers can yield measures capable of consistently differentiating between some consumer behaviour patterns. These demographic and geographic variables, however, do not provide in-depth insights into the reasons why consumers differ in their frequency of use of specific products or services, why consumers choose one variant (i.e., brand) of a product or service over another, or why they vary in their responses to specific brand marketing campaigns. To understand these more subtle factors that might underpin consumer behaviour, we need a different approach. This must be an approach in which questions are asked about why consumers exhibit specific patterns of purchase behaviour and why they develop specific brand preferences. In effect, we need to understand the psychology of the consumer and utilise psychological variables to profile or segment consumers into different types.

The idea of using psychology to determine new sets of measures of consumer classification is not new. Psychology, however, is a complex subject and can be applied in different ways to understand consumers and their product or service choices. Psychological applications can take the form of measures of overt behaviour, techniques designed to measure how consumers respond to types of products and services or variants of them emotionally and cognitively. In other words, psychologists are interested in internal as well as external and directly observable psychological processes and phenomena.

As we have seen in this chapter, psychological tests can be used to produce typologies based on consumers' behaviour patterns linked to their consumer activity. They can also be utilised to measure internal processes such as the motivations, expectations, and perceptions associated with different products and services or specific brand variants. Psychological measures have been applied to consumer populations as a whole without first linking them to any particular product or service purchase patterns or preferences. They have also been utilised to predict or explain consumers' responses in relation to specific products and services.

Note

1   See: https://www.claritas.com/MyBestSegments/Default.jsp?ID=100&menuOption=learnmore.

References

Ajzen, I., & Fishbein, M. (1980) *Understanding Attitudes and Predicting Social Behaviour*. Englewood Cliffs, NJ: Prentice-Hall.
Andreason, A. R. (1984) Life status changes and changes in consumer preferences and satisfaction. *Journal of Consumer Research*, 11, 784–794.
Arndt, J. (1967) The role of product-related conversations in the diffusion of a new product. *Journal of Marketing Research*, 4(3), 291–295.
Boorstin, D. (1974) *The Americans: The Democratic Experience*. New York, NY: Vintage.
Brodmerkel, S., & Carah, N. (2013) Alcohol brands on Facebook: The challenges of regulating brands on social media. *Journal of Public Affairs*, 13(3), 272–281.
Calantone, R. J., & Sawyer, A. G. (1978) The stability of benefit segments. *Journal of Marketing Research*, 15, 395–404.
Costa, P. T., & McCrae, R. R. (1992a) *The NEO Personality Inventory Manual*. Odessa, FL: Psychological Assessment Resources.
Day, G. S. (1990) *Market Driven Strategy*. New York, NY: Free Press.
Demos, J. (1986) *Past, Present, and Personal: The Family and Life Course in American History*. New York, NY: Oxford University Press.
Derrick, F. W., & Lehfield, A. K. (1980) The family life cycle: An alternative approach. *Journal of Consumer Research*, 7, 214–217.
Digman, J. M. (1990) Personality structure: Emergence of the Five-Factor model. *Annual Review of Psychology*, 41, 417–440.
Englis, B. G., & Solomon, M. R. (1995) To be and not to be?: Reference group stereotyping and *The Clustering of America* by B. G. Englis and M. R. Solomon. *Journal of Advertising*, 24, 13–28.
Englis, B. G., & Solomon, M. R. (1997) Where perception meets reality: The social construction of lifestyles. In L. R. Kahle & L. Chiagouris (Eds.) *Values, Lifestyles and Psychographics*, pp. 25–44. Mahwah, NJ: Lawrence Erlbaum Associates, Ch. 2.
Ferber, R. (1979) Comments on paper of life cycle analysis. In W. G. Wilkie (Ed.) *Advances in Consumer Research*, Vol. 6, pp. 146–148. Ann Arbor, MI: Association for Consumer Research.

Fritzsche, D. J. (1981) An analysis of energy consumption patterns by stage of family life cycle. *Journal of Marketing Research*, 28, 227–232.

Frost, W. A. K. (1969) The development of a technique for TV programme assessment. *Journal of the Market Research Society*, 11, 25–44.

Gilly, M. C., & Enis, B. M. (1982) Recycling the family life cycle: A proposal for redefinition. In A. Mitchell (Ed.) *Advances on Consumer Research*, Vol. 9, pp. 271–276. Ann Arbor, MI: Association for Consumer Research.

Green, P. E., Kreiger, A. M., & Schaffer, C. M. (1985) Quick and simple benefit segmentation. *Journal of Advertising Research*, 25, 9–15.

Gunter, B. (2015) *Kids and Branding in a Digital World*. Manchester, UK: Manchester University Press.

Gunter, B., & Furnham, A. (1992) *Consumer Profiles: An Introduction to Psychographics*. London, UK: Routledge.

Haley, R. I. (1968) Benefit segmentation: A decision oriented research tool. *Journal of Marketing*, 30(3), 30–35.

Haley, R. I. (1971) Beyond benefit segmentation. *Journal of Advertising Research*, 11, 3–8.

Haley, R. I. (1984a) Benefit segments: Backwards and forwards. *Journal of Advertising Research*, 24, 19–24.

Haley, R. I. (1984b) Benefit segmentation—20 years later. *Journal of Consumer Marketing*, 1, 5–13.

Homer, P. M., & Kahle, L. R. (1988) A structural equation test of the value-attitude-behaviour hierarchy. *Journal of Personality and Social Psychology*, 54, 638–646.

Kahle, L. R. (1980) Stimulus condition self-selection by males in the interaction of locus of control and self-chance situations. *Journal of Personality and Social Psychology*, 38, 50–56.

Kahle, L. R. (Ed.) (1983) *Social Values and Social Change: Adaptation to Life in America*. New York, NY: Praeger.

Kahle, L. R., Kulka, R. A., & Klingel, D. M. (1980) Low adolescent self-esteem leads to multiple interpersonal problems: A test of social adaptation theory. *Journal of Personality and Social Psychology*, 39, 496–502.

Kammen, M. (1991) *Mystic Chords of Memory: The Transformation of Tradition in American Culture*. New York, NY: Knopf.

Kassarjian. H. H., & Sheffet, M. J. (1991) Personality and consumer behaviour: An update. In H. H. Kassarjian & T. S. Robertson (Eds.) *Perspectives in Consumer Behaviour*, pp. 281–303. Englewood Cliffs, NJ: Prentice-Hall.

Kinnear, T. C., Taylor, J. R., & Sadrudin, A. A. (1972) Socioeconomic and personality characteristics as they relate to ecologically-constructive purchasing behaviour. In *Proceedings of the Third Annual Conference of the Association for Consumer Research*, pp. 34–60. Chicago, IL: Association of Consumer Research.

Koponen, A. (1960) Personality characteristics of purchasers. *Journal of Advertising Research*, 1, 6–12.

Lansing, J. B., & Morgan, J. M. (1955) Consumer finance over the life cycle. In C. H. Clark (Ed.) *Consumer Behaviour*, Vol. 2, pp. 36–50. New York: New York University Press.

Lastovicka, J. L. (1982) On the validation of lifestyle traits: A review and illustration. *Journal of Marketing Research*, 19, 126–138.

Lastovicka, J. L., Murry, J. P. Jr., HJoachimsthaler, E. A., Bhalla, G., & Scheurich, J. (1987) A lifestyle typology to model young male drinking and driving. *Journal of Consumer Research*, 14(2), 257–263.

Lutz, R. J. (1979) A functional framework for designing and pretesting advertising themes. In J. C. Maloney & B. H. Silverman (Eds.) *Attitude Research Plays for High Stakes*, pp. 37–49. Chicago, IL: American Marketing Association.

Matthews, G., Deary, I. J., & Whiteman, M. C. (2003) *Personality Traits*, 2nd Ed. Cambridge, UK: Cambridge University Press.

McKendrick, N., Brewer, J., & Plumb, J. H. (1982) *The Birth of a Consumer Society: The Commercialization of Eighteenth-Century England*. London, UK: Europa Publishing.

Mintz, S., & Kellogg, S. (1988) *Domestic Revolutions: A Social History of American Family Life*. New York, NY: The Free Press.

Moorthy, K. S. (1984) Market segmentation, self-selection and product line design. *Marketing Science*, 3, 288–307.

Murphy, P. E., & Staples, W. A. (1979) A modernized family life cycle. *Journal of Consumer Research*, 6, 12–22.

Murry, J. P. Jr., Lastovicka, J. L., & Austin, J. R. (1997) The value of understanding the influences of lifestyle trait motivations on consumption beliefs. In L. R. Kahle & L. Chiagouris (Eds.) *Values, Lifestyles and Psychographics*, pp. 45–68. Mahwah, NJ: Lawrence Erlbaum Associates, Ch. 3.

Nairn, A., & Hang, H. (2012, December) *Advergames: It's Not Child's Play: A Review of Research*. Available at: www.familyandparenting.org. Accessed 12th June 2013.

O'Guinn, T. C., Allen, C. T., & Semenik, R. J. (2009) *Advertising and Integrated Brand Promotion*. Mason, OH: South-Western Cengage Learning.

Orth, U. R., McDaniel, M., Shellhammer, T., & Lopetcharat, K. (2004) Pormoting brand benefits: The role of consumer psychographics and lifestyle. *Journal of Consumer Marketing*, 21(2), 97–108.

Piner, K. E., & Kahle, L. R. (1984) Adapting to the stigmatizing label of mental illness: Foregone but not forgotten. *Journal of Personality and Social Psychology*, 47, 805–811.

Plummer, J. T. (1974) The concept and application of life style segmentation. *Journal of Marketing*, 38, 33–37.

Raaij, W. F., & Verhallen, T. (1994) Domain specific market segmentation. *European Journal of Marketing*, 28(10), 49–66.

Roberts, M. L. (1998) Gender, consumption and commodity culture. *American Historical Review*, 103, 817–844.

Smith, M. B., Bruner, J. S., & White, R. W. (1956) *Opinions and Personality*. New York, NY: Wiley.

Stampfl, R. W. (1978) The consumer life cycle. *Journal of Consumer Affairs*, 12, 209–219.Wagner, J., & Hanna, S. (1983) The effectiveness of family life cycle variables in consumer expenditure. *Journal of Consumer Research*, 10, 281–291.

Warren, W. E., Stevens, R. E., & McConkey, C. W. (1990) Using demographic lifestyle analysis to segment individual investors. *Journal of Financial Analysis*, 46, 74–77.

Weiss, M. J. (1988) *The Clustering of America*. New York, NY: Harper & Row.

Wells, W. D., & Gubar, G. (1966) The life cycle concept in marketing research. *Journal of Marketing Research*, 3, 355–363.

Yuspeh, S., & Fein, G. (1982) Can segments be born again? *Journal of Advertising Research*, 3, 13–23.

2 Personality Psychology and Consumer Segmentation

The study of human personality has characterised psychology from its earliest days. There have been many different theories of human personality that have derived from different scholarly schools of thought about how to understand human behaviour. Most of these theories were not originally developed with people as consumers in mind. Nonetheless, the marketing world has adopted different psychological models of human personality to produce consumer-profiling frameworks.

An individual's personality reveals more about their character than simply knowing the type of lifestyle they lead or the cultural values they hold most dear. Personality characteristics are moulded by a combination of genetic inheritance and early life experiences. Personality attributes reflect internalised orientations that define consistent patterns of behaviour each of us might display across a range of social settings. The distinctive way each of us responds in a specific situation differentiates us from other people.

If we display consistency in the way we respond to a specific situation, this could be because we have been hardwired to react in a particular way. In the context of marketing, the big question is whether similar consistencies can be found in consumer-related behaviours and preferences that could be signalled by having a particular type of personality. If the answer is 'yes', such consistencies can be found and can be linked back to specific personality traits we have been found to possess via tried and tested clinical tests, then personality variables could have great relevance to marketing professionals in not only describing, but also in explaining and therefore possibly predicting consumer behaviours and preferences.

Over the years, a significant volume of empirical evidence has accumulated from a range of studies carried out around the world to indicate that an understanding of human personality is relevant to a comprehensive understanding of consumer behaviour and of consumers' reactions to brand marketing messages (Koponen, 1960; Plummer, 1985). Over the years, psychologists have discovered many different personality traits and devised a multitude of tests to measure these constructs. They have also conducted a large volume of research designed to validate personality traits in terms of their predictive capabilities linked to human behaviour (Tian, Bearden & Hunter, 2001; Matthews et al., 2003).

This empirical literature is also structured and underpinned by a number of psychological theories about the development and structure of human personality. These theories attempt to provide explanations of how specific personality attributes can control individuals' psychological responses to different environmental stimuli. Some theories have been empirically validated, whereas others have been clinically rationalised. In a further complication, psychologists have sometimes developed different tests to measure the same personality attributes. In this case, there is a further task of determining whether one test is more accurate and valid than another even in a clinical or scientific sense, let alone as a predictor of consumer choices.

This chapter will examine the potential relevance to understanding consumerism of psychoanalytic theory, motivation theory, social theory, trait-factor theory, personal construct and self-concept theory, and the Big Five model of personality. It will then examine some specific examples of the application of personality models to consumer contexts. Perhaps the key development in this sphere in the past 25 years has been the widespread acceptance of the Big Five model. This has represented an attempt to derive a single normative model of human personality. Has it also moved on the usefulness of personality theory in a consumer context?

Key Theories of Personality

Several psychological theories of human personality have influenced thinking about consumers and consumer behaviour. These theories represent sets of explanations about human behaviour and its causes that were developed for the purposes of understanding human psychology in a general sense. These models of human functioning were not developed specifically to help us understand consumer activity, but they can provide insights into how and why certain consumer decisions are made.

The most prominent personality models linked to consumerism are:

(1) Psychoanalytic Theory
(2) Social Neo-Freudian Theories
(3) Trait-Factor Theory
(4) Self-Concept Theory
(5) Big Five Personality Theory

Psychoanalytic Theory

Psychoanalysis developed as a clinically oriented system of analysing, explaining, and understanding human personality. There were a number of key contributors to the field, including Jung, Erickson, and Horney, but the field's most famous theorist was Sigmund Freud. Freud developed one of the most influential theories of personality in psychology. He conceived of human personality and behaviour being shaped by conflict between an unconscious and conscious mind. The 'unconscious' in many ways represented the effects of basic human biological drives that were extensively underpinned by autonomic physiological processes over which individuals have little direct conscious control. The basic biological needs that drive human behaviour are determined by genetic inheritance, and the way they are allowed to become manifest is determined by learned controls acquired through early lifetime experiences. Overriding the demands of the inner needs are societal constraints. Society sets rules and conditions of conduct for human beings to ensure that purely self-centred, base needs are not allowed to control the way people behave, which would result in anarchy. Tensions therefore arise between the internal drives of the individual and the external constraint imposed by society.

For Freud, internal drives were embodied in the concept of the id, which was a source of driving energy (often sexual in nature), and external constraints were defined by the superego. A third concept—the ego—represented a set of psychological processes that mediated between the id and superego, determining which would have the upper hand or perhaps negotiating a compromise outcome that in part satisfied the id's urges and demands and the superego's social and ethical constraints. Together, the interactions between the id, superego, and ego determined behavioural outcomes in different social settings.

Within the Freudian psychoanalytic model, human personality emerged from a sequence of childhood conflicts between the unconscious and conscious components of the psyche. At the centre of these conflicts was sexual tension that was believed to exist in the child in relation to his mother and father. Other base urges also play their parts in determining the emergence of human character through a series of development stages.

At the outset, the infant passes through the Oral Stage, when primary experience involves the mouth and the early pleasures associated with eating and sucking, including on the mother's breast. Initial character-defining tensions arise at the point when the child is weaned off the mother's breast and onto bottle-feeding.

Next comes the Anal Stage, when the main source of pleasure for the child is elimination through urination and excretion. Further tensions arise between child and parents at the point of toilet training. Some children learn that they can experience control (of parents) through deciding whether to hold on to or let go of the waste products of eating.

As the infant turns into a child, a period of sexually oriented pleasure emerges, according to Freud, which he called the Phallic Stage. Freud theorised that at this point the child experiences sexual desire for the opposite-sex parent, that is, sons for their mothers and daughters for their fathers.

Such urges cannot be fulfilled and psychological resolutions must be found to define socially acceptable parent-child relationships. This process was believed by Freud to represent a critical character-forming process.

During the middle years of childhood, the sexual urges of children were conceived to be dormant and did not reawaken until adolescence. For Freud, this was also a largely dormant stage in terms of the child's personality development and was appropriately labelled as the Latency Stage.

Finally, in adolescence, sexual interest usually (although not always) in partners of the opposite sex emerged along with love of objects beyond that of the self and of parents. The emergent young adult experiences many conflicts during this Genital Stage that are sexual in nature and which relate to the definition of personal identity.

The success with which each of us negotiates passage through these development stages determines the type of personality we eventually have as adults. For some individuals, they fail to let go on the tensions experienced at specific stages, and the idiosyncratic urges associated with a specific stage continues to define their personality in later life. Understanding the specific motives associated with different developmental stages that remain present in a person's character can provide insights into the typical patterns of behaviour they might be expected to display in specific social settings. Such insights might extend also to expectations about behaviour displayed in consumer contexts.

Psychoanalysis uses qualitative and open-ended research methods to assess personality. In Freud's case, much of his data derived from extended interviews with patients in clinical sessions in which they talked in their own words about their lives, the ways they might behave in different situations, and their reasons for their behaviours. Projective techniques are also used by psychoanalysts, during which participants describe their thoughts and feelings about abstract visual shapes, interpret pictures, or respond to words or complete unfinished sentences. These techniques can be used with consumers with responses oriented towards motives linked to buying things.

As an example of the way projective methods can be used with consumers, a 1940s American study by Mason Haire presented two almost identical shopping lists to a sample of non-working women. The women were asked to describe the type of person from the shopping list. The only difference between the two lists was that in one case, instant coffee was listed and in the other, it was regular coffee. Consistently, the person with instant coffee in their shopping list was defined as lazy and poor at planning ahead. This finding was significant for its time in that it occurred during an era when 'instant' products such as coffee and cake mix were just coming onto the market and represented a shift in traditional home food and drinks preparation practices from ones involving a lot of effort to new and relatively effortless ones.

Over time, as consumer norms change, so too do the perceptions of certain products and the kind of lifestyle they represent. Thus, when the

Mason Haire study was replicated nearly 30 years later, the original results for instant versus ground coffee makers disappeared. Instant coffee was regarded as normal and therefore not something to be denigrated because it represented a break with a tradition (Webster & Von Pechmann, 1970)

Other marketing research techniques influenced by psychoanalytic thinking have examined so-called 'brand personality'. This concept recognises that product variants defined by distinctive brand names owe their distinctiveness not simply to functional differences, but often to more symbolic features. Thus, specific image characteristics such as 'cheerful', 'exotic', 'gentle', 'mature', and so on can become attached to specific brands, with such images usually shaped by promotional messages in advertising campaigns. These 'personality' features of brands are often difficult to reveal through standard questionnaire surveys and instead require more subtle and sensitive in-depth interviews and observed interactions with brands (see Plummer, 1985a; Berry, 1988; Durgee, 1988).

Neo-Freudian Theories

Freud was not alone in developing a psychoanalytic theory of human personality. Later theorists placed more emphasis on social relationships as the defining aspects of personality, steering thinking away from the Freudian focus on instinct and sexuality. Psychoanalysts following Freud had already begun to move in this direction. From the 1930s to the 1950s, a series of different psychoanalytic models emerged that shifted the emphasis on the drive for superiority (Adler), alleviation of loneliness (Fromm), establishment of positive human relationships (Sullivan), and reduction of anxiety (Horney).

Alfred Adler developed a social theory of psychoanalysis that recognised the importance of rational goals for human beings, which often became manifest in the lifestyle choices made by individuals. In Adler's model, the primary tension was between feeling inferior and superior. People strived through life to feel confident and competent relative to others. As we will see in later chapters, and as noted already in the previous chapter, lifestyles—in turn linked to social values—have been conceived as important signifiers of consumption orientations.

Adler's concept of the inferiority complex as a driving force in human life led him to conclude that the primary drive of human beings is to seek superiority or, at least, to find ways of dealing with feelings of inferiority (Adler, 1964, 1979). The superiority drive led individuals to engage with each other socially and to seek opportunities for self-improvement. This might be achieved through choice of occupation, choice of home, collection of other possessions, and even choice of spouse. In a sense, one might conceive of Adler's theory as the initial articulation of the idea of being upwardly mobile. As such, his theory provides a logical basis for thinking about how personality might influence consumerism.

Adlerian theory embraced the notions of the self and ideal self. The self was often defined by the recognition of weaknesses that needed to be corrected, whereas the ideal self was the improved version of the self the individual sought to achieve. An overly self-centred ideal self—one defined, perhaps, by overly grandiose ambitions—would often be held in check by social and ethical constraints. An individual who sought improvement but failed to take the relevant corrective action to address his or her weaknesses might develop an inferiority complex which could in turn give rise to a range of socially constructive reactions, neutral responses, or more worryingly, destructive reactions, including egocentrism and overdeveloped urges for power and aggressiveness.

Harry Stack Sullivan also extended classical Freudian theory in emphasising the significance to human development of specific, rewarding relationships with important others. Like Adler, Sullivan (1935) conceived that individuals seek to remove or at least to reduce unpleasant tensions such as anxiety in their lives. This could be achieved by attaining greater social competence and establishing relationships with others who could provide relevant sources of social support and reassurance.

Karen Horney was another Neo-Freudian whose model of personality development placed the alleviation of anxiety centre stage. Like Freud, she recognised the significance of parent-child relationships, but conceived that the meaningfulness of these social interactions was not to be found in terms of their explanation of roles of basic biological urges, but rather as setting down the foundations for future social communication and interaction styles. Horney identified three personality types, which she called compliant, aggressive, and detached.

Compliant people seek to be liked and move towards others in search of positive interpersonal relationships. Aggressive people can be argumentative and often move against others, but can transform this drive into positive achievement and attainment in a desire to win the admiration and respect of others. Detached personalities tend to move away from others in that they are driven mainly by a need for independence. This might be underpinned by their confidence in being able to take care of themselves or simply the fact that they wish to lead a life free from obligations and responsibilities (Horney, 1937).

Neo-Freudian thinking has relevance for the understanding of consumer behaviour and can provide a psychological basis for differentiating between consumers. Yet, its direct influence on consumer research has been fairly limited. A personality test based on the work of Horney has been used to predict the product and brand preferences and habits of American college students. Those high in compliance tended to show stronger preferences for the best-known brand names, whereas aggressive types displayed preferences for products with stronger masculine appeals. Detached types showed some product preferences that indicated signs of non-conformism, which in turn signals a desire to be distanced from the masses (Cohen, 1968).

Later tests of the CAD (compliance, aggression, detached) model produced mixed evidence for its explanatory or predictive value in consumer marketing (Woodside & Andress, 1975; Noerager, 1979; Tyagi, 1983). Its measures were found to exhibit consistent and significant statistical relationships with certain other established personality dimensions, such as extraversion (Cohen & Golden, 1972).

Trait-Factor Theory

This approach marks a departure from psychoanalytically based personality theories in that the personality types or 'traits' that it has identified derive from empirical research involving the collection of quantitative data from large samples of people usually via questionnaires. Traits are considered to be attributes of a person's character that predispose them to behave in distinguishable ways across different social settings. Traits are psychological measures that can be used to differentiate one person from another. A trait is regarded as an enduring feature or characteristic of an individual's personality. Traits exert predefined effects on human behaviour such that if two or more individuals are measured as having the same traits, it is expected that they would behave in similar ways in specific social settings. Traits cannot predict precise behavioural responses in any given social situation, but they can indicate where there is a higher probability of one type of response occurring than another.

Traits were measured via the responses people give to verbal statements or terms using linear, numerical scales. Early researchers in the field sought to create a taxonomy of personality types through relevant verbal descriptions of perceived mood states, attitudes, beliefs, and behavioural reports (Allport & Odbert, 1936). Statistical techniques such as factor analysis were then applied to the data yielded by these verbal measures to examine exhaustive correlation matrices in which the responses to each item in a battery of test statements are correlated with responses given to every other item in the list (Cattell, Marshall & Geordiades, 1957). Factor analysis can identify which clusters of items are most closely related in statistical terms, identifying the core 'factors' (or traits) that define personality. The average endorsement scores given to items that loaded highest on a specific factor were aggregated to produce a 'factor score' indicating the strength with which that trait characterised a particular individual. The latter score was then used in further analyses in which personality traits are related to numerically measured patterns of consumer behaviour. Such data were adopted to provide insights into whether certain personality traits are related to specific product preferences or purchase frequencies (Alpert, 1972; Green, Wind & Jain, 1972). More will be said on personality factors or traits and consumer behaviour later in this chapter.

Self-Concept Theory

A number of personality measures have been developed based on the self-concept. Neo-Freudian psychoanalytic theories made reference to the concept of the 'self' and differentiated between different aspects of the self, including the self as actual and the self as ideal. These ideas have been taken forward and developed further by self-concept theorists such as Carl Rogers who have used these constructs to measure how individuals perceive themselves and what they aspire to become. Empirical techniques used to measure self-concept have often been based upon the use of lists of adjectives, such as aggressive, argumentative, confident, dependable, sensitive, sociable, strong, and so on, with respondents being asked to indicate whether or how much each description represents a defining characteristic of their own personality (Rogers, 1951).

The distance between the actual self and the ideal self has frequently been adopted as a key measure because it indicates the extent to which an individual is dissatisfied with their current state. Further examination of specific attributes can reveal more clearly where the key areas of dissatisfaction exist. If an individual is unhappy with his or her character in terms of specific attributes, this dissatisfaction might lead them to seek out ways of improving or changing those aspects of the self they do not like (Rogers, 1961).

In the context of marketing, the discrepancy between the self and the ideal self can indicate where brand promotion messages can offer a means to facilitate change and move towards achieving consumers' ideal self-images. In a classic study, Birdwell (1969) found that car purchases were influenced by the goodness of fit perceived by consumers between their own self-images and the product-image.

Self-concept studies have generally examined the degree of congruence between self-image and product-image (Sirgy, 1980; Sirgy & Danes, 1982). The more these two image concepts are in synchrony, the greater the likelihood that the brand in question will be liked and purchased by the consumer. Some researchers have found that the 'ideal self-image', defined by "what I would like to be" is an important benchmark for comparison with product-image. As the distance between these two perceptions, as measured by aggregate agreement scores on defining descriptive terms, grows smaller, so the perception of similarity increases and this in turn predicts an increased likelihood of preference and purchase (Delozier, 1971; Delozier & Tillman, 1972). This notion of self-image/product-image congruity being critical has not always received empirical support in terms of accurate prediction of product purchases (Green, Maheshwari & Rao, 1969).

Other research has indicated that the 'social self-image', defined by the way an individual would really like to be seen by others, represents a good benchmark for comparison with product-image. As the degree of congruence between these two concepts gets closer, so then the likelihood of product purchase increases (Maheshwari, 1974). Elsewhere, Dolich (1969) found that both the actual self and the ideal self can play a part in product preferences and purchases. He found that for products such as beer, cigarettes, bars of soap, and toothpaste, his participants preferred brands that rated similar to both their actual and ideal self-concepts.

Self-image is a complex concept and it can vary with the social setting in which an individual is present. In other words, individuals can hold different impressions of themselves in different situations. They might, for example, have great self-confidence among certain of their friends, but feel over-awed by others at work. Hence, even though self-image might be an important point of reference for the consumer when considering which of two brands to buy, that self-image could change depending upon whether they are alone or in the company of others with whom they feel confident or inferior.

Some brands are acquired because they have specific symbolic value, often referred to as 'badge value'. This means that it might convey specific impressions about one's taste or status. If that badge value addresses a specific area of the actual self that is perceived to fall short of the ideal self, its acquisition might play a part in enhancing the way the consumer feels about their personality. The importance of symbols and the propensity to take such concepts into account in determining how to behave has been the focus of a branch of social study called symbolic interactionism. This approach to the study of consumer behaviour can provide insights not possible through more standard market research techniques. The reason for this is that it explores the cultural symbolism of products and brands and can define whether some symbols command significant value among some communities. If a product or brand can present can resonate with a key cultural symbol, this could enhance its attractiveness to members of a community who might seek to enhance their own self-concept through its purchase.

Self-confidence is an important aspect of self. It has been shown to be linked to patterns of consumer behaviour and product preferences both directly and via interactions with other aspects of personality. One investigation found that self-confidence interacted with the personality attribute of venturesomeness to influence purchases choices. Items likely to enhance lifestyle and the consumer's own brand image were more sought by college students who were more adventurous and inclined to adopt innovations. Another factor—the tendency of individuals to make rational, thoughtful decisions about what to buy to ensure that they made a good, ordered fit within their lives—drove consumers to seek more information in advance about products before making a decision about which ones to buy (Goldsmith, 1983). The association between higher self-esteem and a tendency to seek new experiences, in turn linked to a tolerance for ambiguity, and seeking more information about products before purchase was confirmed in another study with American women (Schaninger & Sciglimpaglia, 1981)

Big Five Personality Theory

The emergence of the 'Big Five' model of human personality represented an attempt by psychologists to draw together a variety of different enduring psychological dispositions into a more holistic and comprehensive framework of analysis (Costa & McCrae, 1985, 1992; Goldberg, 1992; Wiggins, 1996; John, 1999). The five personality factors are: Extraversion (versus introversion), Agreeableness (or sociability), Conscientiousness (or orderliness), Neuroticism (indicating emotional stability), and Intellect/Imagination (or Openness to Experience).

Extraverts were conceived as outgoing individuals and in need of high levels of stimulation. Their opposites are introverts, who tend to be shy and withdrawn and prefer quieter environments. High scorers on Agreeableness prefer to get along with other people and seek out positive, supportive, and conciliatory relationships, and avoid confrontation. Those high in Conscientiousness are well-organised and prefer order over chaos. They like to plan and work efficiently. Individuals who score high on Neuroticism are sensitive to stressful situations, are prone to get anxious, and can display unstable emotional reactions across a range of circumstances. High scorers on Intellect or Openness to Experience are curious and exploratory individuals who seek to understand the world better and are open to new ways of thinking.

The Big Five model has drawn upon a wide range of personality theory and research. Previous models of personality had been developed that had embraced some, but not all, of the Big Five. The arrival of this five-factor solution for modelling human personality was greeted by widespread acceptance (Larsen & Buss, 2010). This acceptance spread into the consumer field. As this book has shown already, there has been extensive interest in the potential of psychological classifiers of people as an underpinning of models of consumer segmentation. Personality measures in the consumer context were often developed for specific projects with the intention of producing psychological classifications of consumers for specific products or services. Yet, those measures met with mixed success as predictors of eventual consumer preferences and choices.

The adoption of personality measures developed outside the consumer context that had been extensively tested through clinical diagnoses and empirical studies could yield consumer segmentation variables with greater theoretical and methodological robustness and construct validity, and therefore were better able to offer explanations of consumer behaviour. Thus, researchers started to explore these personality trait measures in relation to consumer activities in a number of product fields (Mowen, 2000; Egan & Taylor, 2010; Lin, 2010). The frequent use and testing of personality measures in clinical settings where they were used to explain psychological disorders and abnormal behavioural dispositions meant that it was logical that these individual difference variables would also be extended to the study of abnormal consumer activities, such as compulsive shopping.

Psychographics can reveal important information about consumers that demographics are unable to yield. Most especially, psychological measures can reveal how consumers are motivated to seek out particular products and services and then the features of specific branded commodity variants that make them stand out from the rest. Evidence presented later will show that personality attributes are related to extreme forms of consumer behaviour, such as compulsive buying, and also that in choosing brands, consumers are often drawn to brands that have 'personalities' that match their own.

Two things have been missing from psychological segmentation measures based on personality traits. The first is a consensus among personality psychologists about the core characteristics of human personality. The second is statistical data showing the distribution of personality types across whole populations. The emergence of the Big Five personality framework has represented a movement to address the first of these issues (Costa & McCrae, 1992a; Goldberg, 1992). The second has also been investigated with attempts to produce normative, population-wide data concerning the distribution of these personality traits.

Researchers have explored the distribution of these personality types across cultures (McCrae, 2001; McCrae & Terrecciano, 2008; Schmitt, Allik, McCrae & Benet-Martinez, 2007). Evidence emerged that Extraversion tended to be lower in Asia than other parts of the world. Openness to Experience tended to be highest in Central and South American countries. Meanwhile, in Europe, Neuroticism tended to be higher in eastern and southern European countries than in other European countries (Allik & McCrae, 2004; McCrae, Terracciano & 79 Members of the Personality Profiles of Cultures Project, 2005).

What would also be of interest to professional marketers wishing to utilise these kinds of personality dimensions as normative consumer segmentation tools within national markets are data concerning the distribution of core personality traits across different regions within the same country. One important study has examined regional variations across the United States on a range of political, economic, social, and health indicators. Rentfrow, Gosling, Jokela, Stillwell, Kosinski & Potter (2013) collected data for 48 American states from five samples that totalled nearly 1.6 million people.

Data were collected over time from each sample covering a total time period spanning 1999 to 2010. Different versions of the Big Five Personality Inventory were used across these surveys, with shorter forms being used in some but not in others. Other population statistics were collected for each state using secondary data sources, and these included state populations' demographic profiles, political voting profiles, religious profiles, crime rates, wealth, residential mobility, health status and well-being, and educational and occupational attainment.

State-level scores for each personality trait were calculated and a cluster analysis was used to discover which states exhibited the greatest similarities and differences on specific personality dimensions. Personality and other population data were used to identify three superordinate clusters of states that were labelled as 'Friendly and Conventional', 'Relaxed and Creative', and 'Temperamental and Uninhibited'.

Friendly and Conventional states tended to be located in Middle America and exhibited relatively high levels of Extraversion, Agreeableness, and Conscientiousness and fairly low levels of Neuroticism and very low levels of Openness to Experience. These areas were populated by people with low levels of education, little wealth, economically flat communities, and low social tolerance. Family values were paramount and religiosity was high. The people living in these locations were not generally healthy in their lifestyles and did not welcome change.

Relaxed and Creative states were found mostly along the West Coast and Rocky Mountains. People here were characterised by being relatively low on Extraversion and Agreeableness, very low on Neuroticism, and very high on Openness to Experience. The population here was racially more mixed and people were quite well off, well educated, and had create economically vibrant communities. Their politics was more liberal than conservative. They exhibited moderate religiosity and tended to lead healthy lifestyles.

Temperamental and Uninhibited states were found mainly along the Atlantic Coast and Northeast. People were characterised by being low in Extraversion, very low in Agreeableness and Conscientiousness, very high on Neuroticism, and fairly high on Openness to Experience. Populations here were well educated and affluent and tended also to be older. Religion was observed, but not in the highly conservative way of Middle America, and people were political liberal.

This research will need to be refreshed from time to time to track any changes that might occur as a result of migration, just as is necessary with demographic profiling using census data. An analysis of regional populations that include personality dimensions as well demographic descriptors and social, political, and economic indicators yields a much richer profile for marketers and commercial businesses than traditional population profiles. Given further evidence concerning how the Big Five personality traits can also mediated consumers' buying habits and brand preferences, population-wide personality data can guide marketing decisions in more precise ways by drawing upon the kinds of consumer-related motives and needs that characterise people in different regions.

Big Five and Compulsive Buying

Compulsive buying is manifested as repetitive and uncontrolled buying behaviour over which the consumer seems to have little or no control (Kollat &

Willett, 1960; Ridgway, Kukar-Kinney & Monroe, 2008; Tifferet & Herstein, 2012)). Psychiatrists identified this behaviour in the earliest days of the mass consumer society (Kraepelin, 1915). It was only in the 1980s, however, that systematic research really took form into this phenomenon (Faber & O'Guinn, 1988; O'Guinn & Faber, 1989; Scherhorn, 1990). A great deal of research on this topic has focused on trying to identify the psychological, social, and cultural factors that might cause this behaviour. A number of personality traits have been statistically related to impulsive buying behaviour, including impulsiveness, locus of control, narcissism, and sensation seeking (see DeSarbo & Edwards, 1996; Rose, 2007; Watson, 2009), as well as psychological conditions such as depression (Ergin, 2010). Other characteristics that have been identified with compulsive buying also have indirect links to Big Five personality dimensions. These included approval seeking, dependency, propensity to fantasize, and perfectionism (Nathan, 1988; O'Guinn & Faber, 1989; Peele, 1990).

Neuro-psychology researchers have begun to identify neurobiological systems in consumers that underpin the nature of their reactions to potential buying situations. The Behavioural Inhibition System (BIS) and Behavioural Activation System (BAS) govern responses to settings in which rewards or punishments are anticipated. The BAS, for instance, is sensitive to stimuli that signal potential rewards associated with specific behaviours and also relief from punishment. These conditions create a disposition towards approach behaviour which in a consumer context means an increased probability of trying to make a purchase. The BIS produces the opposite reaction. These systems are hardwired into a person's cognitive neurological apparatus in their brain and represent an enduring physiological characteristic that can serve as an individual difference variable (Rothbart, Ahadi & Evans, 2000).

Individuals who are hardwired to exhibit strong positive reactance towards consumption-related stimuli are more likely to engage in repeat purchases and, in extreme cases, may demonstrate compulsive buying behaviour. It is important to know how to spot individuals with these biological predispositions to react compulsively to marketing-related stimuli because this behaviour is known to be linked to the onset of clinically depressive and other unhealthy symptoms later in life (Rose, 2007; Claes, Bijttebier, Van Den Eynde, Mitchell, Faber, de Zwaan & Mueller, 2010). Further evidence from Germany revealed that two distinct Big Five clusters emerged among individuals already diagnosed with compulsive buying behaviour and the second of these exhibited the strongest compulsive tendencies. These individuals exhibited high scores of Neuroticism and lower scores on the other four personality dimensions compared with those in the first cluster (Mueller, Claes, Mitchell, Wonderlich, Crosby & de Zwain, 2010).

In tests of the Big Five, compulsive buying behaviour was found to be predicted by these personality variables. The first such published test of this type found that consumers that score low in Conscientiousness and Neuroticism (Emotional Stability) and high in Agreeableness were more likely to engage in compulsive purchases (Mowen & Spears, 1999). In a follow-up investigation, just two of the Big Five traits exhibited a significant statistical relationship with compulsive buying behaviour, Agreeableness and Neuroticism (Mowen, 2000). A further study conducted around the same time three of the Big Five factors, high scores on Extraversion and Intellect (Openness to Experience), but lower scores on Agreeableness (contradicting earlier findings) predicted compulsive buying (Balabanis, 2001).

In an attempt to resolve some of the differences between the previous studies' findings, Mikolajczak-Degrauwe, Brengman, Wauters, & Rossi (2012) collected data from nearly 2,300 respondents ages 18 and older in Belgium. The respondents were distinguished into those with high and low propensities to display compulsive buying behaviour. They then completed a short form of the Big Five personality inventory to yield scores on each of the five factors. It was hypothesized in advance that compulsive buyers would score higher on Extraversion and Neuroticism and lower on Agreeableness, Conscientiousness, and Intellect than non-compulsive buyers. These expectations were all confirmed. The agreeableness-compulsive buying outcome disagreed with one earlier study, but this difference was explained by the way in which compulsive buying was measured, with a more general disposition being assessed in the current study.

Big Five and Sustainable Consumerism

There has been a big drive towards responsible consumerism, with a focus on encouraging consumers to buy products that are environmentally sustainable (Barr, 2008; Schrader & Thogersen, 2011). Demographic differences, mostly linked to gender, have emerged in relation to this responsible value orientation towards consumer behaviour. Women have tended to be more environmentally conscious than men when shopping (Eagly, Dickman, Johannesen-Schmidt & Koenig, 2004; Koos, 2011). Evidence has also emerged that personality profiles are important in this context and can differentiate between individuals with strong and weak concerns about the environment (Endler & Rosenstein, 1997; Bosnjak, Bratko, Galesic & Tuten, 2007).

Environmental concern among German consumers was greatest among those with higher scores on the Agreeableness and Openness to Experience dimensions of the Big Five Inventory. In a follow-up experiment with university students, support for sustainable consumer behaviour was not only more prominent, as expected, among women, there was a further tendency for higher scores of Agreeableness, regardless of gender, to be linked to stronger commitment to environmental friendly consumerism (Luchs & Mooradian, 2012)

Big Five and Product Choices

The Big Five personality factors have been examined in relation to several areas of consumerism. These include shopping behaviour and buying a home. The hypothetical possibility that personality dimensions are related to shopping activity is logical given the psychological nature of much of the research into why people shop and how they make their choices. Two key sets of factors directly have been examined that are linked directly to shopping behaviour, and these are consumers' motives and the outcomes that shopping and the consumption of specific products and services can produce.

Consumers may have a number of reasons for shopping, and these can broadly be divided into instrumental or utilitarian purposes and hedonic (often linked to social) reasons. People engage in shopping because they need to make specific purchases for very practical needs. Thus, purchases of food and drink products, household cleaning and personal hygiene products, and household appliances and equipment cater to very basic human needs linked to survival and security. Other practical reasons for shopping may relate to high-level needs such as relationship maintenance and self-identity. Hence, we may buy gifts for family and friends for special occasions or display gratitude for things they may have done for us. We may buy clothes, accessories, and cosmetics to enhance our appearance, appear more attractive to others, or to show off our tastes or make statements about our social status.

We might go shopping as an activity to engage in with family and friends as a social occasion. Shopping then moves beyond being a behaviour that is instrumental in nature in terms of buying products or services for which we have practical needs and becomes a leisure activity or pastime. Very often in this context, shopping is a source of pleasure and this becomes an end goal in itself.

Understanding these different reasons that drive shopping requires some reference to consumer psychology. This means that we need to examine whether such behaviours display consistent patterns over time for specific individuals. If they do, this may reveal something about the character of the individual consumer. The nature of an individual's shopping behaviour not just in terms of the type of products that are purchased, but also in relation to decisions about how to shop, when and where to shop, and who to going shopping with might also reveal deeper-seated characteristics about consumers concerning the type of person they are (Tauber, 1972; Mooradian & Olver, 1996). Further studies have suggested it may be possible to combine personality and lifestyle measures with reported motives for shopping to develop a higher-order model of explanation for consumer behaviour (Mooradian & Olver, 1997)

Some degree of interest has centred on the nature of relationships between core personality factors (such as the Big Five) and instrumental versus hedonic reasons for shopping. Further, researchers have explored whether the Big Five can be clustered into fewer, even higher-order personality variables that then exhibit relationships with these two shopping orientations. Personality research had indicated that personality structure can be even more hierarchical than the Big Five and their constituent components (Digman, 1990, 1997).

Following on from this observation, Guido (2006) conducted small-scale research with consumers in Italy in which they completed a 63-item shopping motives questionnaire and further items designed to measure the Big Five personality dimensions. The five personality factors, Emotional Stability, Openness to Experience, Agreeableness, Extraversion, and Conscientiousness were subsequently related to the factor outcomes of a 12-factor shopping motives solution. The latter were broadly divided into 'instrumental' and 'hedonic' motive types. Guido found that the personality traits of Openness to Experience, Agreeableness, and Extraversion were all positively correlated with 'hedonic' shopping orientations, whereas Emotional Stability and Conscientiousness were positively correlated with 'instrumental' shopping orientations. These findings indicated that consumers characterised by being sociable, outgoing, and experience-seeking sought pleasure from shopping. For these consumers, it appeared, shopping was an enjoyable end in itself. Shoppers who scored higher on Emotional Stability and Conscientiousness were driven more by satisfaction of specific instrumental needs. These consumers went shopping for a specific purpose and with the objective of obtaining specific commodities.

The biggest single purchase most consumers will ever make is buying a home. Acquiring a home is not invariably dependent upon making a purchase because many people rent rather than own their home. The first home a person knows is usually the one in which they are brought up by their parents or carers. Upon reaching adulthood, children leave the 'family' home of their childhood to live independently. At that point, they must reach a decision about where to live. This means deciding on the type of property to move into as well as the location.

The nature of a property usually comes down to whether it is a house or an apartment. It might be an old building or a new building. A house can vary between being detached, semi-detached, or terraced. In a terrace, it can be at the end of terrace or mid-terrace. In a semi-detached arrangement, the degree of attachment to another property can also vary. If the dwelling is an apartment or flat, it can be located in a purpose-built block or in a property that was once a house. In terms of location, the property might be situated in the centre of a large urban area, or in the suburbs, or in a rural setting. In a rural setting, the property might be situated in a small community, or isolated with no neighbours close by. All these different structural and location factors represent a typology that can be used to define people.

The type of property will also give rise to issues linked to patterns of consumerism. In an inner-city location, there may be more acute security issues, which mean that steps must be taken to ensure the property cannot be broken into. The occupant of a property of this type might be in the market to purchase burglar alarms, timer lighting systems, additional locks for doors and windows, and a high fence around the boundary of the property. More of these items might be needed in the case of a house than a flat in a purpose-built block.

The occupant of a property situated in a remote rural location will need their own transportation because public transport may not be available. This occupant will therefore be more likely to need a car than someone living in an urban location with plentiful access to buses and trains.

A suburban dweller living in a house with a large garden will be in the market for plants and garden maintenance products such as garden furniture, a barbeque, a lawn mower, gardening tools, hose pipes and sprinklers, fertilizer, pesticide and herbicide products, and so on. An apartment dweller would usually have less need for these products unless they lived on the ground floor of a conversion that had its own garden.

In the context of the psychology of consumerism, established personality measures have been used to profile the choices people make with their homes. These decisions might concern the type of property acquired and the way the property is decorated and furnished inside and out. Personality factors have also been related to financial arrangements concerning real estate purchases. In the latter case, the significance of personality arises from its relationship to risk taking.

Research has emerged to show that relatively high and low risk-taking personality types differ, in expected directions, in their personal property purchase preferences, particularly in regard to choices of property financing. Thus, whether an individual chooses to rent or buy, and in the case of making a property purchase, whether the buyer chooses to enter into specific types of mortgage arrangements, is related to their personality traits. Ben Shahar & Golan (2014) demonstrated these relationships with micro-level data obtained in Israel and macro-level data from the United States. In both instances, questions about real estate acquisition were used alongside the Big Five Inventory personality test.

The Big Five personality model has identified five dimensions of human personality. This instrument was not developed originally to classify consumers, but it does have some potential relevance as a consumer-typing instrument. The five primary personality dimensions are: Extraversion (versus introversion), Agreeableness (versus antagonism/argumentativeness), Conscientiousness (versus lack of order or direction), Neuroticism (versus emotional stability), and Openness (versus closedness) to new experiences (Costa & McCrae, 1992b; John & Srivastava, 1999).

According to Ben Sharhar and Golan, neuroticism was known to correlate negatively with risk-taking, and they hypothesized that high scorers might be expected to prefer the stability of home ownership over renting. In making property purchases, high scorers on this dimension are also likely to opt for fixed rate mortgages over variable rate agreements because of the greater certainty they offer. High scorers on the Conscientiousness scale seek greater order and efficiency in their lives. These are people who can delay gratification and are therefore likely to prefer longer repayment terms when buying a property with a mortgage.

Those individuals high in openness seek new experiences and welcome fresh ideas for investment. They are likely to feel more comfortable with longer-term investment choices. Individuals scoring high on Agreeableness tend to be warm and forgiving in their nature and seek conciliation or positive social relationships. These attributes were known to correlate with weaker propensities to take risks and so were hypothesized again to encourage the adoption of lower-risk property acquisition and purchase arrangements. With Extraversion, there was no relevant evidence to lead to any specific predictions about how this dimension might shape real estate choices.

Data from just over 1,100 online respondents in Israel and from secondary analyses of American data available through other sources confirmed the predictions made above. Personality types with low-risk propensities, such as high scorers on neuroticism and openness, preferred ownership over renting and fixed-rate mortgages, and prefer property investments over stock investments. Extraversion and openness both correlated negatively with choosing stock investments over property.

For the macro-level analysis, Ben Sharhar and Golan adapted the data collected by Rentfrow et al (2013) reported earlier, which they combined with data on property rental and purchase patterns at a state level across the US. They found a relationship between average state scores on openness and neuroticism and choosing the lower risk option of a lower loan to property value when making property purchases. Higher average levels of Agreeableness were associated with the expected preference for home ownership over renting. In general, personality dimensions associated with low risk taking were found at this macro-level to predict the choice of lower-risk property acquisition arrangements.

Another aspect of consumer decision-making that cuts across product types is the design of a product and its packaging. Research has shown that the Big Five personality traits can predict consumers' preferences based on design attributes. Product appeal is influenced by emotional reactions triggered by design-related attributes. Design features help brands stand apart from their competitors in crowded markets (Desmet, 2003). This visibility can be vitally important at the point of sale, where a brand is positioned physically alongside its rivals. Design features attach aesthetic value to brands which in turn influence the probability of purchase (Hollins & Pugh, 1990; Schmitt & Simonson, 1997).

The relationship between brand design and emotional reactions of consumers has led some theorists to propose that it is pertinent to examine the potential mediating role of personality factors in this relationship (Bloch, Brunel & Arnold, 2003). The use of psychological tests to measure human judgements about the aesthetic quality of objects has been in play across a range of settings since the mid-20th century (Graves, 1948; Meier, 1963; Eysenck, 1983; Gotz, 1985; Bloch, 1995). Research has discovered that aesthetic judgements can indicate whether a product is liked and generates an urge to purchase on the part of a consumer (Bloch et al., 2003).

Early tests using personality scales to predict judgements about visual works of art met with mixed success (Gotz, Borisy, Lynn & Eysenck, 1979; Frois & Eysenck, 1995). Before rushing to dismiss the potential value of personality traits as mediators of aesthetic evaluations of brands, it is important to note that these initial inquiries examined a limited range both of visual stimuli and personality traits. Evidence has emerged that when people judge the aesthetic qualities of works of art, this process is part cognitive and part emotional. It is theoretically reasonable to consider that the emotional part of the judgemental equation in particular could be moderated by specific personality characteristics (Leder, Belke Oeberst &.Augustin, 2004).

In a consumer context, therefore, some researchers have concluded that any study of individual differences in judgements about the appeal of brands should include a comprehensive suite of personality measures to cast the net wide in the hope that some personality traits will emerge that have predictive value in terms of consumers' product-related responses. Myszkowski & Storme (2012) took up this challenge by recruiting a small sample of French college students to complete the Big Five Inventory (John, 1990; John & Srivastava, 1999) and another instrument, called the Visual Product Aesthetics questionnaire, which had been designed to measure the propensity of consumers to choose products on the basis of their aesthetic attributes. The aesthetics judgement instrument had been developed by Bloch et al., 2003).

The Big Five Inventory provided measures of five personality traits: Agreeableness, Conscientiousness, Extraversion, Neuroticism, and Openness. The Visual Product Aesthetics instruments measured the value individuals attached to product design (Value), how much they felt able to evaluate product/brand design (Acumen), and whether design features would make them purchase a product (Response). Scores on these dimensions were then intercorrelated.

Value correlated positively with Agreeableness and negatively with Openness to experience. Thus, outgoing people with less openness to new experiences reported that they attached importance to the product/brand design when judging a product. Lower Openness to experience was also related to self-belief in being able to judge the aesthetic quality of a product or brand design. Finally, people with lower Openness to new experiences also reported having a stronger urge to buy products/brands when confronted by really attractive design features.

This research provided some indicative evidence that personality traits could be linked to the kinds of judgements consumers make about products or brands on the basis of their design features. There are some notes of caution here, however. The sample was both modest in scale, demographically not very diverse, and statistically non-representative of any particular consumer community. The consumption measures focused on personally reported perceptions of the use of product design features to assess those products. There is no evidence of actual purchase behaviour being influenced by such product-related perceptions or mediated by personality characteristics.

The Promise and Limits of Personality Theory

The study of personality is concerned with understanding lasting dispositions that define an individual's character and enduring behaviour patterns. The value of personality theories, models, and related tests to consumer marketing research exists in their ability to not only describe consumer behaviour patterns, but also to explain and predict them. There is a further question to be answered about the relevance of these measures to understanding consumer behaviour.

A personality test that has been extensively clinically and empirically verified might, for instance, be capable of providing a measure of a person's achievement-related orientations. This measure is only of value in consumer settings when 'achievement drive' is a recognisably relevant motive in relation to the purchase of a specific commodity. It is important in the first instance to know that personality measures established in clinical contexts can be effectively used in different settings, such as consumerism (Bowers, 1973). It is then necessary to validate those same measures in terms of their explanatory and predictive capabilities in relation to the use of specific products or services. In the absence of established relevance as such, the usefulness of personality measures in explaining consumers' product preferences and consumption patterns is likely to be limited (Kassarjian, 1973).

What this means is that personality measures need to be tested not simply in relation to blandly stated product variant preferences or reported frequency of use, but perhaps more poignantly, in relation to specific consumer evaluations of a brand, expectations of a product/service, and perceptions of different aspects of performance and gratification. These intermediary measures are important because they represent variables that affect product/service choice and comprise attributes that conceptually can be linked back to personality dispositions.

References

Adler, A. (1964) *The Individual Psychology of Alfred Adler*. H. L. Ansbacher & R. R. Ansbacher (Eds.). New York, NY: Harper Torchbooks.

Adler, A. (1979) *Superiority and Social Interest: A Collection of Later Writings*. H. L. Ansbacher & R. R. Ansbacher (Eds.). New York, NY: W. W. Norton.

Allik, J., & McCrae, R. R. (2004) Toward a geography of personality traits: Patterns of profiles across 36 cultures. *Journal of Cross-Cultural Psychology*, 35, 13–28.

Allport, G. W., & Odbert, H. S. (1936) Trait names: A psycholexical study. *Psychological Monographs*, 47, 211.

Alpert, M. I. (1972) Personality and the determinants of product choice. *Journal of Marketing Research*, 9, 98–92.

Balabanis, G. (2001) The relationship between lottery ticket and scratch-card buying behaviour, personality, and other compulsive behaviours. *Journal of Consumer Behaviour*, 2(1), 7–22.

Barr, S. (2008) *Environment and Society: Sustainability, Policy and the Citizen.* Burlington: Ashgate Publishing.

Ben Shahar, D., & Golan, R. (2014) Real estate and personality. *Journal of Behavioral and Experimental Economics*, 53, 111–119.

Berry, N. (1988) Revitalizing brands: The search for brand personality and value. *Journal of Consumer Marketing*, 5(3), 15–20.

Birdwell, A. E. (1969) A study of the influence of image congruence on consumer choice. *Journal of Business*, 41, 76–78.

Bloch, P. H. (1995) Seeking the ideal form: Product design and consumer response. *Journal of Marketing*, 59, 16–29.

Bloch, P. H., Brunel, F. F., & Arnold, T. J. (2003) Individual differences in the centrality of visual product aesthetics: Concept and measurement. *Journal of Consumer Research*, 16, 461–471.

Bosnjak, M., Bratko, D., Galesic, M., & Tuten, T. (2007) Consumer personality and individual differences: Revitalizing a temporarily abandoned field. *Journal of Business Research*, [Special Issue: Consumer Personality and Individual Differences] 60(6), 587–589.

Bowers, T. A. (1973) Newspaper political advertising and the agenda-setting function. *Journalism Quarterly*, 50, 552–556.

Cattell, R. B., Marshall, M. B., & Geordiades, S. (1957) Personality and motivation: Structure and measurement. *Journal of Personality Disorders*, 19(1), 53–67.

Claes, L., Bijttebier, P., Van Den Eynde, F., Mithcell, J. E., Faber, R., de Zwaan, M., & Mueller, A. (2010) Emotional reactivity and self-regulation in relation to compulsive buying. *Personality and Individual Differences*, 49, 526–530.

Cohen, J. B. (1967) An interpersonal orientation to the study of consumer behavior. *Journal of Marketing Research*, 4, 270–278.

Cohen, J. B. (1968) The role of personality in consumer behaviour. In H. H. Kassarjian & T. S. Robertson (Eds.) *Perspectives in Consumer behaviour*, pp. 220–234. Glenview, IL: Scott Foresman.

Cohen, J. B., & Golden, E. (1972) Informational social influence and product evaluation. *Journal of Applied Psychology*, 56(1), 54–59.

Costa, P. T., & McCrae, R. R. (1985) *The NEO Personality Inventory*. Odessa, FL: Psychological Assessment Resources.

Costa, P. T., & McCrae, R. R. (1992a) *The NEO Personality Inventory Manual*. Odessa, FL: Psychological Assessment Resources.

Costa, P. T., & McCrae, R. R. (1992b) Normal personality assessment in clinical practice. The NEO personality inventory. *Psychological Assessment*, 4(1), 5–13.

Delozier, W. (1971) *A Longitudinal Study of the Relationship Between Self-image and Brand Image*. Unpublished doctoral dissertation, University of North Carolina at Chapel Hill.

Delozier, W., & Tillman, R. (1972) Self-image concepts: Can they be used to design marketing programs. *Southern Journal of Business*, 7, 9–15. DeSarbo, W. S., &

Edwards, E. A. (1996) Typologies of compulsive buying behaviour: A constrained clusterwise regression approach. *Journal of Consumer Psychology, 5*(3), 231–262.

Desmet, P. M. A. (2003) A multilayered model of product emotions. *The Design Journal, 6*(2), 4–13.

Digman, J. M. (1990) Personality structure: Emergence of the Five-Factor model. *Annual Review of Psychology,* 41, 417–440.

Digman, J. M. (1997) Higher-order factors of the Big Five. *Journal of Personality and Social Psychology, 73*(6), 1246–1256.

Dolich, I. J. (1969) Congruence relationships between self-images and product-brands. *Journal of Marketing Research Society,* 6, 80–84.

Durgee, J. F. (1988) Understanding brand personality. *Journal of Consumer Marketing, 5*(3), 21–25.

Eagly, A. H., Dickman, A. B., Johannesen-Schmidt, M. C., & Koenig, A. M. (2004) Gender gaps in socio-political attitudes: A social psychological analysis. *Journal of Personality and Social Psychology,* 87, 796–816.

Egan, V., & Taylor, D. (2010) Shoplifting, unethical consumer behaviour, and personality. *Personality and Individual Differences, 48*(8), 878–884.

Endler, N., & Rosenstein, A. (1997) Evolution of the personality construct in marketing and its applicability to contemporary personality research. *Journal of Consumer Psychology,* 6, 55–66.

Ergin, E. A. (2010) Compulsive buying behaviour tendencies: The case of Turkish consumers. *African Journal of Business Management, 4*(3), 333–338.

Eysenck, H. J. (1983) Visual aesthetic sensitivity and its measurement. In M. Russ (Ed.) *The Arts: A Way of Knowing,* pp. 105–125. Oxford, UK: Pergamon Press.

Faber, R. J., & O'Guinn, T. C. (1988) Compulsive consumption and credit abuse. *Journal of Consumer Policy, 11*(1), 97–109.

Faber, R. J., & O'Guinn, T. C. (1992) A clinical screener for compulsive buying. *Journal of Consumer Research,* 19, 459–469.

Frois, J. P., & Eysenck, H. J. (1995) The visual aesthetic sensitivity test applied to Portuguese children and fine arts students. *Creativity Research Journal,* 8, 277–284.

Goldberg, L. R. (1992) The development of markers for the Big-Five factor structure. *Psychological Assessment, 4*(1), 26–42. Available at: https://robertoigarza.files.wordpress.com/2008/10/art-predicting-personality-with-social-media-golbeck-robles-turner-2010.pdf

Goldsmith, R. (1983) Psychographics and new product adoption: An exploratory study. *Perceptual and Motor Skills,* 57, 1071–1076.

Gotz, K. O. (1985) *VAST: Visual Aesthetic Sensitivity Test,* 4th Ed. Dusseldorf, Germany: Concept Verlag.

Gotz, K. O., Borisy, A. R., Lynn, R., & Eysenck, H. J. (1979) A new visual aesthetic sensitivity test. I. Construction and psychometric properties. *Perceptual and Motor Skills, 49*(3), 795–802.

Graves, M. (1948) *Design Judgement Test.* New York, NY: Psychological Corp.

Green, P. E., Maheshwari, A., & Rao, V. R (1969) Dimensional interpretation and configuration invariance in multidimensional scaling: An empirical study. *Journal of the Market Research Society,* 11, 343–360.

Green, P. E., Wind, Y., & Jain, A. K. (1972) A note on measurement of social-psychological belief systems. *Journal of Marketing Research,* 9, 204–208.

Guido, G. (2006) Shopping motives, big five factors and the hedonic/utilitarian shopping value: An integration and factorial study. *Innovative Marketing*, 2, 57–67.

Hollins, B., & Pugh, S. (1990) *Successful Product Design*. London, UK: Butterworths.

Horney, K. (1937) *The Neurotic Personality of Our Time*. New York, NY: Norton.

John, D. R. (1999) Consumer socialization of children: A retrospective look at twenty-five years of research. *Journal of Consumer Research*, 26, 183–213.

John, O. P. (1990) The 'Big Five' factor taxonomy: Dimensions of personality in the natural language and in questionnaires. In O. P. John, R. W. Robins, & L. A. Pervin (Eds.) *Handbook of Personality: Theory and Research*, pp. 66–100. New York, NY: Guilford Press.

John, O. P., & Srivastava, S. (1999) The Big Five trait inventory: History, measurement and theoretical perspectives. In L. A. Pervin & O. P. John (Eds.) *Handbook of Personality: Theory and Research*, 2nd Ed., pp. 102–138. New York, NY: Guilford.

Kassarjian, H. H. (1973) Personality and consumer behaviour: A review. In H. H. Kassarjian & T. S. Robertson (Eds.) *Perspectives in Consumer Behaviour*, pp. 409–418. Glenview, IL: Scott, Foresman & Company.

Koos, S. (2011) Varieties of environmental labeling, market structures, and sustainable consumption across Europe: A comparative analysis of organizational and market supply. *Journal of Consumer Policy*, 34, 127–151.

Koponen, A. (1960) Personality characteristics of purchasers. *Journal of Advertising Research*, 1, 6–12.

Kraepelin, E. (1915) *Psychiatrie*, 8th Ed. Leipzig: Barth.

Krugman, H. E. (1967) The measurement of advertising involvement. *Public Opinion Quarterly*, 30, 583–596.

Larsen, R. J., & Buss, D. M. (2010) *Personality Psychology: Domains of Knowledge About Human Nature*. London, UK: MacGraw-Hill.

Leder, H., Belke, B., Oeberst, A., & Augustin, D. (2004) A model of aesthetic appreciation and aesthetic judgements. *British Journal of Psychology*, 95, 489–508.

Lin, L-Y. (2010) The relationship of consumer personality trait, brand personality and brand loyalty: An empirical study of toys and video game buyers. *Journal of Product and Brand Management*, 19(1), 4–18.

Luchs, M. G., & Mooradian, T. A. (2012) Sex, personality, and sustainable consumer behaviour: Elucidating the gender effect. *Journal of Consumer Policy*, 35, 127–144.

Maheshwari, A. D. (1974) *Self-Product Image Congruence: A Micro-Level Analysis*. Unpublished doctoral dissertation, University of Michigan, Ann Arbor, Michigan.

Matthews, G., Deary, I. J., & Whiteman, M. C. (2003) *Personality Traits*, 2nd Ed. Cambridge, UK: Cambridge University Press.

McCrae, R. R. (2001) Trait psychology and culture: Exploring intercultural comparisons. *Journal of Personality*, 69, 819–846.

McCrae, R. R., & Terracciano, A. (2008) The Five-Factor model and its correlates in individuals and cultures. In F. J. R. van de Vijver, D. A. van Hemert, & Y. H. Poortinga (Eds.) *Multilevel Analysis of Individuals and Cultures*, pp. 249–283. New York, NY: Taylor & Francis.

McCrae, R. R., Terracciano, A., & 79 Members of the Personality Profiles of Cultures Project (2005) Personality profiles of cultures: Aggregate personality traits. *Journal of Personality and Social Psychology*, 89, 407–425.

Meier, N. C. (1963) *The Meier Art test II, Aesthetic Perception: Preliminary Manual*. Iowa City: Bureau of Educational Research and Service, University of Iowa.

Mikolajczak-Degrauwe, K., Brengman, M., Wauters, B., & Rossi, G. (2012) Does personality affect compulsive buying? An application of the Big Five Personality Model. In G. Rossi (Ed). *Psychology Selected Papers*, pp. 131–144. Ghent, Belgium: Intech.

Mooradian, T. A., & Olver, J. M. (1996) Shopping motives and the Five Factor model: An integration and preliminary study. *Psychological Reports*, 78, 579–592.

Mooradian, T. A., & Olver, J. M. (1997) I can't get no satisfaction: The impact of personality and emotion on postpurchase processes. *Psychology and Marketing*, 14(4), 379–393.

Mowen, J. (2000) *The 3M Model of Motivation and Personality: Theory and Empirical Applications to Consumer Behaviour*. Boston, MA: Dordecht.

Mowen, J., & Spears, N. (1999) Understanding compulsive buying among college students: A hierarchical approach. *Journal of Consumer Psychology*, 8(4), 407–430.

Mueller, A., Claes, L., Mitchell, J. E., Wonderlich, S. A., Crosby, R. D., & de Zwain, M. (2010) Personality prototypes in individuals with compulsive buying based on the Big Five model. *Behaviour Research and Therapy*, 48, 930–935.

Myszkowski, N., & Storme, M. (2012) How personality traits predict design-driven consumer choices. *Europe's Journal of Psychology*, 8(4), 641–650.

Nathan, P. E. (1988) The addictive personality is the behaviour of the addict. *Journal of Consulting and Clinical Psychology*, 56, 183–188.

Noerager, J. P. (1979) An assessment of CAD—a personality instrument developed specifically for marketing research. *Journal of Marketing Research*, 16, 53–59.

O'Guinn, T. C., & Faber, R. J. (1989) Compulsive buying: A phenomonlogical exploration. *Journal of Consumer Research*, 16(2), 147–157.

Peele, S. (1990) *The Meaning of Addiction: Compulsive Experience and Its Interpretation*. Lexington, MA: Lexington.

Plummer, J. T. (1985) How personality can make a difference. *Journal of Advertising Research*, 24(6), 27–31.

Rentfrow, P. J., Gosling, S. D., Jokela, M., Stillwell, D. J., Kosinski, M., & Potter, J. (2013) Divided we stand: Three psychological regions of the United States and their political, economic, social, and health correlates. *Journal of Personality and Social Psychology*, 105(6), 996–1012.

Ridgway, N. M., Kukar-Kinney, M., & Monroe, K. B. (2008) An expanded conceptualization and a new measure of compulsive buying. *Journal of Consumer Research*, 35(4), 622–639.

Rogers, C. (1951) *Client-Centered Therapy: Its Current Practices, Implications and Theory*. London, UK: Constable.

Rogers, C. (1961) *On Becoming a Person: A Psychotherapist's View of Psychotherapy*. Boston, MA: Houghton Mifflin.

Rose, P. (2007) Mediators of the association between narcissism and compulsive buying: The roles of materialism and impulse control. *Psychology of Addictive Behaviours*, 21(4), 576–582.

Rothbart, M. K., Ahadi, S. A., & Evans, D. E. (2000) Temperament and personality: Origins and outcomes. *Journal of Personality and Social Psychology*, 78, 122–135.

Schaninger, C. M., & Sciglimpaglia, D. (1981) The influence of cognitive personality traits and demographics on consumer information acquisition. *Journal of Consumer Research*, 8(2), 208–216.

Scherhorn, G. (1990) The addictive trait in buying behaviour. *Journal of Consumer Policy*, 13(1), 33–51.

Schmitt, B. H., & Simonson, A. (1997) *Marketing Aesthetics: The Strategic Management of Brands, Identity and Image*. New York, NY: Free Press.

Schmitt, D. P., Allik, J. A., McCrae, R. R., & Benet-Martinez, V. (2007) The geographic distribution of Big Five personality traits: Patterns and profiles of human self-description across 56 nations. *Journal of Cross-Cultural Psychology*, 38, 173–212.

Schrader, U., & Thogersen, J. (2011) Putting sustainable consumption into practice. *Journal of Consumer Policy*, 34, 3–8.

Sirgy, M. J. (1980) Self-concept in relation to product preference and purchase intention. In V. V. Bellur (Ed.) *Development in Marketing Science*, Vol. 3, pp. 350–354. Marquette, MI: Academy of Marketing Science.

Sirgy, M. J., & Danes, J. E. (1982) Self-image/product-image congruence models: Testing selected models. *Advances in Consumer Research*, 9, 556–561. Association for Consumer Research.

Sullivan, H. S. (1935) *The Interpersonal Theory of Psychiatry*. New York, NY: Norton.

Tauber, E. M. (1972) Why do people shop? *Journal of Marketing,* 36, 46–49.

Tyagi, P. W. (1983) Validation of the Cad instrument: a replication. In R. P. Bagozzi & A. M. Tybout (Eds.) *Advances in Consumer Research,* Vol. 10, pp. 112–114. Ann Arbor, MI: Association for Consumer Research.

Watson, S. (2009) Credit card misuse, money attitudes and compulsive buying behaviours: A comparison of internal and external locus of control (LOC) consumers. *College Student Journal*, 43(2), 268–275.

Webster, F. E., & von Pechmann, F. (1970) A replication of the shopping list study. *Journal of Marketing*, 34, 61–67.

Wiggins, J. S. (1996) *The Five-Factor Model of Personality: Theoretical Perspectives*. New York, NY: Guilford Press.

Woodside, A. G., & Andress, R. (1975) CAD eight years later. *Journal of the Academy of Marketing Science*, 3, 309–313.

3 Custom-Built Normative Psychographic Consumer Typologies

Many applications of psychological profiling techniques or 'psychographics' to consumer contexts have comprised the development of custom-made instruments designed to measure consumers' interests in and motivations to obtain specific products or services. Rather than taking an established personality test linked to a specific personality theory that was originally developed outside a consumer context, marketing researchers have preferred to utilise psychological techniques to develop new classifications or typologies of consumers based on their attitudes, beliefs, perceptions, and intentions relating to specific types of commodities.

There have also been attempts to produce psychographic typologies that might be applied within commodity categories, but these efforts will be discussed in Chapter 4. This chapter will examine the history of this type of psychological profiling of consumers and its relative successes and failures. It will compare and contrast typologies that have tried to predict and explain domains of consumer behaviour, such as shopping and retail activity, product range typologies, and product-specific typologies.

Psychological theory has often still played an important part in influencing even the custom-built psychographics approaches. This has been especially true of those measures designed to yield normative typologies of consumer populations defined by the lifestyles people lead or aspire to adopt and the values systems they establish to underpin the rules and standards by which they live. Social psychological models of human needs and values have played a part in shaping key values and lifestyles concepts and associated models that have been applied to consumers. Maslow's description of a hierarchy of human needs model and the research on human values by Rokeach have been influential (Maslow, 1954, 1970; Rokeach, 1973).

Maslow's models envisaged a hierarchy of human needs, starting at the bottom with biological needs, followed by security needs, then social needs, esteem needs, and finally, self-actualisation needs. Each successively higher level of needs does not become a focus of attention until needs at the lower level have been satisfied. Biological needs are concerned with survival and drive the human organism to find food and drink to satisfy hunger and thirst. Once the individual has taken care of these needs, he or she then begins to think about finding shelter that offers protection and security from environmental dangers. When no longer preoccupied by hunger and thirst and by personal safety, the next priority becomes establishing social relationships with others. Such relationships address the need for companionship and this, in turn, is linked to survival of the species, which must procreate. After social needs become satisfied, the individual turns his or her attention to self-identity and personal standing in the community that emerge from social activities. Finally, once the individual is no longer driven by the need to acquire self-esteem, attention might then be turned to attaining a high level of excellence in an activity, which becomes a preoccupation and an end in itself (Maslow, 1954).

The influence of Maslow's model of human needs is interesting given the dearth of empirical evidence to support it. Although it offers an elegant description of needs and how they can emerge that seems entirely feasible, it has proven to be a difficult challenge to demonstrate this model scientifically in a consumer setting (Kahle, 1983; Kahle, Boush & Homer, 1989). Evidence that is consistent with Maslow's thinking has emerged from organisational contexts where comparisons of values and needs have been made at different levels of workforces (Moore & Weiss, 1955; Vroom, 1964). This body of research indicated that lower levels in workforces are less concerned about higher-level needs such as self-esteem and self-actualisation because they have not yet satisfied their lower-level needs.

Not all attempts to find supportive evidence have succeeded. One study examined the likelihood that greater success in achieving the satisfaction of lower-level needs and values would drive more attention to achievement of high-level aspirations and vice versa. The statistical relationships between these different need levels and satisfaction levels in each case were not significant (Alderfer, 1969). Even when individuals were deprived of the ability to satisfy lower-level needs, this did not result in a dramatic loss of interest in higher-level need satisfaction, as Maslow's model would predict (Trexler & Schuh, 1971; Graham & Balloun, 1973). Even when a person becomes hungry, it does not then mean that he or she suddenly loses interest in their social relationships with others or maintaining their social status (Kahle, Homer, O'Brien & Boush, 1997).

Rokeach (1973) developed a values survey that comprised 36 items in total, measuring two different types of values: Terminal Values and Instrumental values. Terminal Values measured goals and Instrumental Values measured means by which goals could be reached. Each sub-scale comprised 18 items. Examples of Terminal Values are: 'A comfortable life', 'A world at peace', 'Freedom', 'Happiness', 'True Friendship', 'Wisdom', 'Family Security', 'A sense of accomplishment', and 'Inner harmony'. Examples of Instrumental Values are: 'Ambitious', 'Capable', 'Cheerful', 'Forgiving', 'Helpful', 'Imaginative', 'Logical', 'Loving', and 'Responsible'.

Researchers have had more success demonstrating empirically the usefulness of the Rokeach model in differentiating consumer behaviour than has been the case with the Maslow hierarchy. In one study, consumers' choices of furniture and furniture supplier (traditional story versus discount store) were related to their scores on the Rokeach scales. Personal values were linked to consumer's price sensitivity when making furniture purchases and the type of store from which it was purchased. Price sensitivity was in particular related to rating the instrumental value 'Obedient' higher and the instrumental value 'Broad-minded' lower. Price sensitivity, in turn, led consumers to turn more to the discount store (Becker & Connor, 1982). Further research emerged during the 1970s and 1980s to demonstrate further the efficacy of the Rokeach value measures to differentiate consumers' attitudes and behaviours in useful ways (Munson & McIntyre, 1978, 1979; Reynolds & Jolly, 1980).

Psychographics and Demographics

Psychographics is a collective term that has been used to describe approaches to the understanding of consumer behaviour that examine consumers' stated motives and reasons for exhibiting specific product/service preferences, consumers' expectations of products/services gained from personal experience and second-hand feedback from other consumers, and brand image perceptions derived from marketing and promotional campaigns. Psychographics also places a great deal of attention on lifestyles.

Psychographics comprise descriptive labels of consumers that are distinctive from demographic labels and attempt to go beyond demographics by developing consumer classifiers that offer explanations for consumers' commodity preferences and purchase choices. Because psychographics are measures that are designed to achieve distinctive outcomes in consumer segmentation research from those obtained through demographics, combining the two approaches together was regarded by some marketing scholars as having the potential to provide much richer and more informative profiles of consumers than demographic alone (Lin, 2002).

Demographic measures such as age, household type, socio-economic class, marital status, family status, and nature of occupation can be used to define 'life stage' as a rich and comprehensive compound variable that reveals a great deal about the way consumers live their lives. The concept of 'lifestyle', in comparison, goes beyond life stage by considering not just how individuals live in a physical sense, but also what they think and feel about their current social status. Lifestyle is determined in part by life stage variables, but is also defined by adherence to certain values that underpin lifetime aspirations and goals. These ideas in turn are linked to personal needs—which can also be signalled by life stage—but more importantly in a consumer society that offers many choices, to personal desires.

Hence, psychographics is believed to add richness to demographics not simply in terms of describing consumers, but also in understanding differences among consumers that underpin their consumption patterns and commodity choices (Demby, 1974). There has, however, been debate about whether 'psychographics' and 'lifestyle' are really the same or similar entities. One distinction that has been made is that psychographics refer primarily to an individual's personality attributes and profile, whereas lifestyle relates more to the activity patterns displayed by the individual. Activity patterns have been extended by some theorists and researchers to include interests and opinions. Thus, psychographic profiles and AIO (Activity/Interest/Opinion) profiles are for some distinct types of consumer measurement and for others, they are interchangeable (Reynolds & Darden, 1972b; Darden & Ashton, 1974).

Typing the Typologies

There are different approaches to producing psychologically grounded consumer types. Psychographic analysis is a broad description for a range of measurement methods and types of psychological construct that can be applied to consumers. Demby (1974) attempted one of the earliest taxonomies of psychographics. He differentiated between three classes of psychographic measurement type. These were grounded in: (1) Product attributes, (2) Lifestyle attributes, and (3) Psychological attributes.

Product attributes are based on what the name describes: the core characteristics of products (or services). Consumers may hold many different cognitive constructs that describe and define different functional, appearance, and symbolic features of products. These constructs derive in part from generic definitions of the product or service type and the functions they provide. Some of these defining features might derive from marketing campaigns (i.e., especially those linked to brand image) and others from consumers' own experiences with the commodity in question.

Lifestyle attributes tend to derive from in-depth consultations with consumers that probe how a specific product or service fits into their lives and how a particular variant or brand within a product/service range is differentiated in terms of the meaning it brings to their lives and possibly in the way being associated with it conveys messages about the type of lifestyle a consumer leads or aspires to.

Psychological attributes map onto a product or service feature that derives from the individual consumer and his or her personality. Consumers are divided up according to the reasons they give for using specific commodities and how these reasons might in turn reveal something insightful about the personality of the consumer. Whereas lifestyle attributes might describe the type of life a consumer leads, psychological attributes provide further explanation as to why this is so.

AIO Profiles

Attitude, Interest, and Opinion (AIO) profiles are usually measured using lists of statements with linear, multi-point scales give to respondents to endorse each item on the list. These batteries of items can be administered on questionnaires through the post or websites for self-completion or via telephone or face-to-face interviews. Respondents might be invited to indicate the frequency with which they engage in specific activities, the importance attached to particular interests, or levels of agreement/disagreement with opinion statements. Demographic data concerning geographic location, neighbourhood types, property type, age, gender, occupation, income, marital status, family status, and education are also collected. Multivariate analysis techniques such as factor analysis are used to examine intercorrelations between AIO measures and to produce groupings of items that exhibit the strongest statistical interrelationships with each other (Plummer, 1974; Villani & Lechmann, 1975).

AIO factors have been developed that are product/service-specific and signal the motives, expectations, and benefits perceived to be associated with particular products/services or product/service variants (e.g., brands). AIO profiles have been related to the levels of use of different health care services. The researchers wished to discover whether patients differed in their propensities to show displeasure at the diagnoses and treatments they had received and whether psychographic profiling could provide insights into whether certain types of people were more likely than others to bring malpractice lawsuits if they had just cause. If patients generally believed that doctors are not usually to blame in malpractice cases, they were less inclined to bring such cases themselves. In contrast, if they claimed usually to take good care of themselves or that they tended to get sick more than their friends, they were more dependent on their doctor or more inclined to believe that their ill health was not their own fault and then were quicker to blame health professionals if the treatment they received did not work (Blackwell & Talarzyk, 1977).

Lifestyle and Values Approaches

There have been attempts to broaden out the scope of AIO-style measures to produce more generic types that might fit different markets. We will revisit this psychographic type again in the next chapter when examining studies that tried to establish population-wide norms for the distribution of lifestyle types. One initial approach to this line of investigation administered 300 AIO statements to a sample of respondents who were asked to endorse their agreement or disagreement with each statement along a six-point scale. Factor analysis was then used to examine further whether this long list of items clustered together into a smaller and more manageable number of 'factors' or groups of variables that each represented 'lifestyle constructs' (Wells & Tigert, 1971). Fourteen factors emerged: Price Conscious, Fashion Conscious, Homebody, Community-Minded, Child-Oriented, Compulsive Housekeeper, Self-Confident, Self-Designated Opinion Leader, Information

Seeker, Dislikes Housekeeping, Sewer, Canned Food User, Dieter, and Financial Optimist.

A further study of this type developed a battery of 250 AIO items and 179 frequency-of-use items that concerned different products and services. Each AIO item was endorsed along a linear numerical scale and the data entered into a factor analysis that produced seven lifestyle types: (1) Traditionalists, (2) Frustrated, (3) Life Expansionists, (4) Mobiles, (5) Sophisticates, (6) Actives, and (7) Immediate Gratifiers. There were also seven product use clusters based on the frequency-of-use data: (1) Personal Care, (2) Shelf-Stocker, (3) Cooking and Baking, (4) Self-Indulgent, (5) Social, (6) Children's Products, and (7) Personal Appearance (Cosmas, 1982).

The author of this study also noted that there seemed to be further relationships between the 'lifestyle' types and 'product use' types. Traditionalists were likely to engage in Shelf-Stocking and Cooking/Baking. In contrast, the Frustrated did not seem to know what they liked and displayed a not-clearly-defined pattern to their purchases. Life Expansionism did not yield a clear-cut product preference profile, but some weak inclinations towards Self-Indulgence and Personal Appearance and even Shelf-Stocking were noted. The Mobiles displayed much stronger ties with being Self-Indulgent and had concerns about Personal Appearance and Children. Active types showed preferences for Personal Care, Personal Appearance, and Self-Indulgence. Sophisticates also veered towards Personal Care products and Social products. Lastly, Immediate Gratifiers consumed Personal Care, Cooking/Baking, Social, and Self-Indulgence products.

The Lifestyle construct provides a measure for differentiating between consumers, but is not the same type of consumer classification variable as a personality trait. It is defined by social systems factors, including cultural values, which play an important part in the evaluation of the way people live their lives. Personality traits are shaped by inherited genetic characteristics as well as by environmental learning experiences. Values and Lifestyles characteristics can still be as enduring as personality traits, but they are strongly bound up with the social and cultural setting in which the consumer has lived and been brought up. Socio-cultural influences in the form of codes, conventions, and rules of conduct in social settings often define lifestyle types through the values they manifestly represent. Cultural codes can vary from one country to another. Understanding the distinct cultural values systems of different nation-states has become increasingly important for brand marketers operating on a global scale. The same brand image symbolism and promotional campaigns cannot be expected to work with equal effectiveness in all parts of the world. This is a subject that will be examined in more detail in Chapter 6.

Contemporary marketers have moved back somewhat from using lifestyle concepts as generic markers of consumer types. Even so, it is worth taking a look at the history of research on this subject because it represents an important aspect of the history of consumer profiling based on psychological concepts. Perhaps the most widely discussed system of this kind is the VALS Programme (Mitchell, 1983). Its psychological basis can be traced back to the need hierarchy model of Abraham Maslow (1954) and the social character defining system of Riesman, Glazer, & Denney (1950).

In its first incarnation, VALS assigned all people to nine categories that were determined by a range of psychological factors, including their aspirations, beliefs, desires, hopes, and values. The VALS system combined activity profiles (lifestyle-related) and internal drives (psychological). The initial taxonomy was developed through research with consumers in the United States.

The original nine-type system outlined by Mitchell (1983) were further divided according to four broader drive orientations which reflected Maslow's hierarchy of needs. At the pinnacle of social development was a consumer-type called the Integrated. Below these there were three Outer-Directed types (Belongers, Emulators, and Achievers), three Inner-Directed types (I-Am-Mes, Experientials, and Societally Conscious), and at the bottom of the hierarchy, two Need-Driven types, called Sustainers and Survivors.

Guided by Maslow's need hierarchy, the Survivors and Sustainers are pre-occupied with basic biological and social needs that must be satisfied for the consumer to exist and to be secure. Once these base needs are satisfied, the individual can then turn his or her attention to higher-level needs. In the VALS system, however, there are two pathways (Outer-Directed and Inner-Directed) that an individual can follow at the next level of need gratification. Progression through these need levels represents a type of maturity or advancement in quality of lifestyle. The focus shifts from survival to personal achievement and development. This higher-level development can be manifested in terms of externally visible achievements or internal growth. There is an assumption that people seek to realise their potential and some get further in this respect than do others. As different needs reach ascendancy, so in turn do individuals' interests and preoccupations change, and these changes can be reflected in their consumer activities.

Mitchell (1983) used survey data to estimate the distribution of VALS types in the United States. This population profiling exercise provided marketers with consumer-type definitions that indicated the types of spending priorities one might expect different lifestyle groups to display. The VALS types also indicated the types of promotional messages about brands different consumer groups were likely to be most responsive to. There were clear indications as well that the VALS types often exhibited distinctive demographic profiles.

The Need-Driven types tended to be focused on the basic needs of everyday living. At the bottom of the hierarchy, Survivors tended to be people with lower than average levels of education and income; they also tended to be older people. Hence, economic and health issues frequently dominated their lives. Sustainers were also people with economic constraints limiting their consumer activity, but they tended to be younger and therefore less likely to be preoccupied by health problems. Even so, they were not well off and often felt alienated from mainstream society. Their consumerism was therefore limited to the basic essentials of everyday living.

The Outer-Directed types represented a significant proportion (around two-thirds) of the population. They were economically in better shape than the Need-Driven and more engaged as consumers. Their key overall defining attribute was sensitivity to the opinions of others and wanting to fit in. There were three sub-types: Belongers, Emulators, and Achievers. The Belongers valued family life and traditional values. They sought social stability, valued education, tended to be older (although not old), not highly educated, and had incomes that were below average but still sufficient to explore distinctive tastes in brands.

Emulators tended to be quite young and were driven to do well in life. They were therefore aspirational and their role models often were members of the next group in the hierarchy, Achievers.

Achievers were people who had made something of their lives, whether in business, the professions, or government. This group had a mixed demographic composition, but the most dominant members tended more often to be male, middle-aged, and quite well educated.

The Inner-Directed types are often driven by similar needs to the Outer-Driven, but rather than simply seeking to approval of others, they would be more concerned with finding fulfilment from personal interests that gave them internal gratification. There were three sub-types here: I-Am-Me's, Experientials, and Societally-Conscious.

The I-Am-Me's were judged to comprise only a small fraction of the population, and their behaviour was governed by a mixture of Outer-Directed and Inner-Directed drives. This type comprised young adults with low income who were often still in full-time education. These individuals were idealistic, self-centred and self-absorbed, and preoccupied with their own identities and potential. They are inclined to try new experiences and therefore as consumers might be more open to new products and new brands provided they make a good fit with the type of personal image they wish to develop.

The Experientials comprised another Inner-Directed group. On average, they tended to be a few years older than the I-Am-Me's and were more usually female than male, well educated, and with good incomes for their life stage. They generally sought to expand their life experiences and would seek to get involved with any new activities in which they engaged to get the maximum personal enhancement from them.

Societally Conscious types were the final Inner-Directed category who had moved to a stage of being more idealistic than concerned about individualistic ambitions. They wished to improve their own lives, but in doing so, they also wanted to contribute to making the world a better place as well. These individuals tended to be older than the other two Inner-Directed types, being in their late 30s, and were generally well educated with good incomes.

The Intergrated lifestyle type was positioned at the top of the VALS hierarchy and comprised people that Maslow would have called 'self-actualisers'. These are individuals who are generally middle-aged, well educated, and have successful careers with good incomes. They are driven very much by the need for self-improvement for the express purpose of becoming as good as they possibly can be at whatever they do. This higher-level drive can take over their lives and renders lower-level social needs relatively unimportant. This type represents a tiny proportion of the total consumer base, however, and therefore tends to be of limited interest to marketers.

VALS and Consumer Behaviour

There is some empirical evidence that VALS types can be used to differentiate consumers' product preferences and therefore might yield useful intelligence for marketers when designing promotional campaign for specific brands. Thomas & Crocker (1981) examined purchase levels for a number of product categories and entertainment experiences: imported wine, cold cereals, TV comedy shows, sports magazines, fishing, and museums/galleries.

With imported wines, Survivors, Sustainers, Belongers, and Emulators were lower-than- average users, whereas Achievers, I-Am-Me's, Experientials, and Societally Conscious types were higher-than-average users. With cold cereals, Survivors and Emulators were less likely than average to use these products, whereas Belongers were more likely to do so. The remaining VALS types did not provide any clear pattern of relationship to the use of this product. Sports magazines were read less than average by Survivors, Sustainers, and Belongers, and more than average by Emulators, I-Am-Me's, and Experientials. TV comedy shows were viewed more than average by Sustainers, Emulators, I-Am-Me's, and Experientials, and less than average by Survivors, Achievers, and Societally conscious types. Attendance at museums and galleries was more likely among Achievers, Experientials, and Societally Conscious, and less likely among the other VALS types. Fishing was associated with just four VALS types, being adopted more than average by Sustainers and Belongers and less than average by Survivors and Societally Conscious.

The relevance of these findings for marketers is that they can be used to guide media planning decisions about the placement of advertising campaigns for specific product or service types as well as to provide insights into the kinds of advertising messages that may resonate best with target consumers.

Evolving VALS Systems

VALS research continued through the 1980s into the 1990s, and the original system evolved as the efficacy of the initial model to forecast consumer preferences and choices was tested. A new VALS model was launched at the end of the 1980s (Riche, 1989). As the population profile of the United States changed over this period, the original model was exposed as ill fitted to marketers' evolving needs. The original system had been developed within a consumer market dominated by young adults in their twenties and thirties. By the end of the 80s, this demographic had changed. Accompanied by economic shifts, the original values and lifestyles links outlined by the first model no longer provided sufficiently accurate predictions of consumer behaviour. A new instrument was developed that measured psychological stances on a range of social issues and was tested among two major national surveys of US consumers in 1990.

The second VALS system had a hierarchical format, which again signalled the conceptual influence of Maslow. At the bottom of the hierarchy were the Strugglers. Above these were three pathways defined by status orientation (equivalent to inner-directedness), principle orientation (equivalent to outer-directness), and action orientation (a new pathway concept).

Status-oriented types were sensitive to the views of others and were conscious of their own image. Their purchases therefore played a part in the establishment and maintenance of their personal 'brand'. Principle-oriented types were more idealistic and preoccupied with the status of society and how it could be. Their interests centred therefore on how to make the world a better place and how to contribute constructively to make that happen. Their consumer activities were shaped by these principles and personal branding was not important to them from the perspective of self-image. The action-oriented types were motivated by physical and social activities. Psychologists would call this type 'sensation seekers'. They enjoyed new experiences and risk taking. The two status-oriented types were Achievers and Strivers. The two principle-oriented types were Fulfilleds and Believers. The two action-oriented types were called Experiencers and Makers. At the very top of the hierarchy were the Actualisers, formerly called Integrateds.

Achievers were successful and work-oriented. They respected authority and held somewhat conservative opinions. They were inclined towards conspicuous consumption to acquire branded commodities to show off to others. The Strivers were similarly motivated to the Achievers but lacked their resources. They would still seek to adopt fashions and styles that would enhance others' opinions of them through recognition of their 'good taste', but were limited by their finances in how far they could achieve this outcome.

The Fulfilleds were older, well-educated people, often in well-paid and responsible jobs. They tended to be well informed and clued up about what was happening in the world around them. They valued tradition, but also were willing to embrace change, but not change for the sake of it. They had good incomes and could afford a comfortable lifestyle, but had no interest in wearing their wealth and their possessions as some kind of social brand designed to impress others. The Believers also embraced conservative values and were concerned about society, but had lower incomes than the Fulfilleds and therefore live more modest lifestyles. Family, their local community, their local church, and their national identity were important to them.

The Experiencers were mostly young adults in their twenties who were both physically and socially active. They would spend a lot of their disposable income on going out, on music and clothing and other commodities that also signalled something about their social identity. They were keenly attuned to new social and consumer trends and new brands. The Makers were active but much less brand conscious than the Experiencers. Their resources were usually less than those of Experiencers and they therefore valued cheaper forms of living, often embracing self-sufficiency and alternative lifestyles that were affordable for them. They were unimpressed by material possessions and valued commodities more in terms of whether they served useful, functional purposes.

At the bottom of the hierarchy, the Strugglers had low incomes and limited resources. This meant they had little spare money to spend and focused on catering to their basic needs of food and shelter. Beyond these needs, they had little interest because as consumers, they lacked the resources to be able to choose other than on the basis of price. At the top of the hierarchy were the Actualisers, who tended to be well educated, successful in their careers, and well off. They could indulge themselves in any consumer fantasies, but often did not because they were generally more preoccupied with self-fulfilment and enhancing their personal talents. They were generally not personally image conscious and their consumerism was not part of an aspiration for social status. Instead, they shopped for the best-quality commodities, including luxury items most could not afford, as an expression of their personal interests and taste (see Table 3.1).

The VALS typology was developed further in the 21st century. The model had a similar structure to that shown in Table 3.2. There were a number of typology label changes following new research that resulted in some types being given revised profiles. The three primary drive orientations, previously known as Principle-Oriented, Status-Oriented, and Action-Oriented, became Ideals, Achievement, and Self-Expression. At the foot of the framework, the Strugglers became the Survivors. Under the Ideals driven, the

Table 3.1 The VALS2 Model of Consumer Types

Actualisers		
Principle-Oriented	Status-Oriented	Action-Oriented
Fulfilleds	Achievers	Experiencers
Believers	Strivers	Makers
Strugglers		

Table 3.2 The VALS3 Model of Consumer Types

	Innovators	
Ideals	Achievement	Self-Expression
Thinkers	Achievers	Experiencers
Believers	Strivers	Makers
	Survivors	

Believers remained as they were before, but the Fulfilleds became the Thinkers. Under the Achievement-Oriented and Self-Expression-Oriented, the Achievers, Strivers, Experiencers, and Makers remained as before. At the top of the framework, the Actualisers were re-named the Innovators.

In the 21st century, the Survivors had limited resources and this position in turn meant they led modest lives. It was necessary for them to shop around for good deals, and they tended to remain loyal to trusted and affordable brands. They found it difficult to cope with a rapidly changing world and often felt it was leaving them behind.

Moving up a level, there were three types—Believers, Strivers, and Makers—defined by the primary motivational orientation they represented. Believers were motivated by ideals, but they tended to adhere to traditional beliefs and customs and were generally quite conservative in outlook. They felt most comfortable with established routines and their lives were organised around the family, their local community, and often, local religious organisations.

Strivers were motivated by achievement and were money conscious. How much money you had was the main indicator of your social status for Strivers and they preferred products through which they could show off to others how well they were doing. Their own wealth tended to be limited, but it was important to gain the approval of others through the purchases they made.

Makers were less concerned about tradition and showing off than they were about being able to express themselves in relation to activities they were personally committed to. They were open to new experiences, whether at home or elsewhere. They tended to be practical people, committed to their family, their employer, and the country. They were respectful of others' rights but unimpressed by material possessions.

Moving up to the next level, there were three types, again reflective of the motivational orientations of Ideals, Achievement, and Self-Expression. These types were the Thinkers, Achievers, and Experiencers. Thinkers shared many orientations and values with the Believers, but tended to be better educated, better off, and more successful in their careers. They respected authority while also being open to new ideas. Their incomes afforded them more choices than the Believers. This made they could trade up in their purchases, but still looked for functionality and good value for money. Achievers were committed to their careers and families. They had generally conservative beliefs and led conventional lives. They valued stability over risk yet also had an adventurous side within reason through which they sought to expand their life experiences.

For Achievers, life must have purpose, and this comes through setting goals and achieving them. Experiencers were similarly well to do to Achievers, but were less concerned about impressing other through their achievements and more interested in being able to express themselves through their interests and activities as an end in itself. They sought out good quality in their purchases and could generally afford to indulge their tastes. They were open to new experiences and explored different identities as forms of expression by following the latest fashions.

At the highest level of the VALS framework were the Innovators. This type had previously been called the Actualisers and as with the remainder of the VALS typology, this type was influenced by the motivational model devised by Abraham Maslow in the 1950s. These individuals were well educated, talented, and generally highly successful. This success often translated into wealth, and yet these individuals were not conspicuous consumers and attached no value to impressing others through brands. They were receptive to new ideas, up to date with world affairs and the latest social trends and consumer fashions. They were active as consumers, but bought quality for personal satisfaction and were largely independent in their thinking in this respect and not likely to be swayed by majority fashion trends if these did not fit with their personal tastes. Innovators liked the finer things in life.

Other Values-Based Typologies

The VALS systems are not the only values-based consumer typologies. Researchers from the University of Michigan developed a parallel model with similar intentions called the List of Values (LOV) (Kahle, 1983, 1984; Veroff, Douvan & Kulka, 1981). The LOV was influenced theoretically by a number of social psychological models of attitudes (Feather, 1975), needs (Maslow, 1954), and values (Rokeach, 1973). The list comprises nine values: self-respect, security, warm relationships with others, sense of accomplishment, self-fulfilment, sense of belonging, being well respected, fun and enjoyment in life, and excitement. Security clearly maps onto the security need identified by Maslow, whereas warm relationships with others and sense of belonging mirror Maslow's social needs. Self-respect and being well-respected map onto Maslow's esteem needs, and self-fulfilment, fun and enjoyment in life, and excitement resonate well with self-actualisation.

Different measurement formats were adopted to quantify these values and identify which type a person belonged to. One approach was to ask respondents to identify their two most important values (Veroff et al., 1981;

Kahle, 1983), and another was to ask respondents to rank order the values in terms of their personal relevance (Beatty, Kahle, Homer & Shekhar, 1985). A large-scale survey of consumers across the United States was published by Kahle (1986) using the LOV scale that was an initial attempt to produce normative data about the distribution of different LOV types.

LOV has similarities to VALS. Given that both were influenced conceptually by Maslow's (1954) hierarchy of needs, this is not surprising. There are also distinctive types to each values measurement system. Both LOV and VALS embrace a broad concept of inward-looking and outward-looking bases for values. With VALS, inner-directed and outer-directed pathways were outlined as alternative routes for individuals once they passed through satisfaction of basic needs. This distinction differentiated between consumers in terms of whether their personal growth was driven by individual achievement or the need to do good for others. With the LOV, a distinction was made between internal and external loci of control (after Rotter, 1965). For proponents of the LOV, values could be met through interpersonal relationships, enhancement of self-image, or the acquisition of things as a sign of success.

A nine-value LOV scale was tested with shoppers at two malls in the US. The values comprised: self-respect, security, warm relationships with others, sense of accomplishment, self-fulfilment, sense of belonging, being well respected, fun and enjoyment, and excitement (Perri, 1990). The researcher here found some statistical relationships between values endorsed as ones with which they most identified and types of purchases made. For instance, attaching significance to self-respect, being well respected, and a sense of belonging were each related to buying more health and beauty aids.

In one direct test of Maslow's model with 577 residents of a medium-sized city in the southwestern United States, Kahle et al (1997) presented some evidence derived from self-completion questionnaire measures of reported values and needs that confirmed the needs hierarchy, but there was plenty of further evidence that was inconsistent with it. It was not invariably the case that an apparent lack of need satisfaction at a lower level precluded self-reported satisfaction at a higher level. Furthermore, people with a high-level existence in terms of their affluence could still articulate concerns about threats to lower-level needs as much as people who were socio-economically poorer. The circumstances under which specific need threats, such as to personal security, were described often did vary between these groups, however, and this reflected the different lifestyles they each led. This information was important for brand marketers to bear in mind because devising campaigns to appeal to a specific human need would have to play out different pathways to need satisfaction in social contexts that had the greatest meaning to specific consumer groups.

Elsewhere, evidence emerged that there was little difference between VALS and LOV in their ability to predict with accuracy consumers' purchase choices. Indeed, the power of the LOV depended upon whether a number of demographic measures were included with or excluded from its measurement battery. Taking out the demographics resulted in a dilution of the LOV's predictive capacity. There was some suggestion that the predictive ability of the LOV rested primarily with the demographic measures that had been incorporated within its original form. A conclusion was reached that VALS may prove to be a better consumer segmentation instrument because its psychographic measures are completely independent of demographics (Novak & McEvoy, 1990).

Combining Different Approaches

Some researchers have experimented with combinations of normative and product-specific approaches to consumer segmentation using psychological methods. A step-wise process is sometimes adopted in which researchers use a normative approach, such as values and lifestyles measures, alongside a study of product-specific attitudes and expectations measures (e.g., Hustad & Pessemeier, 1974; Wells, 1974). The order of play here can vary from study to study. The first step might sometimes be a normative profiler followed by a product-specific profiler. There are occasions when this sequence is reversed. By nesting product-specific psychological factors within more normative psychology of consumer profiles, rich data can be obtained that compares consumers with different generic psychologies of consumerism orientations in terms of their dominant expectations about specific products.

Some researchers have examined different lifestyle profiling systems with the same consumer populations to find out how they stack up against each other. In one study conducted in South Africa, Blem, Reekie, & Brits (1989) compared the Values and Lifestyles measures (Mitchell, 1983), Market Research Africa's Sociomonitor (Corder, 1984), and Young and Rubicam's 4C's model (Halley-Wright, 1988). All three sets of lifestyles instruments yielded overlapping consumer categories. These categories reflected the hierarchy of human needs identified by Maslow (1954). For example, the Survivors and Sustainers at the foot of the VALS hierarchy were largely mirrored by the Traditionals and Responsibles in Sociomonitor, and the Resigned and Struggling Poor in the 4C's model. These types therefore persisted across national cultural boundaries and represented something fundamental about the human character (Rousseau, 1990).

The Sociomonitor system recognised the basic needs and the inner-directed and outer-directed orientations that defined the VALS hierarchy. There were different, although overlapping, systems identified, however, for white and black South Africans, which to some extent undermined Rousseau's conclusions about the discovery of culture-independent core human attributes. Among white South Africans, four principal lifestyle types emerged: Responsibles, Branded, Self-Motivated, and Innovators. Among black South Africans, there were Traditionals, Responsibles, Brandeds, I-Am-Me's, and Self-Motivated.

Responsibles were lower-income people concerned about conservation, security, and how they would provide for themselves and their families. They lacked confidence and sought constant reassurance from others. The Branded type sought status and esteem through material possessions, and their identities were often defined by the brands they consumed. Self-Motivated types were often poorly educated but nonetheless aspirational and sought to improve themselves by pursuing personal growth activities. They were driven and individualistic in their outlooks. These three types characterised white and black South African consumers.

Among the white consumers only, the Innovators were well educated and had good jobs and high incomes. They were economically driven but also had a social conscience. They were law-abiding, but were willing to challenge established norms and authorities when they felt this was warranted to bring positive changes to society.

Among black consumers only, the Traditionals were older consumers who tended not to be well educated and were often illiterate and very religious and conservative in their values. They valued the old ways of doing things and were slow to embrace changes in society. The I-Am-Me's were similar to those identified by the VALS system. They were young, self-confident, and pre-occupied with their own image. They were also prickly and could get aggressive if they did not get their own way. They distrusted authority but unlike the Innovators, were unable to produce reasoned challenges to the status quo and were therefore quick to criticise society as being unjust and to class themselves as victims.

Rousseau combined Maslow's need hierarchy, Mitchell's VALS, Market Research Africa's Sociomonitor, and Young and Rubicam's 4C's model to develop a psychographic typology of furniture buyers. This new compound model comprised five types labelled as: Home-Centred, Outer-Directed, Trendsetters, Inner-Directed, and Cultured. This new model, however, was not an attempt to develop a universal or normative psychographic typology covering all consumers. Instead, it was focused specifically on understanding the market for one product range, namely, furniture. Hence, some of the lifestyle types that emerged, such as Home-Centred, Trendsetters, and Cultured, made particular references to furniture purchases. Nevertheless, the new typology provided useful insights into consumer types that were unique to the furniture trade and a tool to classify consumers in terms of the kinds of furniture they were likely to prefer.

Matching Consumer Personality to Brand Personality

Personality measures have been widely used with consumers to segment them across entire markets as well as in relation to specific product or service domains. Marketing researchers have also applied the notion of 'personality' to brands. Just as a consumer's self-image is in part defined by their personality makeup, so too a brand's image depends upon the distinct characteristics assigned to it by consumers. Indeed, it is possible to go further than this and to say that a brand's personality comprises the application of human characteristics to the brand (Gilmore, 1919). Thus, consumers use verbal terms of description and evaluation to define a brand. Brands might be regarded as 'exciting', 'honest', 'tough', or 'reliable'. These are all terms that might be used to describe a person (Keller, 1993).

Conceptions of brands in human terms can be further promoted when celebrities are associated with them. The product or service brands then become imbued with the celebrity's brand, which means that some of the characteristics associated by consumers as fans will become transferred to the product/service brand receiving the celebrity's endorsement (Rook, 1985).

Personality traits might also become associated with product or service brands as a result of transference of the consumer-user's own identity characteristics or of characteristics associated with other known users. Through the experience of using a brand, the consumer develops perceptions and expectations of it and these attributes gradually form into a coherent identity (Plummer, 1985b).

Aaker (1997) explored a new theoretical framework for the classification of brand personality. She took her lead from the application of the Big Five personality factors to consumers. Each of the five personality factors could be further defined in relation to a series of human facets. She gave the example of Extraversion, which other researchers had described variously as representing sub-features such as assertiveness, excitement-seeking, gregariousness, and warmth (see Church & Burke, 1994). A facets list was derived through this analysis of personality factors and tested as brand descriptors among samples of consumers. A factor analysis was used to derive brand personality factors. Five factors emerged in all: Sincerity, Excitement, Competence, Sophistication, and Ruggedness.

These brand personality factors were confirmed among demographic sub-samples and different brand samples. Three of the brand personality factors mapped onto Big Five factors. Excitement matched Extraversion. Sincerity matched Agreeableness. Competence was similar to Conscientiousness. Sophistication and Ruggedness exhibited no Big Five matches.

Subsequent research built upon the work of Aaker and found that brand personality could influence consumers' brand preferences (Zhang, 2007; Chi, Lin, Hsu & Chen, 2011). One of the factors at play was that brand personality factors could boost the amount of trust consumers placed in a brand and this in turn could enhance their loyalty to it (Wysong, Munch & Kleiser, 2004). Confirming the results of Aaker (1997), later researchers found that brand personality comprised more than perceptions of functionality and performance of products or services.

Consumers made a range of judgements about brands, any of which could individually or collectively affect their loyalty to a particular supplier

(Singh, Ehrenberg & Goodhardt, 2008). Loyalty to a brand depended a great deal on the degree to which a brand had an image that matched the consumer's own perception of self. To command regular use, a brand needed to have a 'personality' that reflect important aspects of the consumer's own psychological character and represented an extension of that sense of self (Aaker, 1999; Jamal & Goode, 2001).

The greater the consistency between the consumer's self-concept and his or her perceptions of a brand, the more a consumer would like the brand and want to buy it (Ericksen, 1996; Sirgy et al., 1997). The key factor here was that a brand should permit self-expression. This was far more significant in determining the consumer's choice of brand than simply whether the brand could do what was expected given the type of product or service it represented (Fennis & Pruyn, 2007). A brand's personality is not the same as a human personality and is based on consumers' perceptions and cognitively constructed impressions (Sung & Tinkham, 2005). Even so, human personality factors can facilitate the degree to which consumers perceive a personal connection to a brand (Aaker, Fournier & Brasel, 2004).

Concluding Remarks

There have been numerous attempts to create generic consumer segmentation and classification models beyond demographics and product- or service-related behaviour. As well as psychological measures grounded in classic personality theory, other classifications have drawn upon the ways consumers might be defined in terms of their outlook on the world by the social and cultural settings in which they are brought up. Local sociocultural forces instil in people codes of conduct, often articulated as values, which set the standards by which they should live their lives. Very often, these social standards are implicit and subtle and derived from observing the actions of others, and sometimes they are set down more explicitly in terms of do's and don'ts regarding how a person ought to behave in different social settings.

Marketing professionals have attempted to tap into these cultural values and social standards in the way they promote their brands. Efforts are made through brand promotions to demonstrate how a brand itself resonates closely with dominant values so that by using it, consumers in turn show the world that they are in tune with current social standards and expectations. These standards can derive also from sub-groups within a society that might represent reference sources to which consumers turn for further guidance about how to behave. Such a reference group influences which set sub-cultural standards can be powerful if the group in question is one to which a consumer already belongs or aspires to join.

Marketing researchers have tried to develop consumer classification models and have experimented with empirical instruments that can measure and quantify specific values-based consumer types. These models have then been extended to determine whether they are capable of predicting how consumers are likely to behave in commodity market settings. Such models have proven to have limited predictive power in terms of identifying markets for specific brands or product variants. The challenge of create generic consumer segmentation models based on classification types with which consumers can identify has resulted in rather blunt instruments that can paint a broad portrait of a consumer population but lack the ability to pin down specific patterns of consumer behaviour in relation to product or service types or individual brands.

References

Aaker, J. L. (1997) Dimensions of brand personality. *Journal of Marketing Research*, 34(3), 347–356.

Aaker, J. L. (1999) The malleable self: The role of self-expression in persuasion. *Journal of Marketing Research*, 36, 45–57.

Aaker, J. L., Fournier, S., & Brasel, S. A. (2004) When good brands do bad. *Journal of Consumer Research*, 31(1), 1–16.

Alderfer, C. P. (1969) An empirical test of a new theory of human needs. *Organizational Behaviour and Human Performance*, 4, 142–175.

Beatty, S. E., Kahle, L. R., Homer, P., & Shekhar, M. (1985) Alternative measurement approaches to consumer values: The list of values and the Rokeach value survey. *Psychology and Marketing*, 2, 181–200.

Becker, B. W., & Connor, P. E. (1982) The influence of personal values on attitudes and store choice behaviour. In B. J. Walker, W. O. Bearden., W. R. Darden, P. E. Murphy, J. R. Nevin., J. C. Olson, & B. A. Weitz (Eds.) *An Assessment of Marketing Thought and Practice*, pp. 21–24. Chicago, IL: American Marketing Association.

Blackwell, R. D., & Talarzyk, W. W. (1977) Lifestyle retailing: Competition strategies for the 1980s. *Journal of Retailing*, 51, 7–27.

Blem, N. H., Reekie, W. D., & Brits, R. N. (1989) *Elements of South African Marketing*. Johannesburg: SA: Southern Book Publications.

Chi, K. K. S., Lin, R. J., Hsu, M. K., & Chen, S. C. (2011) Symbolic and functional brand effects for market segmentation. *Australian Journal of Business and Management Research*, 1(6), 75–86.

Church, A. T., & Burke, P. J. (1994) Exploratory and confirmatory tests of the Big Five and Tellegen's Three and Four-Dimensional models. *Journal of Personality and Social Psychology*, 66(1), 460–473.

Corder, C. (1984) *Sociomonitor, Users Manual White*. Johannesburg, SA: Market Research Africa.

Cosmas, S. C. (1982) Life styles and consumption patterns. *Journal of Consumer Research*, 8, 453–455.

Costa, P. T., & McCrae, R. R. (1985) *The NEO Personality Inventory*. Odessa, FL: Psychological Assessment Resources.

Costa, P. T., & McCrae, R. R. (1992a) *The NEO Personality Inventory Manual*. Odessa, FL: Psychological Assessment Resources.

Costa, P. T., & McCrae, R. R. (1992b) Normal personality assessment in clinical practice. The NEO personality inventory. *Psychological Assessment*, 4(1), 5–13.

Costa, T., Rognoni, E., & Galati, D. (2006) EEG phase synchronization during emotional response to positive and negative film stimuli. *Neuroscience Letters*, 406, 159–164.

Coupey, E. (1994) Restructuring constructive processing of information displays in consumer choice. *Journal of Consumer Research*, 21, 83–99.

Crosby, L. A., Bitner, M. J., & Gill, J. D. (1990) Organizational structure of values. *Journal of Business Research*, 20, 123–134.

Darden, W. R., & Ashton, D. (1974) Psychographic profiles of patronage preference groups. *Journal of Retailing*, 50, 99–112.

Darden, W. R., & Perreault, W. D. (1976) Identifying interurban shoppers: Multi-product purchase patterns and segmentation profiles. *Journal of Marketing Research*, 8, 51–60.

Darden, W. R., & Reynolds, F. D. (1971) Shopping orientations and shopping usage rates. *Journal of Marketing Research*, 11, 79–85.

Demby, E. (1974) Psychographics and from whence it came. In W. D. Wells (Ed.) *Life Style and Psychographics*, pp. 9–30. Chicago, IL: American Marketing Association.

Ericksen, M. K. (1996) Using self-congruity and ideal congruity to predict purchase intention: A European perspective. *Journal of Euro-Marketing*, 6(1), 41–56.

Feather, N. (1975) *Values in Education and Society*. New York, NY: Free Press.

Fennis, B. M., & Pruyn, A. T. H. (2007) You are what you wear: Brand personality influences on consumer impression formation. *Journal of Business Research*, 60, 634–639.

Gilmore, G. W. (1919) *Animism*. Boston, MA: Marshall Jones Company.

Graham, W. K., & Balloun, J. (1973) An empirical test of Maslow's need hierarchy theory. *Journal of Humanistic Psychology*, 75, 97–108.

Halley-Wright, A. (1988) Cross-cultural consumer characterisation. Paper presented at the Marketing Mix Conference, Johannesburg, South Africa, 6th October.

Hustad, T. P., & Pessemeier, E. A. (1974) The development and application of psychographic, life style and associated activity and attitude measures. In W. D. Wells (Ed.) *Life Style and Psychographics*, pp. 31–70. Chicago, IL: American Marketing Association.

Jamal, A., & Goode, M. (2001) Consumers and brands: A study of the impact of self-image congruence on brand preference and satisfaction. *Marketing Intelligence and Planning*, 19(7), 482–492.

Kahle, L. R. (Ed.) (1983) *Social Values and Social Change: Adaptation to life in America*. New York, NY: Praeger.

Kahle, L. R. (1984) The values segmentation debate continues. *Marketing News*, 18, 2.

Kahle, L. R. (1986) The nine nations of North America and the values basis of geographic segmentation. *Journal of Marketing*, 50, 37–47.

Kahle, L. R., Boush, D. M., & Homer, P. M. (1989) Broken rungs in Abraham's ladder: Is Maslow's Hierarchy hierarchical? In D. Schumann (Ed.) *Proceedings of Division 23, 1988 Annual Convention of the American Psychological Association*, pp. 11–16. Washington, DC: American Psychological Association.

Kahle, L. R., Homer, P. M., O'Brien, R. M., & Boush, D. M. (1997) Maslow's hierarchy and social adapatation as alternative accounts of value structures. In

L. R. Kahle & L. Chiagouris (Eds.) *Values, Lifestyles and Psychographics*, pp. 111–138. Mahwah, NJ: Lawrence Erlbaum Associates, Ch. 6.

Keller, K. L. (1993) Conceptualising, measuring, and managing customer-based brand equity. *Journal of Marketing*, 57, 1–22.

Lin, C. (2002) Segmentation customer brand preference: Demographic or psychographic. *Journal of Product and Brand Management*, 11(4), 249–268.

Maslow, A. H. (1954) *Motivation and Personality*. New York, NY: Harper & Row.

Maslow, A. H. (1970) *Motivation and Personality*, 2nd Ed. New York, NY: Harper & Row.

Mitchell, A. (1983) *The Nine American Lifestyles*. New York, NY: Warner.

Moore, N., & Weiss, R. (1955) The functioning and meaning of work and the job. *American Sociological Review*, 20, 191–198.

Munson, M., & McIntyre, S. H. (1978) Personal values: A cross-cultural assessment of self values and values attributed to a distant cultural stereotype. In H. K. Hunt (Ed.) *Advances in Consumer Research*, Vol. 5, pp. 160–166. Ann Arbor, MI: Association for Consumer Research.

Munson, M., & McIntyre, S. H. (1979) Developing practical procedures for the measurement of personal values in cross-cultural marketing. *Journal of Marketing Research*, 16, 48–52.

Novak, T. P., & McEvoy, B. (1990) On comparing alternative segmentation schemes: The List of Values (LOV) and Values and Lifestyles (VALS). *Journal of Consumer Research*, 17, 105–109.

Perri, M. (1990) Application of the list of values alternative psychographic assessment scale. *Psychological Reports*, 66, 403–406.

Plummer, J. T. (1974) The concept and application of life style segmentation. *Journal of Marketing*, 38, 33–37.

Plummer, J. T. (1985a) How personality can make a difference. *Journal of Advertising Research*, 24(6), 27–31.

Plummer, J. T. (1985b) Brand personality: A strategic concept for multinational advertising. Paper presented at marketing Educators Conference, New York, Young & Rubicam.

Reisman, D., Glazer, N., and Denney, R. (1950) *The Lonely Crowd: A Study of the Changing American Character*. New Haven, CT: Yale University Press.

Reynolds, F. D., & Darden, W. R. (1972a) An analysis of selected factors associated with the adoption of new products. *Mississippi Valley Journal of Business and Economics*, 8, 31–42.

Reynolds, F. D., & Darden, W. R. (1972b) Intermarket patronage: A psychographic study of consumer outshoppers. *Journal of Marketing*, 36, 50–54.

Reynolds, T. J., & Jolly, J. P. (1980) Measuring personal values: An evaluation of alternative methods. *Journal of Marketing Research*, 17, 531–536.

Riche, M. F. (1989) Psychographics for the 1990s. *American Demographics*, July, 24–26, 30–31, 53–54.

Rokeach, M. (1973) *The Open and Closed Mind*. New York, NY: Basic Books.

Rook, D. W. (1985) The ritual dimension of consumer behaviour. *Journal of Consumer Research*, 12(December), 251–264.

Rotter, J. B. (1965) Generalised expectancies for internal versus external control of reinforcement. *Psychological Monographs*, 80(1), Whole No. 609).

Rousseau, D. (1990) Developing and testing a model of psychographic market segmentation. *South African Tydskrif Sielk*, 20(3), 184–194.

Singh, J., Ehrenberg, A., & Goodhardt, G. (2008) Measuring customer loyalty to product variants. *International Journal of Market Research*, 50(4), 513–530.

Sirgy, M. J., Grewal, D., Mangleburg, T. F., Park, J., Chon, K., Claiborne, C. B., Johar, J. S., & Berkman, H. (1997) Assessing the predictive validity of two methods of measuring self-image congruence. *Journal of the Academy of Marketing Science*, 25(3), 229–241.

Sung, Y., & Tinkham, S. F. (2005) Brand personality structures in the United States and Korea: Common and culture-specific factors. *Journal of Consumer Psychology*, 15(4), 334–350.

Thomas, T. C., & Crocker, S. (1981) *Values and Lifestyles—The New Psychographics*. Menlo Park, CA: SRI.

Thompson, J. R. (1971) Characteristics and behaviour of outshopping consumers. *Journal of Retailing*, 47, 70–80.

Tian, K. T., Bearden, W. O., & Hunter, G. L. (2001) Consumers' need for uniqueness: Scale development and validation. *Journal of Consumer Research*, 28, 50–66.

Tifferet, S., & Herstein, R. (2012) Gender differences in brand commitment, impulse buying, and hedonic consumption. *Journal of Product and Brand Management*, 21(3), 176–182.

Tigert, D. J. (1969) A taxonomy of magazine readership applied to problems in marketing strategy and media selection. *Journal of Business*, 42, 357–363.

Tigert, D. J. (1971) Are television audiences really different? Paper presented at the 54th International Marketing Association meeting, San Francisco, April.

Tigert, D. J., Lathrope, R., & Bleeg, M. (1971) The fast food franchise: Psychographic and demographic segmentation analyses. *Journal of Retailing*, 47, 81–90.

Trexler, J. T., & Schuh, A. J. (1971) Personality dynamics in a military training command and its relationship to Maslow's motivation hierarchy. *Journal of Vocational Behaviour*, 1, 245–253.

Veroff, J., Douvan, E., & Kulka, R. A. (1981) *The Inner American*. New York, NY: Basic Books.

Vigneron, F., & Johnson, L. W. (1999) A review and conceptual framework of prestige seeking consumer behaviour. *Academy of Marketing Science Review*, 9(1), 1–14.

Vigneron, F., & Johnson, L. W. (2004) Measuring perceptions of brand luxury. *Journal of Brand Management*, 11, 484–506.

Villani, K. E., & Lehmann, D. R. (1975) An examination of the stability of AIO measures. In E. M. Mazze (Ed.) *Marketing: The Challenges and the Opportunities*, pp. 484–488. Chicago, IL: American marketing Association.

Visser, E. M., & du Preez, R. (2001) Apparel shopping orientation: Two decades of research. *Journal of Family and Consumer Research*, 29, 72–81.

Vitz, P. I., & Johnson, D. (1965) Masculinity of smokers and the masculinity of cigarette images. *Journal of Applied Psychology*, 49, 155–159.

Vrechopoulos, A., Siokos, G., & Doukidis, G. (2001) Internet shopping adoption by Greek consumers. *European Journal of Innovation Management*, 4(3), 142–152.

Vroom, V. (1964) *Work and Motivation*. New York, NY: Wiley.

Wagner, J., & Hanna, S. (1983) The effectiveness of family life cycle variables in consumer expenditure. *Journal of Consumer Research*, 10, 281–291.

Wallace, D. J. (1995) Shopping online: A sticky business. *Advertising Age*, April, p. 20.

Wansink, B. (1997) Developing useful and accurate customer profiles. In L. R. Kahle & L. Chiagouris (Eds.) *Values, Lifestyles and Psychographics*, pp. 183–198. Mahwah, NJ: Lawrence Erlbaum Associates, Ch. 9.

Warren, W. E., Stevens, R. E., & McConkey, C. W. (1990) Using demographic life-style analysis to segment individual investors. *Journal of Financial Analysis*, 46, 74–77.

Watkins, D., Akande, A., Fleming, J., Ismail, M., Lefner, K., Regmi, M., Watson, M., Yu, J., Adair, J., Cheng, C., Gerong, A., McInerney, D., Mpofu, E., Singh-Sengupta, S., & Wondima, H. (1998) Cultural dimensions, gender, and the nature of self-concept: A fourteen country study. *International Journal of Psychology*, 33, 17–31.

Watson, S. (2009) Credit card misuse, money attitudes and compulsive buying behaviours: A comparison of internal and external Locus of Control (LOC) consumers. *College Student Journal*, 43(2), 268–275.

Wells, W. D. (1974) *Life Style and Psychographics*. Chicago, IL: American Marketing Association.

Wells, W. D., & Tigert, D. (1971) Activities, interests and opinions. *Journal of Advertising Research*, 11, 27–35.

Wysong, S., Munch, J., & Kleiser, S. (2004) This brand's for you. An exploratory look at how individual variables can influence brand personality perceptions. *American Marketing Association Conference Proceedings*, 15, 239–246.

Zhang, M. (2007) Impact of brand personality on PALI, a comparative research between two different brands. *International Management Review*, 3(3), 36–47.

4   The Search for Psychology-Based Predictors of Purchase Preferences

As the previous two chapters have discussed, marketing professionals have tried to develop more normative psychographic typologies that are not linked to specific product ranges or types of consumer activity. These have derived both from established scales designed to measure human 'personality traits' and developed in non-marketing settings and also from custom-built scales designed specifically for application in consumer contexts. The latter instruments purport to measure constructs often referred to as 'lifestyle traits'.

The aim of that research was to establish instruments that can be used to classify entire consumer populations and generate a parallel taxonomy to the standard demographic dimensions that are more generally used in this context. By establishing measures grounded in psychological variables and testing these with large 'establishment' samples it was hoped to create normative data that would not only differentiate between consumers on the basis of psychological constructs, but also produce normative data that revealed the distribution of each type for entire populations.

Marketing researchers have long recognised that an understanding of consumers from the perspectives of their personal (that is, psychological) characteristics and lifestyle attributes (based on an appreciation of their cultural values) can provide valuable insights into their consumer behaviour and brand preferences across a range of commodity and service settings (Raaij & Verhallen, 1994; Gonzalez & Bello, 2002; Harcar & Kaynak, 2008).

There is substantial research literature on the topic of psychographics that has focused on the development of psychology-based measures designed to help marketers understand more narrowly defined consumer-related behaviours. In fact, the great majority of psychographics applications have had far less grand ambitions than producing normative typologies for entire consumer populations. Thus, research exercises such as those linked to VALS (Mitchell, 1983) and the LOV (Kahle, Beastty & Homer, 1986) are the exception rather than the rule. Instead, most early research into consumer-typology building using psychology as its basis focused on delivering a better understanding of specific types of consumer behaviour such as the propensity to purchase new items in the market (Tigert, 1969; Donnelly, 1970; Coney, 1972), or to make impulse purchases (Kollat & Willett, 1960), or to buy from catalogues (Reynolds, 1974).

Other psychology-based measures have been used to produce typologies of styles of consumer behaviour such as the way people approach shopping. Then, psychographics and personality psychology have been used to study propensities to use specific product or service types or to differentiate consumers of different variants of a specific product or service range. In addition, psychological measures have been applied to classify consumers in relation to their media consumption behaviours. The latter studies are important for better understanding how to position advertising campaigns for specific products and services given the psychological nature of their consumer communities. This chapter will review research that has applied psychographics to a number of specific domains of consumer activity.

Psychological Types and Shopping

Traditionally, most consumer activity can be described as being a form of shopping. In the 21st century, 'shopping' can take place in a number of different settings and increasingly occurs with consumers sitting with a computer screen on a desk, in their lap, or in their hand, and requires surfing through a few pages of a website and then making a few clicks on the screen icons. Many people still use real, physical shops, although even here, the nature of shopping behaviour has evolved with the week-to-week basics being bought in a single large store—the local supermarket— rather than the old-fashioned way of visiting different shops for different commodities. When seeking to purchase more occasional items, such as clothing, accessories, furniture and other major household items, electronics goods, and other big ticket items, consumers increasingly prefer the comfort of the mall to the high street, where they might have to brave the cold or venture out into the rain.

One typology that emerges from these observations is one based on the people's general shopping setting preferences, such as being an 'in-home shopper' versus an 'out-of-home shopper' (Thompson, 1971). Another distinction might be made between the 'supermarket shopper' who likes to drive to a single location and complete the weekly shop and the 'high street shopper' who does not mind shopping on foot and visiting a number of different local stores that each specialises in selling specific types of products (e.g., cosmetics, household cleaning products, food, etc).

These divisions have been used in marketing research and have conventionally been linked to demographic types. Variables such as age, education, income, and socio-economic class have often been found to differentiate between shopping types (Sexton, 1974). A factor associated with the type of shopping setting preferred is the perception of how the best bargains can be achieved. Hence, shopping patronage is influenced by knowing that specific outlets give the best deals. If these are to be obtained in a supermarket or in specific department stores in the mall, these are the place to which shoppers will turn and return (Prasad, 1975).

Demographic factors provide useful descriptive tools but do not explain why consumers make specific choices. Psychographics, in contrast, can measure the motives that drive consumers to specific shopping locations and can link in other psychological measures, such as consumers' perceptions and evaluations of stores, and the extent to which they cater to their needs and provide for a pleasant shopping experience (Tigert, Lathrope & Bleeg, 1971; Reynolds & Darden, 1972; Darden & Ashton, 1974; Moschis, 1991).

Even before psychographics became recognised as a discipline that offered a distinctive approach to classifying consumers, marketing researchers noted that the decisions that people made about shopping represented psychological constructs (Stone, 1954). This early research was conducted on a small scale with little over 100 women in Chicago. Stone identified four shopper types that he called Economic, Personalising, Ethical, and Apathetic. Each of these shopper types was defined by specific concerns, decision-making, and shopping styles.

The Economic Shopper was a socially aspiring type who preferred known brands and patronised stores that were convenient and also competitive in their pricing. She would visit large department stores to get the best deals. The Personalising Shopper was not so concerned with always getting the best-known brands and would shop around different locations, especially locally, to get the best-value buys. She enjoyed shopping in local stores where she could get to know shopkeepers personally, and for this shopper type, the personal touch was an important aspect of capturing her patronage.

The Apathetic Shopper did not like to shop and exhibited no loyalty to any shopping outlet, whether large or small, local or not. Shopping was a chore and something that needed to get done as quickly as possible with the least inconvenience. The Ethical Shopper was strongly bound to her local shopping environment and developed enduring loyalty to shopkeepers she knew. This behaviour stemmed not simply from convenience, but from a sense that the local shopkeeper was an important part of the community and deserved support to combat the effects that large department stores were having on the local high street.

These vignettes of shopper types provide a much richer impression of personalities than their demographic profiles can yield. They somehow make shoppers seem more like real people. How useful such typing is to marketing campaign design or for predicting product preferences and purchase patterns remains an open question. The shopper types described above derived from research with a small and non-representative sample of American women who were homemakers. To what extent these types could have been generalised to the wider population of consumers in the United States at that time is debatable. There is a further question also about how stable these shopper types were. Confirming that shopper types of this kind could change even within a few years, one of the researchers involved in that research produced a different looking typology of women supermarket shoppers just a few years later.

This research was extended many years later by Darden & Reynolds (1971). Once again, they applied the four shopper categories devised by Stone to a slightly larger sample of women shoppers in the health and personal product field. They were able to confirm that these types still held up.

From a series of interviews with 116 'housewives' from one suburban area, Darden & Ashton (1974) identified seven shopper types. These were labelled: Apathetic shopper, Demanding shopper, Quality shopper, Fastidious shopper, Stamp Preferred shopper, Convenient location shopper, and Stamp Haters. The researchers expressed each type as a percentage of the total sample, but given the modest sample size, such percentages are probably misleading and should not be taken as giving a compelling indication of the wider distribution of these shopper types.

Once again, descriptive profiles were provided for each type, but whether they had any significant predictive validity in terms of purchase preferences was not proven. We were told, for instance, that the Apathetic shopper had no shopping location preferences, as observed in the earlier study from which this type emerged, and apparently liked supermarkets with a lot of choice and competitive prices. What we do not know is whether these self-reported preferences would translate into real behaviour. For the Quality shopper, fresh produce was important, especially with meat, but beyond that, there was little to define this type. The Demanding shopper also looked for quality but was not concerned about collecting trading stamps, which were important during that era.

In fairness to the authors of this study, they advised caution against generalising from its findings. Their typology, they claimed, might be used to provide general guidance and to generate hypotheses for further empirical investigation. The data it yielded might be used by supermarkets to guide decisions about product mix and displays provided they had data on the distribution of these types across their known patrons.

Further research from the United States in the 1970s produced a similar shopping typology with grocery shoppers that retained Apathetic shoppers who were contrasted with Involved shoppers and joined by Price shoppers and Convenience shoppers. The latter two categories exhibited many of the qualities observed in earlier studies among 'Economic shoppers' (Williams, Painter & Nicholas, 1978).

Later research explored the generalisability of psychographic shopper types across different geographical locations. The research instrument used here was a hybrid that combined general lifestyle types with more specific shopping-related orientations. Seven shopper types were defined: Inactive shoppers, Active shoppers, Service shoppers, Traditional shoppers, Dedicated Fringe shoppers, Price shoppers, and Transitional shoppers.

The researchers found considerable consistency in the emergence of these shopper types across 17 different geographic markets in the United States (Lesser & Hughes, 1986).

The initial typology was refined further, with two-category and three-category typologies emerging. Bellenger & Korgaonkar (1980) focused on Economic versus Recreational shoppers. These were shoppers with a specific purpose versus those who were not instrumentally driven by particular product needs and simply viewed shopping as a leisure pursuit. In a study of older consumers, shoppers were divided into 'Active', 'Economic', and 'Apathetic'. Once again, the characteristics of these types mirrored those outlined by earlier research—the active leisure seekers, the price conscious, and the disinterested (Lumpkin, 1985).

In extending this research, Lumpkin, Hawes, & Darden (1986) concentrated on consumers in rural locations and differentiated between 'inactive inshoppers', 'active outshoppers', and 'thrifty innovators'. The first type had little interest in shopping and restricted their purchases to local stores. The second type was much more engaged and adventurous as shoppers, exploring different outlets and enjoying the experience. The final category was confident in their tastes and led the way as early adopters of product and service innovations and new brands.

The major limitation of these early studies was that they produced typologies of shoppers that were not fully validated in terms of accurate behaviour predictions (Samli, 1975). If psychographics are to be used to predict shopping outcomes, one approach to adopt is to compare the profiles of patrons and non-patrons of specific retail outlets. One study that adopted this approach included measures of demographics, media habits, and psychographics to differentiate between consumers who were established as users or non-users of four types of retail outlets: convenience store, department store, discount store, and fast-food franchise (Bearden, Teel, & Durand, 1978).

Five psychographics types were identified: Traditionalist (with old-fashioned tastes), Outgoing/Individualist (believes in being self-sufficient/DIY-oriented), Quality Service (searches for best-quality providers), Socially Conscious (prefers fashionable brands rated by other people), and Other-Directed (needs advice and recommendations of others to guide purchase decisions). Combinations of demographics, media habits, and psychographic factors differentiated patrons/non-patrons of each story type. With convenience stores, users were less traditional, less outgoing, and less socially conscious. With department stores, users were more quality conscious and more outer-directed. Discount store customers were less traditional, less outgoing, and less socially conscious than non-users. Fast-food users were more outgoing and more socially conscious than non-users.

This kind of profiling can have a number of benefits for marketers. Demographic profiles combined with media habits profiles can provide guidance in terms of placement of marketing campaigns. Psychographics can then reveal more about the kinds of values and product-related expectations consumers hold dear. These data can be used as input to guide decisions about the designs of branding and packaging and the nature of promotional appeals used in advertisements.

In a further attempt to validate psychographic measures as predictors of shopping orientations, research has been carried out into the motives that underpin local versus non-local shopping. Initial research in this field focused mostly on classification schemes for markets based on their spatial locations and layouts (Converse, 1949; Reilly, 1953). Such factors were discovered from early on to influence consumers' choices of where to shop (Huff, 1964; Bucklin, 1966, 1967, 1971; Dommermuth & Cundiff, 1967; Moore & Mason, 1969; Haines, Simon & Alexis, 1971).

As major shopping centres together with large department stores and supermarkets developed, the catchment areas of specific retail locations grew bigger. People came from greater distances to buy both their weekly shop and more specialised goods (Herman & Beik, 1963, Thompson, 1971). These changes to the geographical and physical structures of retailing posed challenges to smaller retailers that had been dependent upon local trade for their business viability. As more of their customers migrated out of the immediate vicinity in which they lived and abandoned local high street shops, many local retail businesses closed. As with most innovative patterns of behaviour, the adoption of out-of-town shopping was characteristic of younger and better-educated people at first, but eventually spread across most demographics. Shopping malls were attractive because they contained a wide variety of retail outlets that catered to short-term and long-term consumer needs. They offered the convenience of stores positioned relatively close together and the comfort of a controlled environment in which to shop all the year around.

It was not simply their demographic profile that differentiated the initial adopters of out-of-town mall shopping, but also their psychographics. Comparisons of 'in-shoppers' (who stayed within their local shopping area) and 'out-shoppers' (who travelled farther afield) have revealed a number of specific types of consumer. One American study of housewives who lived in the suburbs of a medium-sized town identified five types: Inshoppers, Big-Ticket Outshoppers, Furniture Outshoppers, Appearance Outshoppers, and Home Entertainment Outshoppers (Darden & Perreault, 1976).

Inshoppers, as we have seen already, tended to do most or all of their shopping locally. The other four types travelled beyond their immediate locality to obtain specific products and were variants of the outshopper defined by the specific product type they travelled out of town to buy. Big-Ticket Outshoppers went outside their own locality to get expensive items such as major appliances for their homes. Furniture Outshoppers are a self-explanatory type. Appearance Outshoppers travelled out of town for fashion items and jewellery. Home Entertainment Outshoppers travelled out of their immediate community for goods such as TV sets, radios, and other electronic equipment.

Outshoppers in general tended to be more fashion conscious and more innovation oriented than inshoppers, and this influenced their interest in known and trendy branded items regardless of the product type. Home Entertainment Outshoppers were the most fashion conscious of all. Outshoppers generally were also more financially optimistic than were Inshoppers, although not always more self-confident. Outshoppers were found to get a lot of enjoyment from shopping itself that goes beyond simply needing to make specific purchases.

Fashion Shopping

Another field in which psychographics has been used is fashion shopping (Visser & du Preez, 2001). Clothing is one of life's essentials, after food and drink. In a modern consumer context, however, shopping for clothes and for other associated items such as accessories, cosmetics, and jewellery is driven by more than basic needs. It represents a realm of self-expression for consumers, with branded items being worn as identity badges that comprise symbolic messages about the wearer's social status and lifestyle. It is understandable, therefore, that a psychological dimension to understanding consumer behaviour was explored by early marketing researchers (King & Ring, 1975).

People can purchase fashion merchandise through many different outlets. These include major department stores, specialist fashion boutiques and other outlets, catalogues, websites, and television shopping channels. There are many factors that can influence fashion choices, including price, premium offers, outlet service quality, and convenience, but branding factors linked to the product itself and the outlet through which it is bought are frequently among the most critical. For many people, fashion choices represent an important aspect of their own identity. What they wear can say a lot about the kind of person they are. It is not surprising, therefore, that while fashions are designed with a specific demographic in mind, manufacturers and retailers must also take into account psychographic factors because these also play a key role in determining consumers' personal selections.

Consumers for whom fashion consciousness is important tend to turn to fashion opinion leaders, including designers and celebrities, for ideas and inspiration. Researchers have examined psychographic variables in relation to fashion choices and retail choices for fashion purchases (Grubb & Grathwold, 1967; Berry, 1969; Lazer & Wyckham, 1969; Summers, 1970; Darden & Reynolds, 1974; Hirschmann & Mills, 1979).

Early attempts to relate generic lifestyle traits to fashion-related behaviour met with mixed success. Understanding how individuals lived their lives in a general sense often proved to lack the focus needed to predict specific purchases they might make (Wind & Green, 1974). Evidence did emerge, however, that when lifestyle and value measures were more closely tailored to the fashion market, they could provide some useful indications of how consumers make choices and of the specific choices they are most likely to make. One American study that involved a survey of over 6,000 women in Los Angeles uncovered seven lifestyle types associated with fashion: Leaders, Followers, Independent, Neutrals, Uninvolved, Negatives, and Rejectors (Gutman & Mills, 1982).

Leaders were consumers for whom fashion consciousness is centrally important to their lives and who make a point of being up to speed with the latest designs. Hence, among their peers, they like to be ahead of the pack with new fashion styles and brands. Having said that, Leaders tend to feel most comfortable with established brand names and look out for new lines produced by these companies.

Followers also have an acute sensitivity to being fashionable, but depend upon Leaders for guidance about which styles are 'in'. Independents embrace fashions but seek to plough their own furrow in that they seek neither to lead nor follow others. Often this type will reject mainstream brands in favour of styles rejected by the masses as a badge of independence of thought and taste. The Neutrals like to be fashionable to a point, but this is not for them a defining and core aspect of their lives. The Uninvolved, in comparison, have little or no interest in fashion. Negatives attach meaning to fashion but do not wish or seek to be led and are more functional in their tastes that brand-image driven. For this type, it is important to look good in the sense of being neat and tidy, but not to seek social status through brands. The Rejectors not only share the Neutrals' relative disinterest in fashion, but are completely unconcerned about what they wear or how they appear.

It is clear from the above psychographic typology that some fashion 'types' are more interested in fashion than are others and among those with fashion consciousness, the types of brands each might prefer are not the same. Such data provide marketers with broad-brush portraits of consumer types that can guide decisions about marketing strategies, brand design, and promotional campaigns. They are probably unable to pinpoint exactly the product or brand choices individual consumers will make, but they can narrow down options about how to persuade them.

A typology emerged from one study that was based on the idea that some consumers are more engaged with clothes shopping than are others. Shim & Kotsiopulos (1993) differentiated women apparel shoppers into those who were highly involved, apathetic, and convenience oriented. The highly involved shoppers were concerned about their personal appearance and chose brands carefully to establish the right kind of image. Apathetic shoppers were driven by these concerns and had little interest in fashion or shopping for apparel. The convenience shoppers had some interest in apparel, but were not willing to put themselves out to shop for this type of product. They sought easier solutions, and many were keen catalogues shoppers.

Boedeker (1995) observed that consumers can vary in terms of whether shopping is regarded as a fun experience or something that is functional.

In a research study with a sample of shoppers, he found that the two most prominent types were 'traditional' shoppers and 'new-type' shoppers. Demographically these two types were very similar, but they differed more markedly in their motives for shopping and expectations of the benefits they would receive from the experience. New-type shoppers more often conceived of shopping as a recreational activity and thus sought to go shopping in environments that catered to that need. While this type, as with the traditional shoppers, sometimes had functional shopping needs, shopping was a much broader lifestyle experience.

Psychographic measures have been found useful in differentiating consumer types in the clothing market around the world. Research in India among college students ages 18 to 23 found two fashion-related psychographic factors called fashion consciousness and innovativeness. These two factors combined with the Inner-directed and Outer-directed of the LOV model to predict clothing choices. There were no direct statistical relationships between LOV dimensions and fashion purchases, and instead the fashion-related psychographic factors served as mediating variables (Roy, 2007).

Not all research into fashion consciousness has supported the premise that psychological shopping orientations can significantly predict clothing purchases. One study found that psychographic predictors performed unsuccessfully with mature consumers (Huddleston, Ford, & Bickle, 1993). More generally, however, evidence accumulated across the 1950s to the 1990s to show that psychographics can provide useful indicators of shopping orientations linked both to brand preferences and purchase choices (Visser & du Preez, 2001).

Psychological Types and Product Choices

Psychographics and personality psychology have been used to classify consumers in relation to their product and service preferences. At this level of analysis, psychological responses, including attitudes and opinions, beliefs and perceptions, motives and behavioural intentions, are measured in direct relation to product/service types or to specific products or services. The aim of this type of research is to discover the reasons consumers might have for wanting to buy and use a specific product or service. Going deeper still, this research approach can be used to find out why one product/service variant or brand is preferred over others in the same commodity range.

Typologies have been developed for air travel (Behaviour Science Corporation, 1972), bank charge cards (Plummer, 1971), cosmetics (Wells & Tigert, 1971), food products (Tigert, Lathrope & Bleeg, 1971; Wells & Tigert, 1971), hand soap (Plummer, 1971), motor vehicles (Young, 1973), and many others. It is worth taking a closer look at some of these typologies and whether they deliver valuable marketing insights. Psychographics have tended to comprise both custom-built psychological typologies and the adaptation of personality scales originally developed outside a marketing context.

Household Furnishings

Establishing a home is one of the most important aspects of daily living. In terms of human needs, the home caters to our security and safety needs that are positioned just one step up from the biological needs (Maslow, 1970). Once a location and property have been found, the next step is to convert the physical structure into a personalised space that can be called 'home'. This process involves choosing how to furnish the property. In modern, 21st century societies, consumers are confronted with many options in relation to different types of furniture. Given the significance of the home and the way it is presented to its occupants' personal identities, it is essential for marketers working in this product field to understand the psychology of their target markets.

General values and lifestyle characteristics and specific psychographic attributes have been linked to household furnishing choices in different parts of the world. Research from Malaysia, for instance, reported that lifestyle distinctions could be distinguished between ethnocentric and polycentric lifestyle orientations and between shopping orientations. The lifestyle orientations signalled whether consumers sought to create a traditional household interior that was associated with their ethnic and cultural origins or a more modern and contemporary look. Consumers were further differentiated into Personalising shoppers and Apathetic shoppers. The former sought to buy furniture that enabled them to create an atmosphere in their home that projects messages about their own character. The latter were not motivated in this or any other way by furniture shopping (Hassan, Muhammad & Bakar, 2010).

Motor Vehicles

Evans (1959) used an established personality profiler called the Edwards Personal Preference Schedule to differentiate between owners of Chevrolet and Ford cars. This personality test yielded some differences of note, but for the most part was fairly insensitive to differences between owners of these two car brands. The conclusion reached here was that personality was of little use in predicting car brand choices. A more circumspect position might be that this particular personality test—which was one among many that were already available at the time of this research—was unable to provide useful distinctions in relation to car brand choices.

Other research demonstrated that psychographics could provide useful insights into the reasons why people might choose a particular brand of car, and that these data could be used to ensure that the way a brand was promoted contained appeals of relevance to the most likely buyers. Young (1973) examined the use of psychographics among people in the market for a Ford Pinto. The Pinto was a small car and had been promoted as a product that was not only small, but also 'carefree and romantic'. It was manufactured for the American market to compete with smaller cars being imported at that time from overseas manufacturers in Europe and the Far East. Psychographic research revealed that the original advertising appeals were not all relevant to consumers' perceptions of the Ford Pinto. In particular, the idea of this model as 'romantic' did not make a good fit for many potential buyers. More important attributes were power, reliability, economical to run, and functionality. As a result of this research, which redefined the psychological profile of Pinto customers, Ford changed its advertising accordingly and enjoyed growth in market share.

Prescription Drugs

In another product field, of prescription drugs and medicines, psychographics were used to produce product-specific psychological types. In a study of prescription drug users, an extensive battery of attitude statements yielded data that were factor analysed to produce four different customer types. Realists were concerned about taking control of their health personally and not relying only on a doctor. Authority Seekers also believed that health could be taken under control and not left to fate, but they also believed that specialists such as doctors and other health professionals should be listened to because they had authority in the field. Sceptics were not generally concerned about their health and were unlikely to resort to medicines if they caught a cold. Hypochondriacs had a lot of concern about their health and believed they were prone to get ill. They were in the market for any possible remedies out there. Research showed that Hypochondriacs were heavy users of prescription drugs, whereas Sceptics were light users, with the other two types falling in between (Ziff, 1971).

Similar research was conducted among consumers of a stomach remedy. Once again, respondents completed a battery of items that measured a combination of measures of symptom frequencies, perceived benefits of different brands, attitudes concerning treatments, and other beliefs about different ailments. Following a series of analyses, the researcher described four consumer types: Severe Sufferers, Active Medicators, Hypochondriacs, and Practicalists.

Severe Sufferers tended to be young adults, well educated, and to have children. They were anxious people and their concerns often revolved around health issues. They would take ailments seriously and seek appropriate forms of treatment without delay and were willing to try new products. The Active Medicators were similar demographically to the Severe Sufferers, although they were not as anxious. Yet, they still used remedies to relieve aches and pains. Hypochondriacs were usually older and not as well educated and often female. They were concerned about their state of health and at the same time lacked the confidence to self-medicate, preferring instead to depend upon the advice of medical authorities. Practicalists were older, well educated, emotionally adjusted people, and not generally overly concerned about their health. They would accept occasional aches and pains or illness as part of life and would not constantly seek remedies (Pernica, 1974).

Psychographics have been used to differentiate between consumers for cosmetics and toiletries. In relation to men's toiletries, for example, Furse & Greenberg (1975) measured men's attitudes and identified two broad consumer types. They labelled these as 'Mr. Practical' and 'The Fun-Loving Routine User'. 'Mr. Practical' was mostly concerned about the functional aspects of aftershave products and was usually less impressed by the inflated symbolic appeals of advertising. Members of this psychographic type were more impressed by appeals that resonated with their personal experience with the products. 'The Fun-Loving Routine User' regarded toiletries such as aftershave and cologne as good fun and as capable of giving off pleasant sensations. They were not taken in by claimed psychological reasons for using these products, such that their use signalled something about the personality of the user, for example, that users were men who did not take themselves too seriously. They did believe, however, that the use of these products could enhance a man's sexual attractiveness by making him smell nice.

The most important insights of this research derived from perceptions of advertising messages. Understanding the psychographics of consumers for these products could indicate whether certain types of advertising would be seen as persuasive. Another dimension of persuasion was the style of cognitive information processing adopted by male consumers. Furse and Greenberg also included an analysis of this attribute. They discovered that consumers could vary in the ways they preferred to receive information about products. Some preferred to receive written information, and others liked to see images of the product and scenarios in which it might be used. Others liked to experience the physical sensations of the product, such as its texture, smell, and colour. These data could provide some guidance concerning how best to promote these products to different psychographic types, but psychographics alone did not emerge as a significant predictor of eventual purchase patterns.

Another study with women consumers of eye makeup and shortening found that heavy and light users of these products differed demographically and in terms of their psychographics (Wells & Beard, 1974). Heavy users were young, well educated, and lived in metropolitan areas. They were also heavy users of other cosmetics products, such as face makeup, lipstick, hairspray, and perfume. In addition, they were more likely to be smokers. In terms of psychographic measures, these consumers valued being attractive and presentable, especially to men, and regarded their makeup as an important aspect of their self-image. They were willing to explore the market and try new products, liked to go out for dinner, enjoyed the ballet and foreign travel. They were not traditional homebodies and regarded their home as an extension of their self-image and therefore in need of the same care and attention.

Many householders have pets. This also represents a large market for animal foodstuffs and accessories. There has been an interest in whether consumer psychographics can provide useful insights into purchase patterns and choices for these products. In 1970, one of the major pet food manufacturers in the United States, General Foods, undertook a study of dog food buyers. Six types of dog owners were identified that were defined by a mixture of demographic, life stage, and lifestyle variables. Two of these types were seen as representing the best potential market categories for a new dog food product. One type, consisting mainly of childless women who lived in apartments in inner-city areas, owned dogs as baby substitutes. They devoted a lot of resources to their pet, bought premium brands, and spoiled their pets, often changing brands. The second type, called 'the nutritionalists', were well-educated dog owners with high incomes. Dogs were important companions and it was important to these owners to keep their pets healthy, and this meant being careful about the types of pet food they bought.

One research study examined the market for cameras and identified three types based on demographics and psychological measures (Hughes, 1978). Self-attributed psychological traits were found to be related to the type of camera owned. Some consumers bought expensive products and big brand names, and others went down a more practical and economical route. The brand in focus was Nikon, and owners of this make of camera regarded themselves a broad-minded, discriminating and intelligent, and also as reserved and conformist.

Psychographics have also been linked to people's propensities to engage in certain activities, such as playing the lottery. Researchers in the United States compared groups of people who were regular or occasional lottery ticket purchasers and those who never took part (McConkey & Warren, 1987). A sample of people were asked to completed a battery of around 200 psychographic items that were subsequently analysed to identify a smaller number of response clusters that represented different psychographic types. Heavy lottery ticket buyers tended to be more likely to live in inner-city areas, to be over-eaters, and to not be particularly health conscious. Even so, they liked to travel and were keen to go overseas to explore the world more so than occasional lottery ticket purchasers and non-purchasers.

People who did not play the lottery tended to be less optimistic than those who bought tickets and had more conservative values. They observed traditional gender stereotypes about the women's place being in the home and the man's role being the breadwinner. They were more health conscious that heavy lottery players, watched their diets, and drank alcohol occasionally.

Those who played the lottery occasionally mostly fell in between the other two groups in most of these different respects. They were, however, more optimistic than heavy players and less interested in foreign travel than non-players.

Financial Products and Investment Choices

Psychological profiles have been found to differentiate between the investment choices people make in different parts of the world. Deciding which financial products to purchase is a matter that frequently entails weighing up risk. Some financial product consumers are more inclined to take risks than are others and this propensity can be signalled by individuals' personality profiles. Investors who are both active and inclined to commit with large sums tend to score higher on risk-taking measures (Barnewell, 1987). Heavy investors have also been marked out as more non-conformist than are light investors (Warren, Stevens, & McConkey, 1996).

Much of this evidence has derived from the United States. Even in Eastern cultures, however, it has been found that people who invest more heavily in financial products tend to be more adventurous and are also more innovative, fashion conscious, and have a greater sense of optimism (Lim, 1992).

Subsequent Malaysian research conducted with investors sampled from the capital city, Kuala Lumpur, confirmed that active and passive investors differ in their personalities (Ghazali & Othman, 2004). In this instance, 'active' investors were people who played the stock market at least three times a month, and 'passive' investors were less frequently engaged in playing the financial market. The researchers utilised psychographic measures derived from a number of earlier American studies (Wells & Tigert, 1971; Darden & Ashton, 1974; Wells, 1975; Kinnear & Taylor, 1976). A further battery of items was used to measure after-work activities.

A factor analysis was used on the raw psychographic data and identified four significant clusters of psychological measures, which defined the Independent/Self-confident type, careful spenders, the risk-oriented type, and debt avoiders. The Independent/Self-confident believed in their personal abilities and judgement. Careful spenders tended to use cash to by most items, occasionally using a credit card. The risk-oriented were innovative and liked to seek out new experiences. The debt avoiders disliked accumulating debt and believed in spending within their means.

Responses to after-work activities items were also factor analysed to yield three significant factors, labelled: knowledge seeker, outdoor lover, and outgoing/entertaining. Knowledge seekers engaged in reading and other pursuits concerned with learning. Outdoor lovers pursued lots of outdoor activities and liked to travel, whereas the outgoing/entertaining liked to go to parties and socialise a lot.

In this study, as elsewhere, active investors more than passive investors were found to be knowledge seekers and also to enjoy going out, enjoying new physical experiences and meeting new people (see also Barnewell, 1987; Warren et al., 1990). In relation to the psychographic measures, however, one only factor—risk-taking—significantly differentiated between active and passive investors. As expected, the active investors were more inclined to take risks than were the passive investors.

The Allianz Life Insurance Company conducted a study with over 3,200 American adults ages 44 to 75 years to identify a number of psychologically and demographically defined preretirement and retirement population segments (Allianz, 2010). The outcome was a five-fold typology of financial personality types. These were labelled as 'overwhelmed' (32%), 'iconic' (20%), 'resilient' (27%), 'distracted' (7%), and 'savvy' (14%). The 'overwhelmed' were not prepared for retirement and operated barely above survival mode. In contrast, the 'iconic' felt they were well prepared financially for their retirement years and believed in the American Dream.

The 'resilient' were fairly confident they had prepared as much as they could for the future, but experienced residual uncertainties about whether they had done enough to secure themselves financially throughout their retirement years. They felt they might need to work longer to compensate for any shortfalls in their financial needs from their current savings.

The 'distracted' had made plans like the 'resilient' and hoped they had done enough to secure a comfortable lifestyle during retirement, but felt they might not have done enough and were unsure what to do about it.

The 'savvy' were confident they had done enough for their retirement or, if not yet, then they would. They believed they would be well placed through diverse investments to enjoy a comfortable lifestyle after they finished working, and such was their self-confidence that they were even prepared to take some risks with their investments to get a bigger return.

Personal Commodity Choices

We have already seen that psychographics have been applied to differentiate shopper types and that these typologies have been applied to shopping for fashion items. The research examined previously was concerned with general consumer orientations towards shopping rather than the role played by psychological factors in decisions concerning types of products to purchase. Psychographics have been investigated in relation to product choices with fashion (Visser & du Preez, 2001).

Young consumers who were regular buyers of clothes exhibited different psychological profiles from those who engaged in fashion shopping much less often. Clothes were much more important to the heavy clothes shoppers, who regarded themselves as more knowledgeable about fashions and as more innovative in their tastes to the point of conceiving themselves as fashion opinion leaders among their friends. For the heavy shoppers, clothes represented an aspect of self-expression and personal identity (Goldsmith, 2002).

The purchase of cosmetics is important to some consumers because of the part they play in representing the outward appearance of the self. Choices of products in this domain therefore are especially important to those consumers who wish to project a specific image of themselves. Women consumers in India were found to classify cosmetics in terms of personality profiles that they identified as having importance to their own preferred image. Some openly admitted that product choices depended upon whether they made a good fit for they preferred self-image or for the way they perceived their own personality. Others made choices they were sure would be approved by their social reference groups (Hema, Bakkapa & Somashekkar, 2012).

Holiday and Tourism Choices

Gonzalez & Bello (2002) examined the experiences of tourists in Spain and developed a psychographic model for consumer segmentation that was conceptually guided by Maslow's (1954) hierarchy of human needs. This model had also influenced custom-built, normative models of consumer segmentation such as the various iterations of the Values and Lifestyles model (see Beatty, Homer, & Kahle, 1988; SRI, 2006). The different needs and interests of tourists were identified, such as the type of holiday, preferred location and setting, distance from home, and combination of work trips with vacation trips. Statistical analyses of the data yielded from this investigation produced five psychographic types: Home-Loving, Idealistic, Autonomous, Hedonistic, and Conservative.

Home-Loving types, as their label would suggest, liked to take holidays close to home. This did not mean they eschewed opportunities to travel, but when they did, they sought out destinations where the location and accommodation reminded them of home. These consumers had conservative tastes, enjoyed life's simple pleasures, and sought good value for their money. They also enjoyed holidaying with lots of family members.

The Idealistic type shared the simple, conservative tastes of the Home-Loving type, but enjoyed physically active holidays, such as walking trips. Understandably, therefore, they preferred rural holidays over city breaks and enjoyed short trips over long ones.

The Autonomous type consisted of pleasure seekers and sought holiday destinations that offered variety and especially a good nightlife. They were happy on short city breaks as well as longer holidays in the sun, and generally liked the longer breaks to be near the coast. Whereas Home-Loving types would be happy to stay in the homes of family or friends, the Autonmous types preferred to stay in hotels and were always keen to get away for an overseas break, whether short or long.

The Hedonistic type also sought holidays that offered personal pleasure, but they were driven by higher pursuits that enabled them to engage in self-expression rather than mindless enjoyment. Often these were individuals who travelled with friends rather than family members and often sought out new and unusual destinations to visit that would set them apart from normal holidaymakers. The Conservative type comprised family-oriented individuals with a sense of materialism. They liked predictability and order in their lives and preferred quiet holidays with their family or close friends, usually to places with which they were familiar.

This research revealed that tourists could be helpfully classified in terms of holiday aspirations and expectations that were in turn linked to deeper-seated values and needs. Understanding more about the psychology of consumers as tourists could uncover reasons why holidaymakers could be differentiated in ways that could help service providers cater more effectively to their needs. Demographic factors lacked this type of sensitivity, and psychographics frequently cut across specific demographic categories.

Luxury Brand Choices

There have been attempts to construct tailor-made consumer segments linked to specific categories of consumption based on value types. One body of research of this type examined psychographic categories associated with definitions of luxury brands. 'Luxury' represents a specific kind of concept in consumerism and is linked to a wide range of product and service categories. Yet, there are often underlying ideas and values that define luxury wherever it is applied. It generally conveys impressions about quality and exclusivity (Furnham & Bunyon, 1986; Dubois & Laurent, 1994; Tsai, 2003; Vigneron & Johnson, 1999, 2004).

Luxury has been found to have a multidimensional structure that embraces function, personal needs, and culturally symbolic components (Widemann, Hennigs & Siebels, 2009). One model of luxury value differentiated between four dimensions: financial, functional, individual, and social. The financial dimension classified products and product variants in terms of price and the messages that that attribute conveyed about the status of the commodity. The functional dimension considered the benefits to the consumer of having a specific product or brand. The individual dimension was concerned with whether the product made a good fit for the consumer in terms of their self-image and personal value. The social dimension represented the reputational value of a product or a variant of it to the consumer's social reference group (Widemann, Hennigs & Siebels, 2007).

Other luxury value-related dimensions have emerged from other research. Some brands have rarity value, for instance, and this lends them a degree of uniqueness and exclusivity. Other brands have a reputation built on reliability in the dependability in delivery of what they were made for. Such characteristics define them as standout products of the highest quality of their type (O'Cass & Frost, 2002). In the case of some brands that have luxury status, they are desired by consumers through the conspicuous use and purchase of them. Such brands serve as status symbol badges to be worn by consumers so as to convey messages to others about their own social status and distinctive taste (Mason, 1981; Bearden & Etzel, 1982; Tian, Bearden & Hunter, 2001). Brands then acquire prestige value because of their status relative to their rivals (O'Cass & McEwen, 2004).

Luxury goods are important to consumers who can afford them because of the self-image many wish to project to others, especially to members of the reference groups to which they belong or aspire to join. Even then, there must be a degree of congruity between the image of a brand—even a luxury one—and the consumer's sense of self to encourage its purchase and use (Puntoni, 2001). Consumers will study promotional messages for luxury brands to assess this brand-image to self-image congruity (Graeff, 1996). A consumer's attachment to luxury brands can also emerge from positive experiences with their products or services, which can create an appealing hedonic tone around the brand, pulling the consumer back to it again and again (Kapferer, 1997; Dubois & Czellar, 2002). To work effectively, however, these emotional responses must occur to products and services that match a consumer's internal and enduring needs which define their personalities (Tian et al., 2001; Tsai, 2005)

Psychographics and Shopping in the Digital Era

The 21st century has witnessed dramatic technological developments that have changed the way people live their lives. These developments have taken root in the way products and services are promoted, discovered, and purchased. More shopping can be carried out remotely via the Internet. Most leading retailers operate their own websites not simply to promote their businesses, but also as sites of transactions with their customers. Marketing researchers have directed increased attention to the digital world as an environment in which consumer activity occurs. Their efforts have included the study of psychological consumer typologies that have emerged within the new world of digital consumerism.

Online shopping did not emerge from nowhere. Long before the Internet became public, consumers shopped remotely using catalogues. In-home shoppers were differentiated from those who resorted only to out-of-home shopping mostly in terms of their demographic profiles. American researchers found, for example, that catalogue shoppers were more likely to be women who were not in paid employment (i.e., housewives) and women in part-time employment with young children, unmarried males under the age of 40, and households with a female head aged 40 to 49 (Darian, 1987).

The emergence of the online shopper has created an interest in finding out more about this behaviour and the people who engage in it. Just as typologies have been discovered for different types of 'offline' or traditional shopping, so, too, have they been defined for online shoppers. Some researchers have defined consumer typologies that segment both adopters and non-adopters of online shopping. Initially, there were doubts about whether the Internet would emerge as a transactional shopping platform and was regarded by some as acting as little more than a price comparison site (Wallace, 1996). For many consumers, shopping was conceived as an enjoyable leisure activity that would not deliver the same level of satisfaction when conducted online (Rowley, 1996). Instead, if transactions were going to occur on this platform, it was a location that would appeal most to the Apathetic shopper who had little interest in shopping per se.

Yet, within a few years of the Internet going 'public', it was being adopted around the world not simply as a shop window, but as a site of making purchases for a wide range of goods (Dholakia, 1999; Vrechopoulos, Siomkos & Doukidis, 2001; Dholakia & Uusitalo, 2002; Goldsmith, 2002). With the emergence of wireless Internet connections, consumers quickly latched on to mobile shopping that could be conducted both outside and inside the home (Coursaris & Hassanein, 2002; Vrechopoulos, Siokos & Doukidis, 2001; Balasubramanian, Peterson & Javenpaa, 2002; Bigne, Ruiz, Sanz, 2005).

Despite the earlier research with 'outshoppers', that is, consumers who leave their home to shop, research with home shoppers, especially when this migrated onto the Internet, initially revealed little evidence of specific motives linked to this style of retail activity (Hagel & Armstong, 1997; Korgaonkar & Wolin, 1999). There were distinctive demographic profiles linked to Internet shopping. These shoppers were more likely to be better off and older than non-online shoppers and more likely to be male (Donthu & Garcia, 1999; Korgaonkar & Wolin, 1999). There were some early signs of distinctive psychological characteristics associated with Internet shoppers, such as being more variety seeking and less risk averse (Donthu & Garcia, 1999).

One of the reasons frequently identified for home shopping has been its convenience for the consumer (Gehrt & Carter, 1992; Blakney & Sekely, 1994). Yet this apparently logical explanation for this behaviour is not always supported by empirical evidence. This is true not just for catalogue shopping, but also for Internet shopping (Gehrt, Yale & Lawson, 1996; Rowley, 1996; Jarvenpaa & Todd, 1997). Although convenience is not being dismissed as a motive for remote shopping, whether conducted offline or online, growing evidence has emerged that there are other motives that underpin the online shopping behaviours of some consumers. Many of these 'other' motives, however, are not new. Research on catalogue and Internet shopping has reproduced shopping motives identified originally by much earlier investigations of 'brick-and-mortar' shopping.

It will be recalled that Stone (1954) identified four shopper orientations: Economic, Personalising, Ethical, and Apathetic. Later studies sometimes reduced and sometimes extended this number of orientations. Despite these variances, some consistent threads ran through all this empirical work (Westbrook & Black, 1985; Lesser & Hughes, 1986). Some shoppers were driven by price consciousness and the need to get a good deal, which for them offered the 'best value' (Stephenson & Willett, 1969; Williams et al., 1978; Shim & Mahoney, 1992). Others enjoyed shopping as an end in itself as an extension of their leisure and social lives. In other words, shopping was a form of recreation, whether it took place in a mall or while browsing through a catalogue (Stephenson & Willett, 1969; Bellenger & Korgaonkar, 1980; Gehrt & Carter, 1992). Others sought out premium brands for self-identity purposes. Others could not care less about shopping. The Apathetic shoppers have not drawn much attention from researchers, perhaps because they have essentially opted themselves out (Brown & Reid, 1997). However, it might be just as insightful to know why some people do not enjoy shopping as to study the reason why some cannot leave it alone.

Shopping orientations, representing shopping-related psychographic attributes, were found to vary between consumers from different demographic categories, but also independently differentiated those who engaged in online shopping and those who did not. Gender, education, and household income were important factors linked to the propensity to engage in online shopping, but also significant were convenience and recreational shopping orientations. Consumers motivated by convenience needs were more likely than others to shop online. It is interesting also to note that recreational shoppers, who enjoyed shopping in general, had also embraced online shopping. Online shopping was also differentially adopted for different product types (Girard, Korgaonkar & Silverblatt, 2003).

A online survey conducted with over 9,600 American consumers identified seven clusters of online shoppers: Personalising, Recreational, Economic, Involved, Convenience-oriented, Community-oriented, and Apathetic, Convenience-oriented shoppers (Brown, Pope & Voges, 2003). These findings confirmed consumer types already demonstrated by earlier studies of offline shoppers. There are consumers who are motivated to shop for personal needs that range from essentials to identity- or image-related. There are consumers that are price-conscious and seek good deals. There are others for whom shopping is a chore and they seek methods that add to making the experience less troublesome and more convenient. There are those for whom shopping is a pleasurable leisure activity in its own right. There are those whose shopping habits are shaped by other social purposes, such as supporting local community retailers. These types of consumer were found to exist among online shoppers as much as they had been among offline shoppers.

Despite this typology of consumers being identified, weaker evidence occurred that these consumer types served as indicators or predictors of purchase intention or actual purchase behaviour. Subsequent research among British online consumers confirmed many of these consumer types, but again found that they did not predict consumption choices or actual purchases

(Jayawardhena, Wright & Dennis, 2007). These findings also indicated that online consumers cannot be considered a breed apart from offline consumers in their psychological nature or in respect of the factors that shape their purchase behaviours (see also, Min & Wolfinbarger, 2005)

Alfred, Smith, & Swinyard (2006) identified three online shopper types called socializers, e-shopping loves, and e-value leaders and three non-online shopper types labelled as fearful conservatives, shopping averters, and technology muddlers. Socializers were active and enthusiastic shoppers, both online and offline. E-shopping lovers had shifted over to online shopping and this now predominated over traditional shopping. E-value leaders were even more committed to online shopping and devoted a lot of time to it along with other online activities that dominated their lives. The fearful conservatives were not at all comfortable with computer technology or the online world. Shopping averters were still committed to traditional forms of shopping. Technology muddlers were not inherently against online shopping, but their lack of digital world competence meant they simply were unable to take advantage of it.

Concluding Remarks

There is a long history of using psychological measures to differentiate between consumers in marketing research and practice. In some instances, marketing researchers have developed original instruments to measure psychological orientations on the part of consumers towards specific areas of consumer activity or to specific product and service domains. In other instances, established psychological scales have been utilised to explain why some consumers are drawn to particular products and services.

Psychographics that have been targeted at specific domains of consumer activity have enjoyed greater success in terms of predicting and explaining consumer behaviours than models that have attempted to produce generic typologies for entire populations. One reason for this could be that custom-built psychographic measures have comprised items that measure specific motivational orientations towards specific products. These instruments therefore comprised measures that were directly relevant to decisions about the target product or service. More generic psychographic models lack this element and provide very generic descriptions of consumers that indicate highly generalised commodity orientations, but few if any insights into why consumers might wish to purchase specific products/ services or brands.

The benefits of psychographics to marketing professionals when applied to an understanding of markets for specific product or service types are found in the insights such consumer segmentation can provide in reasons why consumers might approach or avoid specific products/services or variants of products and services. These reasons might be couched in terms of motives, needs, aspirations, attitudes, beliefs, and other perceptions that could also help marketers shape promotional messages that will resonate with consumers' reasons for making specific purchases. Demographic dimensions provide useful heuristic devices to describing consumer populations, but offer no explanatory insights into consumers' behavioural choices. As the next chapter will show, although demographics remain useful in terms of some aspects of market segmentation, such as defining products that might be best suited to one gender, a specific age group, or a specific racial category, psychographics can add further important insights within demographic categories about how the consumer behaviours and choices, even of members of the same demographic group, can manifest great diversity.

References

Alfred, C. R., Smith, S. M., & Swinyard, W. R. (2006) E-shopping lovers and fearful conservatives: A market segmentation analysis. *International Journal of Retail and Distribution Management*, 34(4/5), 308–333.

Allianz (2010) *Reclaiming the Future: The Five Financial Personalities White Paper*. Minneapolis, MN: Allianz Life Insurance Company. Available at: https://www2.allianzlife.com/content/public/Literature/Documents/ENT-1093-N.pdf

Balasubramanian, S., Peterson, R. A., & Javenpaa, S. L. (2002) Exploring the implications of M-commerce for markets and marketing. *Journal of the Academy of Marketing Science,* 30(4), 348–361.

Balasubramanyan, R., Cohen, W. W., Pierce, D., & Redlawsk, D. P. (2011) What pushes their buttons? Predicting polarity from the content of political blog posts. In *Proceedings of the ACL-11 Workshop on Language in Social Media*, Portland, Oreg, 23 June, pp. 12–19.

Barnewell, M. M. (1987) Psychographics characteristics of the individual investors. In M. M. Barnewell (Ed.) *Asset Allocations for the Individual Investors*, pp. 125–140. Homewood, IL: Dow Jones Irwin.

Bearden, W. O., & Etzel, M. J. (1982) Reference group influence on product and brand purchase decisions. *Journal of Consumer Research*, 9, 183–194.

Bearden, W. O., Teel, J. E. Jr., & Durand, R. M. (1978) Media usage, psychographics and demographic dimensions of retail shoppers. *Journal of Retailing*, 54, 65–74.

Beatty, S. E., Homer, P. M., & Kahle, L. R. (1988) Problems with VALS in international marketing research: An example from an application of the empirical mirror technique. *Advances in Consumer Research*, 15, 375–380.

Behaviour Science Corporation (1972) *Developing the Family Travel market*. Des Moines, Iowa: Better Homes and Gardens.

Bellenger, D. N., & Korgaonkar, P. K. (1980) Profiling the recreational shopper. *Journal of Retailing*, 56(3), 77–92.

Berry, L. L. (1969) Components of department store image: A theoretical and empirical analysis. *Journal of Retailing*, 51, 3–20.

Bigne, E., Ruiz, C., & Sanz, S. (2005) the impact of internet user shopping patterns and demographics on consumer mobile buying behaviour. *Journal of Electronic Commerce Research*, 5(3), 193–209.

Blakney, V. L., & Sekely, W. (1994) Retail attributes: influence on shopping mode choice behaviour. *Journal of Management Issues*, 6(1), 101–118.

Boedeker, M. (1995) New-type and traditional shoppers: A comparison of two major consumer groups. *International Journal of Retail and Distribution Management*, 23(3), 17–26.

Brown, M., Pope, N., & Voges, K. (2003) Buying or browsing? An exploration of shopping orientations and online purchase intention. *European Journal of Marketing*, 37(11/12), 1666–1684.

Brown, S., & Reid, R. (1997) Shoppers on the verge of a nervous breakdown. In S. Brown & D. Turley (Eds.) *Consumer Research: Postcards from the Edge*, pp. 79–149. London, UK: Routledge.

Bucklin, L. P. (1966) Testing propensities to shop. *Journal of Marketing*, 30, 22–27.

Bucklin, L. P. (1967) The concept of mass in intra-urban shopping. *Journal of Marketing*, 31, 37–42.

Bucklin, L. P. (1971) Trade area boundaries: Some issues in theory and methodology. *Journal of Marketing Research*, 8, 30–37.

Coney, K. A. (1972) Dogmatism and innovation: A replication. *Journal of Marketing Research*, 9, 453–455.

Converse, P. D. (1949) New laws of retail gravitation. *Journal of Marketing*, 14, 339–344.

Coursaris, C., & Hassanein, K. (2002) Understanding m-commerce: A consumer-centric model. *Quarterly Journal of Electronic Commerce*, 3(3), 247–272.

Darden, W. R., & Ashton, D. (1974) Psychographic profiles of patronage preference groups. *Journal of Retailing*, 50, 99–112.

Darden, W. R., & Perreault, W. D. (1976) Identifying interurban shoppers: Multiproduct purchase patterns and segmentation profiles. *Journal of Marketing Research*, 8, 51–60.

Darden, W. R., & Reynolds, F. D. (1971) Shopping orientations and shopping usage rates. *Journal of Marketing Research*, 11, 79–85.

Darian, J. C. (1987) In-home shopping: Are there consumer segments? *Journal of Retailing*, 63(3), 163–186.

Dholakia, R. R. (1999) Going shopping: key determinants of shopping behaviours and motivations. *International Journal of Retail and Distribution Management*, 27(4), 154–165.

Dholakia, R. R., & Uusitalo, O. (2002) Switching to electronic stores: Consumer characteristics and the perception of shopping benefits. *International Journal of Retail and Distribution Management*, 30(10), 459–469.

Dommermuth, W. P., & Cundiff, E. W. (1967) Shopping goods, shopping centres and selling strategies. *Journal of Marketing*, 31, 32–36.

Domzal, T. J., & Kernan, J. B. (1983) Television audience segmentation according to need gratification. *Journal of Advertising Research*, 10, 37–49.

Donnelly, J. H. Jr. (1970) Social character and acceptance of new products. *Journal of Marketing Research*, 7, 111–113.

Donthu, N., & Garcia, A. (1999) The internet shopper. *Journal of Advertising Research*, 39, May-June, 52–58.

Douglas, S. P. (1975) *Working Wives and Nonworking Wives: Families as a Basis for Market Segmentation*, pp. 75–114. Cambridge, MA: Marketing Science Institute.

Douglas, S. P., & Craig, C. S. (2006) On improving the conceptual foundations of international marketing research. *Journal of International Marketing*, 14(1), 1–22.

Dubois, B., & Czellar, S. (2002) Prestige brands or luxury brands? An exploratory inquiry on consumer perceptions. In *Proceedings of the 31st European Marketing Academy Conference*, 31st Conference, Braga, Portugal. pp. 1–9.

Dubois, B., & Laurent, G. (1994) Attitudes toward the concept of luxury: An exploratory analysis. In S. Leong & J. Cole (Eds.) *Asia Pacific Advances in Consumer Research*, pp. 273–278. Provo, UT: Association for Consumer Research.

Evans, F. B. (1959) Psychological and objective factors in the prediction of brand choice: Ford versus Chevrolet. *Journal of Business*, 32, 340–369.

Furse, D. H., & Greenberg, B. A. (1975) Cognitive style and attitude as a market segmentation variable: A comparison. *Journal of Advertising*, 4, 39–44.

Gehrt, K. C., & Carter, K. (1992) An exploratory assessment of catalog shopping orientations: The existence of convenience and recreational segments. *Journal of Direct Marketing*, 6(1), 29–39.

Gehrt, K. C., Yale, L. J., & Lawson, D. A. (1996) A factor-analytic examination of catalog shopping orientations in France. *Journal of Direct Marketing*, 10(4), 19–28.

Ghazali, E., & Othman, M. N. (2004) Demographic and psychographic profile of active and passive investors of KLSE: A discriminant analysis. *Asia pacific Management Review*, 9(3), 391–413.

Girard, T., Korgaonkar, P., & Silverblatt, R. (2003) Relationship of type of product, shopping orientations, and demographics with preference for shopping on the internet. *Journal of Business and Psychology*, 18(1), 101–120.

Goldsmith, R. (2002) Some personality traits of frequent clothing buyers. *Journal of Fashion Marketing and Management*, 6(3), 303–316.

Gonzalez, A. M., & Bello, L. (2002) The construct lifestyle in market segmentation the behaviour of tourist consumers. *European Journal of Marketing*, 36(1/2), 51–85.

Graeff, T. R. (1996) Using promotional messages to manage the effects of brand and self-image on brand evaluations. *Journal of Consumer Marketing*, 31(4), 4–18.

Grubb, E. L., & Gathwold, H. L. (1967) Consumer self-concept, symbolism and market behaviour: A theoretical approach. *Journal of Marketing*, 31, 22–27.

Gutman, J., & Mills, M. K. (1982) Fashion lifestyle, self-concept, shopping orientation and store patronage: An integrative analysis. *Journal of Retailing*, 58, 64–86.

Hagel, J. III, & Armstrong, A. (1997) *Net Gain: Expanding Markets Through Virtual Communities*. Boston, MA: Harvard Business School Press.

Haines, G. H., Simon, L. S., & Alexis, M. (1971) The dynamics of commercial structure in central city areas. *Journal of Marketing*, 35, 10–18.

Harcar, T., & Kaynak, E. (2008) Life-style orientation of rural US and Canadian consumers: Are region-centric standardized marketing strategies feasible? *Asia-Pacific Journal of Marketing and Logistics*, 20(4), 433–454.

Hassan, Y., Nik, N. M., & Bakar, H. A. (2010) Influence of shopping orientation and store image on patronage of furniture store. *International Journal of Marketing Studies*, 2(1), 175–184.

Hema, P., Bakkapa, B., & Somashekkar, I. C. (2012) An empirical stud of personality and cosmetics consumer behaviour. *Research Journal of Management Sciences*, 1(4), 12–15.

Herman, R. O., & Beik, L. L. (1963) Shoppers' movements outside their local retail area. *Journal of Marketing*, 32, 45–51.

Hirschmann, E. C., & Mills, M. K. (1979) Women's occupational status, innovativeness, opinion leadership and innovative communication. In R. S. Franz, R. M. Hopkins, & A. Toma (Eds.) *Proceedings, Southern Marketing Association Annual Conference*, pp. 270–275. Lafayette: South Western Louisiana University.

Huddleston, P. H., Ford, I. M., & Bickle, M. C. (1993) Demographic and lifestyle characteristics as predictors of fashion opinion leadership among mature consumers. *Clothing and Textiles Research Journal*, 11(4), 26–31.

Huff, D. L. (1964) Defining and estimating a trading area. *Journal of Marketing*, 23, 34–38.

Hughes, G. D. (1978) *Marketing Management.* Reading, MA: Addison-Wesley.

Jarvenpaa, S. L., & Todd, P. A. (1997) Is there a future for retailing on the internet. In R. A. Peterson (Ed.) *Electrojic Marketing and the Consumer*, pp. 139–156. Thousand Oaks, CA: Sage.

Jayawardhena, C., Wright, L. T., & Dennis, C. (2007) Consumers online: Intentions, orientations and segmentation. *International Journal of Retail and Distribution Management*, 35(6), 515–519.

Kahle, L. R., Beatty, S. E., & Homer, P. (1986) Alternative measurement approaches to consumer values: The List of Values (LOV) and Values and Lifestyles (VALS). *Journal of Consumer Research*, 13, 405–409.

Kapferer, J. N. (1997) Managing luxury brands. *Journal of Brand Management*, 4(4), 251–260.

King, C. W., & Ring, L. J. (1975) Retail fashion segmentation research: Development and implementation. Paper presented at the annual meeting of the Marketing Division of the Canadian Association of Administrative Sciences, University of Alberta, 2–3 June.

Kinnear, T. C., & Taylor, J. R. (1976) Psychographics: Some additional findings. *Journal of Marketing Research*, 13, 422–425.

Kollat, D. T., & Willett, R. P. (1960) Customer impulse purchasing behaviour. *Journal of Marketing Research*, 1, 6–12.

Korgaonkar, P. K., & Wolin, L. D. (1999) A multivariate analysis of web usage. *Journal of Advertising Research*, 39(2), 53–68.

Lazer, W., & Wyckham, R. (1969) Perceptual segmentation of department store markets. *Journal of Retailing*, 45(Summer), 3–14.

Lesser, J. A., & Hughes, M. A. (1986) The generalizability of psychographic market segments across geographic locations. *Journal of Marketing*, 50, 18–27.

Lim, C. F. (1992) Demographic and lifestyle profiles of individual investors in the KLSE. Unpublished MBA thesis, University of Malaysia, Kuala Lumpur.

Lumpkin, J. R. (1985) Shopping orientation segmentation of the elderly consumer. *Journal of the Academy of Marketing Science*, 13(2), 271–289.

Lumpkin, J. R., Hawes, J. M., & Darden, W. R. (1986) Shopping patterns of the rural consumer: Exploring the relationship between shopping orientations and outshopping. *Journal of Business Research*, 14, 63–81.

Maslow, A. H. (1954) *Motivation and Personality.* New York, NY: Harper & Row.

Maslow, A. H. (1970) *Motivation and Personality,* 2nd Ed. New York, NY: Harper & Row.

Mason, R. (1981) *Conspicuous Consumption: A Study of Exceptional Consumer Behaviour.* Aldershot, UK: Gower Publishing.

McConkey, C. W., & Warren, W. E. (1987) Psychographic and demographic profiles of state lottery ticket purchasers. *Journal of Consumer Affairs*, 21(2), 314–327.

Min, S., & Wolfinbarger, M. (2005) Market share, profit margin, and marketing efficiency of early movers, bricks and clicks, and specialists in e-commerce. *Journal
of Business Research*, 58, 1030–1039.

Mitchell, A. (1983) *The Nine American Lifestyles*. New York, NY: Warner.

Moore, C. T., & Mason, J. B. (1969) A research note on major retail centre patronage. *Journal of Marketing*, 33, 61–63.

Moschis, G. P. (1976) Shopping orientations and consumer uses of information.
Journal of Retailing, 52, 61–70.

Moschis, G. P. (1991) Marketing to older adults: An overview and assessment of
present knowledge and practice. *Journal of Consumer Marketing*, 8(4), 33–41.

O'Cass, A., & Frost, H. (2002) Status brands: Examining the effects of non-product
brand associations on status and conspicuous consumption. *Journal of Product
and Brand Management*, 11, 7–8.

O'Cass, A., & McEwen, H. (2004) Exploring consumer status and conspicuous
consumption. *Journal of Consumer Behaviour*, 4(1), 25–39.

Pernica, J. (1974) The second generation of market segmentation studies: An
audit of buying motivations. In W. D. Wells (Ed.) *Lifestyle and Psychographics*,
pp. 277–313. Chicago, MI: American Marketing Association.

Plummer, J. T. (1971) Lifestyle patterns and commercial band credit card usage.
Journal of Marketing, 35, 34–41.

Prasad, V. K. (1975) Socio-economic product risk and patronage preferences of
retail shoppers. *Journal of Marketing*, 39, 42–47.

Puntoni, S. (2001) Self-identity and purchase intention: An extension of the theory
of planned behaviour. *European Advances in Consumer Research*, 5, 130–134.

Raaij, W. F., & Verhallen, T. (1994) Domain specific market segmentation. *European Journal of Marketing*, 28(10), 49–66.

Reilly, W. J. (1953) *The Law of Retail Gravitation*. New York, NY: W. J. Reilly &
Co.

Reynolds, F. D. (1974) An analysis of catalogue buying behaviour. *Journal of Marketing*, 38, 47–51.

Rowley, J. (1996) Retailing and shopping on the internet. *International Journal of
Retail and Distribution Management*, 24(3), 26–37.

Roy, S. (2007) Structural equation modelling of value-psychographic trait-clothing
purchase behaviour: A study on the urban college-goers of India. *Young Consumers: Insights and Ideas for Responsible Marketers*, 8(4), 269–277.

Rubin, A. (1979) Television use by children and adolescents. *Human Communication Research*, 5, 109–120.

Rubin, A. (1981) An examination of television viewing motivations. *Communication Research*, 8, 141–165.

Rubin, A. (1983) Television uses and gratifications: The interactions of viewing patterns and motivations. *Journal of Broadcasting*, 27, 37–51.

Samli, A. C. (1975) Use of segmentation index to measure store loyalty. *Journal of
Retailing*, 51, 53.

Sexton, D. E., Jr. (1974) A cluster analytic approach the market research function.
Journal of Marketing Research, 11, 109–114.

Shim, S., & Kotsiopulos, A. (1993) A typology of apparel shopping orientation segments among female consumers. *Clothing and Textiles Research Journal*, 12(1),
73–85.

Shim, S., & Mahoney, M. Y. (1992) The elderly mail-order catalog user of fashion products: A profile of the heavy purchaser. *Journal of Direct Marketing*, 6(1), 49–58.

SRI (2006) European SRI Study 2006. Available at: http://www.eurosif.org/publication/european-sri-study-2006/. Accessed 12th September 2015.

Stephenson, P. R., & Willett, R. P. (1969) Analysis of consumers' retail patronage strategies. In P. R. McDonald (Ed.) *Marketing Involvement in Society and the Economy*, pp. 312–322. Chicago, IL: American Marketing Association.

Stone, G. P. (1954) Observations on the social psychology of city life. *American Journal of Sociology*, 60, 36–45.

Summers, J. O. (1970) The identity of women's clothing fashion opinion leaders. *Journal of Marketing Research*, 7, 178–185.

Thompson, J. R. (1971) Characteristics and behavior of outshopping consumers. *Journal of Retailing*, 47, 70–80.

Tian, K. T., Bearden, W. O., & Hunter, G. L. (2001) Consumers' need for uniqueness: Scale development and validation. *Journal of Consumer Research*, 28, 50–66.

Tigert, D. J. (1969) A taxonomy of magazine readership applied to problems in marketing strategy and media selection. *Journal of Business*, 42, 357–363.

Tigert, D. J., Lathrope, R., & Bleeg, M. (1971) The fast food franchise: Psychographic and demographic segmentation analyses. *Journal of Retailing*, 47, 81–90.

Tsai, S. (2005) Impact of personal orientation on luxury-brand purchase value. *International Journal of Marketing Research*, 47(4), 429–454.

Vigneron, F., & Johnson, L. W. (1999) A review and conceptual framework of prestige seeking consumer behaviour. *Academy of Marketing Science Review*, 9(1), 1–14.

Vigneron, F., & Johnson, L. W. (2004) measuring perceptions of brand luxury. *Journal of Brand Management,* 11(6), 169–186.

Visser, E. M., & du Preez, R. (2001) Apparel shopping orientation: Two decades of research. *Journal of Family and Consumer Research*, 29, 72–81.

Vrechopoulos, A., Siokos, G., & Doukidis, G. (2001) Internet shopping adoption by Greek consumers. *European Journal of Innovation Management*, 4(3), 142–152.

Wallace, D. J. (1995) Shopping online: A sticky business. *Advertising Age*, April, p. 20.

Wallace, D. (1996) Experiential learning and critical thinking in nursing. *Nursing Standard*, 10(31), 43–47.

Warren, W. E., Stevens, R. E., & McConkey, C. W. (1996) Using demographic lifestyle analysis to segment individual investors. *Journal of Financial Analysis*, 46, 74–77.

Wells, W. D. (1975) Psychographics: a critical review. *Journal of Marketing Research*, 12, 209–229.

Wells, W. D., & Beard, A. D. (1974) Personality and consumer behaviour. In S. Ward & T. S. Robertson (Eds.) *Consumer Behaviour, Theoretical Sources*, pp. 144–199. Englewood Cliffs, NJ: Prentice-Hall.

Wells, W. D., & Tigert, D. (1971) Activities, interests and opinions. *Journal of Advertising Research*, 11, 27–35.

Westbrook, R. A., & Black, W. C. (1985) A motivation-based shopper typology. *Journal of Retailing*, 61(1), 78–103.

Widemann, K. P., Hennings, N., & Siebels, A. (2007) Measuring consumers' luxury value perception: A cross-cultural framework. *Journal of Academy of Marketing Science*, 11, 1–21.

Widemann, K. P., Hennigs, N., & Siebels, A. (2009) Value-based segmentation of luxury consumption behaviour. *Journal of Psychology and Marketing*, 26, 625–651.

Williams, R. H., Painter, J. J., & Nicholas, H. R. (1978) A policy-oriented typology of grocery shoppers. *Journal of Retailing*, 54(1), 27–42.

Wind, Y., & Green, P. E. (1974) Some conceptual measurement and analytical problems in life style research. In W. D. Wells (Ed.) *Life Style and Psychographics*, pp. 99–126. Chicago, IL: American Marketing Association.

Young, S. (1973) Research both for strategic planning and for tactical product use revisited: An exploration with personality research form. In *Proceedings of the 19th Annual Conference of the Advertising Research Foundation*, New York, pp. 13–16.

Ziff, R. (1971) Psychographics for market segmentation. *Journal of Advertising Research*, 11, 3–10.

5 Psychological Profiles Within Demographics

Consumer markets have always been segmented according to demographic categories. Thus, marketers have long been interested in understanding the distinctive consumer tastes and choices of different age groups, each gender, and consumers differentiated in terms of their geographical location, family, social, and economic status, level of education, and other non-psychological factors that might define the type of person they are and the way they live their lives.

Physical characteristics such as whether a consumer is male or female can be used to map specific types of consumption behaviours, but they do not directly explain why particular product or service choices are made. To know about this, we need to understand consumers' motivations and also the nature of their personalities that might in turn shape the way they respond to different social and environmental experiences, as well as the way they process information from their environment.

Demographic categories can enable marketers to decide in a broad sense on their main target market, but they still need to understand in competitive markets which factors influence different individuals even from the same demographic group to make different brand selections. Psychographics can provide a source of relevant information, and consumer segmentation based on psychological profiling can be applied within demographic groups to provide a finer-grained understanding of consumers' brand-related attitudes and behaviours. This chapter will examine how psychological profiling has been applied in this way and how the psychographics has evolved over time.

Psychographics measures consumers' needs and motives, their expectations about products and services, and their own position with the wider world. Psychological measures have been used to produce normative profiles of consumer populations as well as to define market segments for specific product or service types. These measures have sometimes been development specifically for consumer profiling purposes, and sometimes they have derived from psychological tests developed outside the marketing world. Psychographics have distinctive value, but their proponents have generally not endorsed them as a substitute for demographics. Instead, psychological measures can supplement and often enhance demographic details by linking product or service use back to internal decision-making processes rather than simply to descriptive profiles.

Although psychographics may claim to provide comprehensive profiles of entire populations of national markets or of the markets for specific product/services, the reality is that such profiles often interact with demographic differences among consumers within those specified markets. For example, a psychographic typology might claim to classify the readers of a specific magazine, but those readers might also be differentiated by demographic attributes. Even when the magazine is designed specifically for women, the types of women who consume it could vary in terms of their age, their socio-economic background, whether they are married, whether they have children, and so on. These women might also differ in terms of their hobbies and interests, their activity profiles, and their values. They might also vary in their positions of personality dimensions, such as Extraversion-introversion, Conscientiousness, Neuroticism, Sociability, and Open-mindedness.

For marketers, it might be useful to know whether old and younger women readers have the same values or the same personality traits, or whether younger readers are more outgoing than older readers, or whether all readers regardless of age tend to be high in conscientiousness. Such profiling details could help guide decisions about layout, content, and the types of advertising to carry.

In broader social terms, there is value to knowing whether specific demographic groups have displayed any changes over time in their values or personality profiles. If they have, how can these changes be explained, and what are their implications for marketers? If the grey market (that is, those over 50) shows signs of becoming more extraverted over time, for instance, this might have implications for their propensities to seek out new experiences and even to take more risks.

Gender and Psychographics

Gender is one of the core consumer segmentation variables. There are product and service ranges that are targeted at both genders and many more that are aimed at just one of them. Even for those ranges that are targeted at both genders, the promotional campaigns used to reach men and women can differ in their persuasive styles and appeals. There are often underlying assumptions about each gender, frequently shaped by social and cultural stereotype, that influence the tactics used by marketers to reach women and men. These stereotypes comprise long-conditioned beliefs about the personalities of men and women and about the roles in society to which they each best suited. There has been extensive research conducted in both developed and developing nations around the world into the use of psychographics specifically with women consumers that has identified a range of motives, values, and personality traits linked to purchase preferences and choices

(Prakash, 1986; Bakewell & Mitchell, 2003; Hanzaee & Aghasibeig, 2010; Akturan, Tezcan & Vignolles, 2011; Tifferet & Herstein, 2012; Goi, 2015).

Such stereotypes have been manifested in advertising in the way women are depicted. Certain product categories have been deemed women's products by advertisers—even though they are not—largely because some social roles have traditionally been occupied by women. A good example of this is advertising for household cleaning products that conventionally featured women as product users on the grounds that housework was women's work. As social roles have evolved over time, not least with the increased presence of women in the workforce, home-making roles that were traditionally associated with 'housewives' are more often shared in domestic settings in which both the man and woman of the household have careers.

Within the consumer segmentation context, the social changes just alluded to have created another division among women, between those who work and those who do not. As the social roles of women have evolved in developed countries, social values have also shifted in relation to the treatment of genders. Marketers have also recognised that these demographic changes have triggered shifts in social beliefs about gender and the outlooks that members of each gender can have about their lives and the opportunities that might come their way. These social shifts have in turn given rise to new consumer segments that can be defined via psychographics. One example of this is illustrated by the aspirations of women and whether they perceive that there are as many opportunities for them as there are for men. Some women embrace these new outlooks, and others prefer to adhere to a more traditional view of womanhood. One researcher expressed these types as 'Traditional' versus 'Expanding Outlook' (Bryant, 1977).

Women with a modern or 'expanded' outlook believed that girls should have the same aspirations as boys and while not abandoning ideas of entering into traditional institutions such as marriage and motherhood, they should also recognise that they can balance these aspects of their lives with also having a career and a life outside the home. It has emerged that these distinctions and the psychographic labels attached to them do not simply describe changing social systems: they can also predict different consumption preferences and behaviours. Thus, women with career aspirations who embrace a modern concept of their gender exhibit different brand preferences from women with more traditional worldviews in relation to product ranges aimed at their gender, such as cosmetics (Reynolds, Crask & Wells, 1977).

Women's shopping patterns also varied depending on whether they lived traditional or expanded lives. In the pre-Internet era, working women would tend to go to the same retail outlets for their weekly shop and to have a specific day on which they shopped (*Editor and Publisher*, 1972). These differences in shopping behaviour were not all that surprising given that 'housewives' could go shopping any day of the week, whereas women in employment would have more restricted opportunities for shopping.

Quite apart from the employment status of women, however, their out-look on life also made a difference to their shopping attitudes and behav-iours. Although life outlook was correlated with employment status, this was not a perfect match. Even some women who did not have careers and did not go out to work could still embrace modern views about woman-hood. Equally, some employed women might continue to adhere to many traditional views about the importance of marriage and family in defining a woman's identity.

Women who held liberal perceptions about their gender were found to make more shopping trips each week than women with non-liberal (or tra-ditional) views and women who were not sure where they stood (Anderson, 1972a). Non-liberated women were also less concerned about convenience shopping and with simply getting the shopping done as quickly and effi-ciently as possible. It is likely that such women were mostly not in employ-ment and that they therefore had more time available to shop around. Certainly, the same researcher found that women who went out to work made fewer shopping trips and were more brand loyal (Anderson, 1972b). Further evidence emerged that when women had paid employment, they might shop more than once, just as stay-at-home women did, but employed women were less likely to use shops close to home (presumably instead using ones close to work if they commuted to their job). The husbands or employed women were also likely to do more of the weekly shopping than did those married to stay-at-home wives (Douglas, 1975).

Further studies confirmed that demographic factors and life stage were important differentiating factors in the women's market, although there could also be an interplay between psychographic and demographic fac-tors in the determination of store and brand loyalties. Women who rated the maternal role of their gender lower tended to be more brand loyal and to shop in the same stores (Carmen, 1974). Women who were mothers and had teenage children showed a greater than average propensity to buy con-venience foods. This propensity was also found to be higher among women who were employed than among those who were not (Anderson, 1971, 1972b). What we might be seeing here is mainly a life stage effect with women who go out to work and also raise families having busy lives and tight time constraints placed on specific activities such as shopping. It is easier and quicker to purchase from outlets where one is already familiar with the store layout and therefore to buy the same products over and over.

While the consumer behaviour of women in regard to commodities designed for use by both genders (e.g., food, drink, household cleaning products) is undoubtedly shaped by life stage, which in turn is defined by a combination of certain demographic variables, there is a psychological dimension to their consumerism as well. This fact has been confirmed by studies conducted over several decades. During this period, the nature of consumer activity and the diversity and complexity of marketing have both evolved considerably.

In the early 1970s, one researcher identified six different psychographic types among women consumers. This research was carried out with American housewives and the psychographic types were derived through statistical clustering techniques that were applied to data from women's responses to a large series of attitude statements. The six types comprised: Outgoing Optimists, Conscientious Vigilants, Apathetic Indifferents, Self-Indulgents, Contented Cows, and Worriers (Ziff, 1971).

Descriptions of these types explained their psychological differences and also other drives that underpinned their consumerism preferences. Thus, Outgoing Optimists were outgoing and community oriented and were concerned about personal grooming and how they appeared. Conscientious Vigilants liked orderly lives and valued cleanliness, home cooking, and shopping around for the best produce and deals. Apathetic Indifferents tended to be withdrawn, but in terms of their involvement with their community and their family, could be irritable, were not concerned about their appearance, but were into home cooking in big way. Self-Indulgents had a relaxed outlook on life, were family oriented, liked home cooking, and valued home making. Contented Cows were also relaxed and did not worry about things, were not house proud, and could be a bit complacent about cleanliness and looked out for good deals when making purchases. Worriers were generally negative about and dissatisfied with their lives, did not really look after themselves, could be selfish, and sought convenience and economy when shopping.

A subsequent American study investigated women who were employed or stay-at-home housewives and further differentiated working women into those who worked out of financial necessity versus those who were career oriented. Stay-at-home types were more traditional in their outlook, especially in regard to their perceptions about the roles of women; they valued being a homemaker, planned their shopping trips carefully, and looked for good deals. The career-oriented type were the most liberal and outgoing of the women surveyed and were more likely than the others to indulge in impulse buying, treats, and eating away from home. Those women who worked for the money were concerned about their health and showed the highest use of convenience foods (Satow & Johnson, 1977).

Psychographics has been used to distinguish between women on the basis of their food preparation habits (Roberts & Wortzel, 1979). Women were differentiated into those with traditional and contemporary outlooks on life. The traditional types valued their role as homemakers and readily saw the man as the chief breadwinner in the household. Contemporary women held more egalitarian views about the social roles of the gender. They felt that men and women should share household chores and any decisions made about the home and family. Contemporary women, who were more likely to be employed outside the home, were also concerned about efficiency and saving time.

Two further typologies of these women were created, one of which was based on food preparation habits and the other in shopping behaviour orientations. Five food preparation types were defined: the Joy of Cooking type, the Service Role type, the Anti-Cooking type, the Sensory Orientation type, and the Food Is Fuel type. The three shopping orientation types were: Concern for Time type, Concern for Price type, and Concern for Quality type. The shopping types are self-explanatory, but the food preparation types need further explanation.

Joy of Cooking types liked to create new dishes. Service Role types were most concerned with cooking to please their families. Anti-Cooking types were interested in meals that could be prepared quickly and easily. Sensory Orientation types liked to use herbs, sauces, and spices with unusual dishes. Food Is Fuel types were health conscious and concerned about the nutritional quality of foods they prepared.

Traditional women embraced Service Role and Food Is Fuel values and rejected those of the Anti-Cooking type. For traditional women, the aim of cooking was to please their families rather than to indulge in some form of personal pleasure or fulfilment. Contemporary women, in contrast, were more likely to be Anti-Cooking or Joy of Cooking types. For some career-oriented women, cooking was a chore and something they had little time for. For other career-oriented women, cooking was embraced as an extension of their aspiration-oriented drives for self-improvement that defined their careers and extended into other parts of their lives.

Personality differences associated also with gender have been examined in relation to problematic consumer behaviour such as the propensity to make impulsive purchases. Making consumer choices depends upon the ability to weigh up information received about products and services and then to use this information to evaluate brands and make purchase decisions in retail settings (Capon & Davis, 1984; Coupey, 1994). Rational purchase decisions are therefore characterised by consumers being able to process complex information that is then compared with outcome experiences with the purchases they make (MacInnis, Moorman & Jaworski, 1991).

In reality, however, not all purchase decisions are rational in this way. Furthermore, not all consumers are inclined to adopt a rational approach to shopping. Purchase decisions can be made on impulse, and some consumers are found to be more inclined than are others to behave this way (Cobb & Hoyer, 1986; Beatty & Ferrell, 1998; Dholakia, 2000). In extreme cases, consumers can become addicted to impulsive buying and are driven by their compulsions to make unplanned purchases on a regular basis (O'Guinn & Faber, 1989; Faber & O'Guinn, 1992; Nataraajan & Goff, 1992).

Such impulsiveness has been linked to underlying and enduring psychological conditions in the individual. People who display impulsivity in different aspects of their lives are often characterised by a trait that predisposes them to process information in an idiosyncratic way—often referred to as attention deficit hyperactivity disorder (ADHD). People with this condition experience difficulties processing information comprehensively in settings in which their senses are bombarded with multiple stimuli. Impulsivity represents part of this condition with sufferers displaying poor self-control over their behaviours. At the same time, these individuals can display hyperactivity that often manifests itself as restlessness and an inability to focus their concentration on one thing for very long (Jaska, 1996).

There is a gender dimension to the question of consumer impulsivity. ADHD has been thought to afflict males more than females. There has been dispute about this conclusion, however, and one explanation for it has been that there are differences between the methods used with the sexes to diagnose this problem (Nadeau, Littman & Quinn, 1999). There is a concern that the diagnosis of females with attention deficit disorders is flawed and often misses cases (Jaska, 1996). With boys, ADHD can be manifested in disruptive behaviour, which is very visible. Girls can display different symptoms such as withdrawing into themselves and this is not always so immediately apparent (Solden, 1995). Even with girls, though, ADHD can produce a greater likelihood of overt disorder in their behaviour than is normally found among members of their own gender (Gershon, 2002).

The presence of impulsivity in general behaviour can be a precursor to its appearance in consumer activity. People with attention deficit disorder process information from their surrounding environment differently from other people (Schroder, Drive & Streufert, 1967). Sufferers can experience problems processing information presented as a sequence even when efforts have been made to give the information order and structure (Melini, 1987). This means that in serial presentations, individuals with attention deficit disorder end up processing less information than do others (Holdnack, Moberg, Arnold, Gur & Gur, 1995).

Hypothetically, these findings indicate that in a consumer context, individuals with attention deficit disorder will process information from brand marketing differently from other consumers. When consumers can handle large volumes of diverse information about brands effectively, they are better placed to make informed decisions about brand choices. When confronted with information overload, any consumer might experience poorer-quality decision-making about brands simply because they have less information on which to base those decisions (Jacoby, Speller & Kohn, 1974a; Jacoby, Speller & Kohn-Berning, 1974b).

There has been debate about whether more information invariably results in better choices being made (Malhotra, Jain & Lagakos, 1982). Yet, knowing that attention deficit disorder can trigger a psychological orientation to processing environmental experiences whereby the individual can easily be distracted by irrelevant stimuli, it seems feasible that sufferers will experience poorer-quality processing of brand information than other consumers. Those with this disorder might then in turn display greater impulsivity in their purchases because they found planned consumerism more of a challenge (Kaufman-Scarborough & Cohen, 2004).

Age and Consumption

Marketers use age as a key consumer segmentation variable. Age is often interrelated with gender and also with variables such as marital status, family status, and occupational status to define the concept of 'life stage'. Life stage is correlated with age, but not exactly so. In others words, two people can be at different life stages at the same age or the same life stage at different ages. For example, two individuals could be married with two children aged eight and 10, have similar jobs and similar incomes, yet one has achieved this by the age of 35 and the other is aged 50. Another example might be two individuals both aged 40, one of whom has the same family setup as just described, whereas the other is single and lives alone. Despite the age differences in the first example, those two individuals could have similar consumption needs. Yet, in the second example, despite being the same age, these two individuals may have quite different consumption needs. It is entirely likely that in the first example, the two individuals will have similar lifestyles and associated values whereas in the second case, both their lifestyles and values will be quite different.

With regard to age per se, it is possible to define consumer segments by age group that will have value in marketing strategy. Thus, there are products developed specifically for children that only children use. Marketing appeals may have to take into account adult reactions where parents, for instance, are the financial gatekeepers and will decide on behalf of their children whether to buy a particular children's product. Ultimately though, a product must appeal to the age group at which it is primarily targeted and intended.

Marketers and advertisers in mainstream media have been known over many years, and certainly during the era of commercial broadcast television, to place much emphasis on the young and middle-aged adult markets. This is one reason why in the United States, television audience ratings among the 18 to 49s is such an important metric in judging the success of programmes in terms of their value to advertisers. Yet, there was growing recognition across the last decade of the 20th century that has continued into the 21st century that adult markets aged 50 and over have great value as well (Gunter, 1998). This value can be found for providers not simply of age-specific products and services, but also for more generic product and service sectors not least because the older adult market—often referred to as the 'grey market'—often has more disposable income than younger adult markets. Other important market changes are that people in developed countries are living longer (which means they have more years as consumers) and are staying healthier later in life (which means they are active in diverse markets for longer).

Older consumers are active media users. Their media consumption patterns differ from those of younger generations. These differences have been observed over many decades (Steiner, 1963; Bernhardt & Kinnear, 1976;

Stephens, 1982). They persist to this day even though the older generations have developed more diverse media habits as the media landscape has evolved with digital technology developments. The over-60s remain big users of television and radio, are avid readers of newspapers and magazines, but also have also begun to embrace digital interactive media and mobile communications in greater numbers. The traditional mass media therefore remain important marketing platforms for the grey market and more so than is the case for young adults, where attention is increasingly devoted to new online media applications such as social media sites. Furthermore, older consumers continue to be loyal users of traditional reception technologies, such as TV sets, whereas younger generations also attach much significance to a range of other devices and especially to ones they can carry around (Ofcom, 2015).

Grey Market Psychographics

There has been debate about where the grey market begins in terms of biological age. A further complication lies with the fact that as observed above, people are living longer and staying more youthful and healthy and active into their later years. Claims that '50 is the new 30' grab headlines and can be effective attention grabs for public relations campaigns, but also serve to illustrate changes to the health status of populations in developing countries. If 60 is also the new 40, should 'old age' begin at 70 or 80? For convenience, the age taken here will be 50. This remains the cut-off age for 'non-greys' used by advertisers in economically powerful nations such as the United States. It is also the minimum age for membership of organisations that market services to the older age groups such as Saga in the United Kingdom.

The 50 and over age range, however, cannot be regarded as comprising a single, homogeneous consumer segment. People in the 50 to 59 age bracket will tend to be far more active than those aged 80+. In general, the younger end of the grey market spectrum will comprise many people still in full-time employment, many at the peak of their careers. It will also comprise individuals who have taken early retirement. As people grow progressively older, in the 50+ range, they will progressively withdraw from the employment market and may experience a downturn in their incomes. Furthermore, they will include different generations. Two generations within the same family, one in their sixties and the other in their eighties, could both be 'retired' in terms of employment status, but lead different lifestyles and adhere to different sets of social values. These differences in turn could drive them towards different consumer interests, needs, and activities.

Psychographics can therefore have considerable value to marketers seeking to understand a diverse category of consumers. The grey market has considerable economic power and therefore cannot be ignored by most major sectors of manufacturing and service supply. Age has become a psychological concept as much as a chronological one and this means that understanding the psychological processes which underpin the interests, tastes, and decision-making of older consumer has crucial significance to brand designs, promotions, and marketing strategies (Schiffman & Sherman, 1991).

The application of psychographics with older consumers has taken on a number of perspectives. These have include attempts to combine psychographics with demographics, studies of generic lifestyles traits, and product specific psychological typologies (see Day, Davis, Dove & French, 1987; Huddleston, Ford & Bickle, 1993).

Values and lifestyles measures have been used to develop generic psychographic typologies of older consumers. Day et al (1987) were interested in finding out whether older consumers could be segmented in terms of lifestyles attributes and what kinds of marketing messages specific psychological segments would be most receptive to. This research obtained data from a small sample of 112 married women aged over 65 who had retired. They were presented with an extensive AIO statements battery to complete and the researchers derived 21 initial clusters of responses from these data. Further clustering analysis was conducted on the data for the 21 clusters to yield two superordinate factors that were labelled as 'Self-Sufficient' and the 'Persuadable'.

The first group was characterised psychologically by exhibiting a strong internal locus of control, a variable which measured an enduring trait indicating the extent to which people believe they are in control of events in their lives (internal control) or that such events are largely determined by forces such as chance or fate that are outside their personal control (external control). The second group was more prone to risk-taking and exhibited an external locus of control.

The 'Self-Sufficient' were further sub-divided into two sub-groups named 'Active Integrated' and 'Disengaged'. The former group was opinionated, politically conservative, and confident they could handle most situations by themselves. They were driven and ambitious and believed that through hard work, a person could achieve anything they wished. The latter group were confident about controlling events in their own lives but were more content with their lives as they were. They liked to keep informed about the world and socially engaged, but they were not aspirational in the same way as the 'Active Integrated'.

The 'Persuadables' were also further divided into two sub-groups, called the 'Passive Dependent' and the 'Defended Constricted'. The former adopted a rather complacent and almost resigned approach to life. They had little concern for their image and appearance, were often socially isolated, and focused their attention on their own home. These individuals had frequently not enjoyed successful working lives and many had never worked outside the home. The latter group, in contrast, was outgoing and sociable, sought out new social contacts and experiences, and had an openness to life that carried over from their earlier years into their later life. They were not always self-confident, but they were willing to make an effort with others to ensure they did not become socially isolated or disconnected from everyday life.

These profiles provided important information for advertisers that were intent on targeting the grey market. They revealed the psychographic heterogeneity of this age range. Advertising appeals needed to distinguish between older women who demographically appeared to be fairly homogeneous in terms of psychological measures that revealed that even women who appeared on the surface to be similar could have very different orientations towards the outside world. Variances in attributes such as self-confidence, openness to fresh experiences, sociability, and risk taking meant that advertisements designed to appeal to women high on these factors might not work well with women who scored low on them.

In another American study with older people, Gollub & Javitz (1989) examined the lifestyles and values of older adults, drawing upon earlier research into VALS. The research combined demographics, psychographics, and health status data to produce six consumer types. These types were used to differentiate between older people in respect of the ways they wished to live out their lives. Key differences emerged that were related to the types of properties in which older Americans wished to live. Some preferred single-family homes, others opted for apartment dwelling, and some preferred to live in retirement complexes or communities that could provide special support. Some older people wished to live in settings that provided community and recreational amenities, and others wished to be situated close to health care facilities.

Four psychological dimensions were identified that could be used to differentiate these older consumers in terms of psychographic factors. These dimensions were: autonomy-dependence, introversion-extraversion, self-indulgence/self-denial, and openness to change. Utilising responses on these scales and health status data, six psychographic segments were distinguished: Explorers, Adapters, Pragmatists, Attainers, Martyrs, and Preservers.

Explorers were self-reliant and independent. They liked to control their own lives and live life their way. They could be introverted, but sought autonomy, and their distrust of institutions meant they were inclined to deny help from others.

Adapters were outgoing and extraverted types. They enjoyed new experiences and were open to change. Yet, they could also be very dependent types. For that reason, personal relationships were important to them and their self-identity was often defined through their material possessions. They were well educated and generally enjoyed good health, but they were also self-indulgent. Even so, they did not expect members of their family to run around after them in their old age, but they were open to moving if necessary to a setting where relevant support could be obtained as they grew older.

Pragmatists were also outgoing and sociable, although not as well educated or as wealthy as Adapters. They were also more willing to put pressure on family members for support, perhaps because they lacked the resources to buy it in. They tended to be conformists with conservative political orientations and would take practical decisions about their lives based on what was feasible.

Attainers were a relatively young 'elderly' psychographic segment. They were also the most active, autonomous, healthy, and well-off segment. They preferred to believe they were and could remain independent of their children as they grew older. They sought new experiences and still had objectives to achieve in life. They were more likely than any other psychographic type to own their homes, most likely to live with a spouse, and most likely still to have children living at home. They were socially and culturally active, but had reached a point where, upon becoming empty nesters once the kids had gone, they would consider downsizing their home.

Martyrs had a 'stick-in-the-mud' mentality. They were resistant to change, often well educated but with a strong sense of dependency and entitlement. They believed that children had an obligation to support parents as the latter grew old. They were inward looking, not very sociable, and more inclined than any other types to live a somewhat ascetic life of denial.

Preservers were characterised by being in poor health. They were change resistant, highly dependent, and willing to take help from any source—family members or outside support systems or agencies. They were the most likely to consider moving into retirement communities or sheltered housing.

What was clear again from these psychographic profiles was that they provide a richness of description of older consumers and also identified a number of specific characteristics not revealed by demographics that would make these groups differentially sensitive to the same marketing campaigns. These psychographic types revealed different classes of lifestyle, different values about how to live, and different need states that could underpin quite diverse consumer behaviour profiles.

In relation to fashion, research found that there were three psychographic dimensions defined by lifestyle traits that shaped the fashion tastes and choices of older consumers. These were related to how outgoing consumers were in their approaches to shopping, whether they were socially active, and whether they tended to build up credit. Even when placed alongside demographic variables such as educational level, income level, and occupational status, these psychographic measures were significant indicators of fashion orientations and behaviour (Huddleston et al., 1993).

Another investigation of lifestyle types among older people defined six clusters or factors: Self-Reliants, Quiet Introverts, Family-Oriented, Active Retirees, Young and Secure, Solitaires (Sorce, Tyle & Loomis, 1989). The authors argued that it was important for marketing professionals to recognise these distinctions and to use the psychological profiles associated with them to inform promotional campaigns for their brands. Other scholars critiqued this typology and the research that underpinned it and questioned whether these psychographic types had predictive validity in relation to consumers' product and brand choices (Moschis, 1991).

It is important in this context to examine closely how specific demographic and psychographic factors interact to determine specific consumer purchase orientations and outcomes. For example, older people have often been characterised as being economically better off than younger people because they have lower costs and fewer debts to service and in some instances may have benefited from inheritances from their own elderly parents. Having more disposable income does not automatically mean that the older consumer will be a more profligate spender. If, psychologically, they have a thrifty mentality, they may be motivated most of all to control their outgoings and seek cheap deals or premium offers.

Age as a Matter of Perception

Chronological age reveals how long a person has been alive, but it does not show how old they feel. Two people can be the same age and yet feel quite different in terms of their relative youthfulness. This difference is especially likely to occur in the grey market where everyone has accumulated a significant number of years. Yet, two 60-year-olds might display significantly different energy levels and outlooks on life. Such perceived differences are often underpinned by the varying life experiences of these individuals, but also more profoundly by their health status and fitness level. Some people remain youthful a lot longer than others. As a result, some people 'feel' older than others, and this in turn influences how they behave in different settings.

Hence, older consumers can be differentiated in terms of their 'objective' age (that is, the actual chronological age) and their 'subjective' age (that is, how old they feel inside). In addition, differences can be found in the age at which people are believed to have become 'old'. For someone aged 30, a 50-year-old might seem 'old'. For a 50-year-old, someone aged 70 might be perceived as old. Thus, as we grow older, we often push back the age at which we believe 'old age' begins. These perceptions can also be influenced by how well a person adjusts to getting older. For some individuals, a state of denial emerges and 'old age' is continually pushed backed further the older they get. This adjustment to one's fate in terms of getting older can serve as a segmentation variable in the consumer context (French & Fox, 1985).

As people enter an older age bracket, research has shown over time that several key variables consistently emerge as influential in determining how members of the grey market are likely to behave. These are discretionary income, health status, activity level, discretionary time, and response to others (Bone, 1991). When older consumers have more money to spend, more time on their hands to do so, have the energy through keeping active and healthy to engage in various shopping excursions, and do not become too stuck in their ways in terms of how they think others perceive them, they retain a youthful consumer activity profile.

This self-image they establish has been called 'cognitive age' (Barak & Schiffman, 1981). While chronological age can be a good indicator of some purchase patterns, cognitive age can give rise to behaviour that does not always match chronological age expectations (John & Cole, 1986; Abrams, 1990; Cole & Gaeth, 1990). Older consumers with a 'young' cognitive age can often display consumer behaviours more usually associated with chronologically younger people (Underhill & Cadwell, 1983; Sherman, Schiffman & Dillon, 1988).

There is evidence that 'cognitive age' or the age that older consumers perceive themselves to be can be a better predictor of consumption outcomes than actual chronological age (Yoon et al., 2005). Cognitive age is believed to be more closely linked to the way people think about themselves and this in turn is related to the lifestyles they lead or aspire to and the decisions they make about the products and services they desire and the brand variants they like most (Cleaver & Muller, 2002; Iyer, Reisenwitz & Eastman, 2008; Myers & Lumbers, 2008; Ying & Yao, 2010).

The concept of cognitive age can display a degree of psychological fluidity in the sense that the 'age' at which people place themselves can vary with the way the question is asked, any objects or social circumstances in relation to which the question is asked, and even the time of day when it is asked. It is also important to map the cognitive age nominated by a person with their actual age. Cognitive age could have different implications for the prediction of consumer activity in general or specific brand choices depending upon the actual age of the person giving it. A 50-year-old may say he or she feels like a 30-year-old, as indeed might a 70-year-old. However, these two individuals might make different fashion choices, taking into account also the perceived reactions of others. A 50-year-old woman who has retained her figure might still feel comfortable wearing a short dress more usually associated with someone aged 30, whereas a 70-year-old woman might not even though she feels youthful inside (Stephens, 1991). Apparently, older people feel more youthful in the morning than later in the day and this factor alone can affect the cognitive age they give for themselves (Yoon, 1997). More generally, the cognitive age that an older consumer might acknowledge will also depend upon how their self-confidence. Greater self-esteem can trigger feelings of youthfulness (Sherman, 1990).

It seems that even self-confidence is not a stable attribute, however. There have been ongoing debates about the enduring nature of a 'cognitive age' as a consumer attribute. Despite having been classed as a 'trait', it is apparently one that can shift over time as a person gets older. This is not a perfect correlation whereby as an individual grows older chronologically, so too does the age they give as the one they currently feel like (Kleinspehn-Ammerlahn, Kotter-Gruhn & Smith, 2008).

Self-concept has been found to be sensitive to external events (Bailey, 2003). This means that it can be 'up' at one point in time and 'down' at another (Gao, Wheeler & Shiv, 2009). A 'shaken self' whereby the individual has experienced a momentary blow to his or her self-confidence can influence self-perceptions (including cognitive age) and consumer behaviour (Gao et al., 2009). A key factor here also could be that the loss of a feeling of youthfulness among older consumers can result in them feeling generally less happy and that that response in turn can blunt their enthusiasm to buy certain types of products or services (Mogilner, Aaker & Kamvar, 2012).

Researchers have found that cognitive age estimates can vary with the physical and social circumstances in which they are made. Guido, Amatulli & Peluso (2014) questioned people aged 65 and over about the age they felt they were. Cognitive ages ranged from 30 to 90, with a mean of just over 48 years. Respondents were asked to indicate their cognitive age in relation to three sets of circumstances: six different physical contexts ('at a resort', 'in the countryside', 'in a park', 'in a shop or mall', 'in a church', 'in a senior centre'); four social contexts ('in the company of suitors', 'in the company of an attractive person', 'in the company of children or grandchildren', 'in the company of friends') and four product categories ('using sportswear', 'sports equipment', 'food items', 'technology').

A Youth Age Index (YAI) was calculated in each case by subtracting the cognitive age given from the respondent's chronological age. The average cognitive age was found to be significantly lower than the chronological age in relation to all these different settings or circumstances. What was also interesting was that the YAI—or the index of how youthful a person felt—was bigger in more hedonistic settings such as 'at a resort', 'in the countryside', 'in the presence of suitors', or 'in the company of an attractive person'. The YAI was also bigger in relation to sportswear products than food and technology items.

Regardless of the context-related relativity of cognitive age, it is an influential factor in the behaviour of older people, including their consumer-related activity. Older people who also perceive themselves to be 'old' tend to be less active in their lifestyles, have been shown to attend cultural events less often, have less interest in keeping up with the latest fashions, and are less inclined to engage in newer retail activities such as online shopping (Iyer et al., 2008).

Knowledge that context factors can give perceived youthfulness a boost when carefully chosen could guide marketers in terms of how to manipulate the settings of brand promotions. If older consumers are more likely to respond positively towards a brand when it is associated with circumstances that make them feel younger, such enhancements to cognitive age might make them more likely to make purchases, especially of products or services they might sometimes feel are not age appropriate.

Young Consumers

Understanding how consumerism develops in childhood has attracted much research attention. Children have emerged as a primary target market for brand marketers in many product and service categories. Children are a secondary target group in numerous other sectors where they may form part of a joint decision-making process in the family home. Knowing how children come to understand what brands are, how they react to brand promotions, and how they can be encouraged to make purchases or requests to purchase from others have become important goals for brand marketers. There are in addition more general social concerns about children being absorbed into consumption-driven cultures and the degree to which they become defined by materialism in their lives. There have been critical treatises written on this subject with accusations that governments have failed to accord sufficient protection to children as inexperienced consumers, that the commercial world has too often taken unfair advantage of children's immaturity, and that even parents could do more to guard their children against advertisers (Linn, 2004, Palmer, 2006).

Definitions of 'childhood' can vary, but in simple demographic terms, children are generally defined as people aged under 18 years. Yet, even this age group cannot be regarded as a homogeneous community. Apart from the usual gender, ethnic, and socio-economic class differentials, children can be differentiated by their age, which is in turn related to their level of psychological and physical development. Before the age of five, children have a fairly crude understanding of the world around them and as consumers, their comprehension of 'brands', 'advertisements', and money are extremely limited (Gunter & Furnham, 1998; Gunter, Oates & Blades, 2005). In addition, to these developmental differences, children can vary in their personality profiles. These psychological differences can influence how they respond to the world around them.

There is further evidence that a combination of development factors and psychographic factors can define the nature of child consumers, in particular in relation to their orientations towards materialism (Achenreiner, 1997; LaBarbera & Gurhan, 1997; Buijzen & Valkenburg, 2003; Kasser, 2005). There has been further concern about whether materialism leads to a contented happy life or represents a root cause of childhood disenchantment and depression. Evidence has been examined that when children become deeply involved with consumer culture, it creates more problems than it solves. Relationships between children and their parents can become strained and children grow more anxious about their own position in their social milieu (Schor, 2004).

Against this backdrop, materialism itself has been defined less as a reaction of socio-cultural circumstances and more as an individual difference factor. The importance that consumers attach to material possessions can systematically vary from on person to the next (Belk, 1984). At the same time, materialism remains an aspect of the cultural milieu in which the individual consumer resides and embraces a set of principles or values by which he or she lives their lives (Richins, 1987; Richins & Dawson, 1992). This 'psychographic' dimension can be measured quantitatively and a number of marketing researchers have developed scales for this purpose (Belk, 1985; Richins, 2004).

Although some materialistic values scales were designed for children (Kasser, 2005), many have been developed with adult consumers. These have often centred on the aspirational needs of individuals and have been culturally restricted, with much of the research being conducted in the United States, and directed towards a more individualistic values culture with core measures focusing on concepts such as 'the American Dream' (Kasser & Ryan, 1993, 1996; Kasser & Ahuvia, 2002). Legitimate questions have been raised about whether concepts of materialism, when measured against adult concepts, can be properly understood by children (Nairn, Griffin & Gaya Wicks, 2008).

Materialism scales have been developed specifically for children (Achenreiner, 1997; Goldberg, Gorn, Peracchio & Bamossy, 2003; Kasser, 2005). These scales have been tested for their content and construct validity, the internal reliability of their items, and their dimensional structure. This literature produced evidence that materialism is a construct that can be measured and used to differentiate between young consumers. Materialism in children is often associated with a similar trait being present in parents (Goldberg et al., 2003). Much evidence has also supported the idea that there is a single dimension of materialism (Kasser, 2005). At least one author has challenged this position, however.

Schor (2004) put forward a Consumer Involvement model that distinguished three types of items called 'Dissatisfaction', 'Consumer Orientation', and 'Brand Awareness'. The first dimension represented children's perceptions of their own possessions and whether they had everything they wanted or whether they felt short-changed compared to their friends. The second dimension reflected the centrality of consumerism to children's lives. The third dimension indicated the extent to which children were brand conscious and how important brands were to personal identity. This model has been empirically confirmed by other researchers (Bottomley, Nairn, Kasser, Ferguson & Ormrod, 2010).

Lifestyle and psychographics indicators of consumer behaviour have been shown to vary with the time period within which people were born. Although family, friends, and community factors can shape young consumers' product and brand preferences, there are specific generational factors defined by the era in which young people live that determine contemporary tastes across a range of product and service types (Bakewell, Mitchell & Rothwell, 2006).

The emergence of shopping malls created a new type of shopping experience that was embraced by most consumers, but especially by younger generations that adopted these spaces as extensions of their social lives. As such, shopping became more than a purposeful and instrumental experience determined by specific product-related needs and instead was integrated with the young consumer's social milieu. Judgements about where to shop were therefore influenced not simply by perceptions of retailer reliability and product or service quality, along with price, premium incentives, and value for money, but also by where were the most favoured places to hang out and be seen (Stoltman, Gentry & Anglin, 1991; Shim & Kotsiopulos, 1992a, 1992b, 1993; Lee, Ibrahim & Hsueh-Shan, 2005). These judgements and perceptions can be gathered and analysed to generate psychographic types and lifestyle traits linked to shopping behaviour, often revealing generational and life stage differences in shopping orientations even across fairly narrow age spans (du Preez, Visser & Zietsman, 2008).

Concluding Remarks

Demographics have represented standard classifiers in marketing practice and market research almost since the time mass marketing began. This is not surprising in light of the tradition of population censuses to break down national populations in terms of specific demographic factors such as age, gender, ethnicity, marital status, and socio-economic class. Such population descriptors can be used to identify differences in behaviour patterns among consumers. Yet these descriptors offer no explanations for why any such behavioural differences occurred.

When it comes to the way commodity and service markets are constructed, some direct their wares at everybody, whereas others target specific population sub-groups. On many occasions, such sub-groups are defined in terms of demographic factors. Hence, there are products that are made exclusively for women and those that are made exclusively for men. Within specific product ranges, there will again sometimes be variants targeted at one gender rather than the other. Clothing products are targeted at both genders, but clothing styles of men and women differ. Some clothes tend to be worn predominantly by women (e.g., dresses) and others mostly by men (e.g., ties). Other clothing items, such as gloves, hats, shoes, socks and suits, are used by both genders, but in each case, there are gender-specific styles.

Similarly, there are products that might be targeted at older people and those aimed at younger people (e.g., children). Most toy products are designed for children, although there are adult toys. Similarly, there may be financial products targeted at many adult age groups, but some specific products designed exclusively for people over a specified age (e.g., 50 or 60 years). Yet, within these demographically defined product markets, there are further variations in the attitudes, beliefs, aspirations, interests, and motivations of consumers that could affect their product or service choices. There may also be personality differences that mediate the ways they might respond to specific brand designs or promotional campaigns. Thus, even when marketing professionals identify good reasons for narrowing their focus on specific target demographics, they may still find it advantageous to understand the variances that can occur within specific demographic groups in their consumption preferences.

References

Abrams, M. (1990) Inequality among the over 55s. Paper presented at an Admap/Campaign Seminar, Gold Amongst the Grey, London, UK, 25th October.

Achenreiner, G. B. (1997) Materialistic values and susceptibility to influence in children. In M. Brucks & D. J. MacInnis (Eds.) *Advances in Consumer Research*, Vol. 24, pp. 82–88. Provo, UT: Association for Consumer Research.

Akturan, U., Tezcan, N., & Vignolles, A. (2011) Segmenting young adults through their consumption styles: A cross-cultural study. *Young Consumers*, 12(4), 348–366.

Anderson, B. B. (1972a) Are we missing the MS? In *Proceedings of the Third Annual Conference of the Association for Consumer Research*, Provo, Utah, pp. 436–445.

Anderson, B. B. (1972b) Working women versus non-working women: A comparison of shopping behaviours. In *Combined Proceedings*, Chicago, IL: American Marketing Association, pp. 355–359.

Anderson, W. T. Jr. (1971) Identifying the convenience oriented customer. *Journal of Marketing Research*, 8, 179–183.

Bailey, J. A. II (2003) Self-image, self-concept, and self-identity revisited. *Journal of the National Medical Association*, 95, 383–386.

Bakewell, C., & Mitchell, V. W. (2003) Generation Y female consumer decision-making styles. *International Journal of Retail & Distribution Management*, 31(2), 95–106.

Bakewell, C., Mitchell, V. W., & Rothwell, M. (2006) UK Generation Y male fashion consciousness. *Journal of Fashion Marketing and Management*, 10(2), 169–180.

Barak, B., & Schiffman, R. G. (1981) Cognitive age: A nonchronological age variable. In K. B. Monroe (Ed.) *Advances in Consumer Research*, Vol. 8, pp. 601–606. Ann Arbor, MI: Association for Consumer Research.

Beatty, S. E., & Ferrell, E. M. (1998) Impulse buying: Modelling its precursors. *Journal of Retailing*, 74, 169–191.

Belk, R. W. (1984) Three scales to measure constructs related to materialism: reliability, validity and relationships to measures of happiness. In T. Kinnear (Ed.) *Advances in Consumer Research*, Vol. 11, pp. 291–297. Provo, UT: Association for Consumer Research.

Belk, R. W. (1985) Materialism: Trait aspects of living in the material world. *Journal of Consumer Research*, 12, 265–280.

Bernhardt, K. L., & Kinnear, T. C. (1976) Profiling the senior citizens' market. In B. Anderson (Ed.) *Advances in Consumer Research*, pp. 449–452. Chicago, IL: American Marketing Association.

Bone, P. F. (1991) Identifying mature segments. *Journal of Consumer Marketing*, 8(4), 19–32.

Bottomley, P. A., Nairn, A., Kasser, T., Ferguson, Y. L., & Ormrod, J. (2010) Measuring childhood materialism: Refining and validating schor's consumer involvement scale. *Psychology & Marketing*, 27(7), 717–740.

Bryant, B. E. (1977) *American Women Today and Tomorrow*. Washington, DC: US Government Printing Office.

Buijzen, M., & Valkenburg, P. M. (2003) The unintended effects of television advertising: A parent-child survey. *Communication Research*, 30, 483–503.

Capon, N., & Davis, R. (1984) Basic cognitive ability measures as predictors of consumer information processing strategies. *Journal of Consumer Research*, 11, 551–562.

Carmen, J. M. (1974) Some generalisations and problems regarding consumer problem solving in grocery store channels. In J. N. Sheth (Ed.) *Models of Buyer Behaviour*, pp. 70–87. New York, NY: Harper & Row.

Cleaver, M., & Muller, T. (2002) I want to pretend I'm eleven years younger: Subjective age and senior's motives for vacation travel. *Social Indicators Research*, 60, 227–241.

Cobb, C. J., & Hoyer, W. D. (1986) Planned versus impulse purchase behaviour. *Journal of Retailing*, 62, 384–409.

Cole, C. A., & Gaeth, G. J. (1990) Cognitive and age-related differences in the ability to use nutritional information in a complex environment. *Journal of Marketing Research*, 27, 175–184.

Coupey, E. (1994) Restructuring constructive processing of information displays in consumer choice. *Journal of Consumer Research*, 21, 83–99.

Day, E., Davis, B., Dove, R., & French, W. (1988) Reaching the senior citizen market. *Journal of Advertising Research*, 28, 23–30.

Dholakia, U. M. (2000) Temptation and resistance: An integrated model of consumption impulse formation and enactment. *Psychology & Marketing*, 17, 955–982.

Douglas, S. P. (1975) *Working Wives and Nonworking Wives: Families as a Basis for Market Segmentation*. Chicago, IL: Marketing Science Institute.

du Preez, R., Visser, E. M., & Zietsman, L. (2008) Lifestyle, shopping orientation, patronage behaviour and shopping mall behavioura study of South African male apparel consumers. *European Advances in Consumer Research*, 8, 279–280.

Editor & Publisher (1972) Working women's food buying traits revealed, 105, 62.

French, W. A., & Fox, R. (1985) Segmenting the senior citizen market. *Journal of Consumer Marketing*, 2(1), 61–74.

Gao, l., Wheeler S. C., & Shiv, B. (2009) The "shaken self": Product choices as a means of restoring self-view confidence. *Journal of Consumer Research*, 36(1), 29–38.

Gershon, J. (2002) A meta-analytic review of gender differences in ADHD. *Journal of Attention Disorders*, 5, 143–154.

Goi, C-L. (2015) The impact of personality on Generation Y buying behaviour: Perception of females on fashion. *International Journal of Social Science and Humanity*, 5(1), 6–9.

Goldberg, M. E., Gorn, G. J., Peracchio, L. A., & Bamossy, G. (2003) Understanding materialism among youth. *Journal of Consumer Psychology*, 13, 278–288.

Gollub, J., & Javitz, H. (1989) Six ways to age. *American Demographics*, 11, 28–57.

Guido, G., Amatulli, C., & Peluso, A. M. (2014) Context effects on older consumers' cognitive age: The role of hedonic versus utilitarian goals. *Psychology & Marketing*, 31(2), 103–114.

Gunter, B., & Furnham, A. (1998) *Children as Consumers: A Psychological Analysis of the Young People's Market*. London, UK: Routledge.

Gunter, B., Oates, C., & Blades, M. (2005) *Advertising to Children on TV: Content, Impact and Regulation*. Mahwah, NJ: Lawrence Erlbaum Associates.

Hanzaee, K. H., & Aghasibeig, S. (2010) Iranian Generation Y female market segmentation. *Journal of Islamic Marketing*, 1(2), 165–176.

Holdnack, J. A., Moberg, P. J., Arnold, S. E., Gur, R. C., & Gur, R. E. (1995) Speed of processing and verbal learning deficits in adults diagnosed with attention deficit disorder. *Neuropsychiatry, Neuropsychology & Behavioural Neurology*, 8, 282–292.

Huddleston, P. H., Ford, I. M., & Bickle, M. C. (1993) Demographic and lifestyle characteristics as predictors of fashion opinion leadership among mature consumers. *Clothing and Textiles Research Journal*, 11(4), 26–31.

Iyer, R., Reisenwitz, T. H., & Eastman, J. K. (2008) The impact of cognitive age on seniors' lifestyles. *Marketing Management Journal*, 18, 106–118.

Jacoby, J. J., Speller, D. E., & Kohn-Berning, C. A. (1974a) Brand choice behaviour as a function of information load. *Journal of Marketing Research*, 11, 63–69.

Jacoby, J. J., Speller, D. E., & Kohn-Berning, C. A. (1974b) Brand choice behaviour as a function of information load—replication and extension. *Journal of Consumer Research*, 1, 33–41.

Jaska, P. (1996) What is ADD/ADHD? Interview with Peter Jaska. Ph.D. Meninger Clinic Seminar, Online Psych Forum. Available at: www.add.org

John, D. R., & Cole, C. A. (1986) Age differences in information processing: Understanding deficits in young and elderly consumers. *Journal of Consumer Research*, 13, 297–315.

Kasser, T. (2005) Frugality, generosity and materialism in children and adolescents. In K. A. Moore & L. Lippman (Eds.) *What Do Children Need to Flourish? Conceptualising and Measuring Indicators of Positive Development*, pp. 357–374. New York, NY: Springer Science.

Kasser, T., & Ahuvia, A. C. (2002) Materialistic values and well-being in business students. *European Journal of Social Psychology*, 32, 137–146.

Kasser, T., & Ryan, R. M. (1993) A dark side of the American dream: Correlates of financial success as a central life aspiration. *Journal of Personality and Social Psychology*, 65, 410–422.

Kasser, T., & Ryan, R. M. (1996) Further examining the American dream: Differential correlates of intrinsic and extrinsic goals. *Personality and Social Psychology Bulletin*, 22, 280–287.

Kaufman-Scarborough, C., & Cohen, J. (2004) Unfolding consumer impulsivity: An existential-phenomenological study of consumers with attention deficit disorder. *Psychology & Marketing*, 21(8), 637–669.

Kleinspehn-Ammerlahn, A., Kotter-Gruhn, D., & Smith, J. (2008) Self-perceptions of aging: Do subjective age and satisfaction with aging change during old age? *Journal of Gerontology*, 63, 377–385.

Kluckhohn, C., & Strodbeck, F. (1961) *Variations in Value Orientations*. Evanston, IL: Row, Peterson.

Knutson, B., Rick, S., Wimmer, G. E., Prelec, D., & Loewenstein, G. (2007) Neural predictors of purchases. *Neuron*, 53, 147–156.

Kocak, A., Abimbola, T., & Ozer, A. (2007) Consumer band equity in a cross-cultural replication: An evaluation of a scale. *Journal of Marketing Management*, 23(1–2), 157–173.

Kollat, D. T., & Willett, R. P. (1960) Customer impulse purchasing behaviour. *Journal of Marketing Research*, 1, 6–12.

Koos, S. (2011) Varieties of environmental labeling, market structures, and sustainable consumption across Europe: A comparative analysis of organizational and market supply. *Journal of Consumer Policy*, 34, 127–151.

Koponen, A. (1960) Personality characteristics of purchasers. *Journal of Advertising Research*, 1, 6–12.

Korgaonkar, P. K., & Wolin, L. D. (1999) A multivariate analysis of web usage. *Journal of Advertising Research*, 39(2), 53–68.

Kraepelin, E. (1915) *Psychiatrie*. 8th Ed. Leipzig: Barth.

Krugman, H. E. (1967) The measurement of advertising involvement. *Public Opinion Quarterly*, 30, 583–596.

Laaksonen, P. (1994) *Consumer Involvement: Concepts and Research*. London, UK: Routledge.

LaBarbera, P. (1999) Marketing on the Internet: The role of cognitive style in user attitudes and behaviour. In *Proceedings of the 28th European Marketing Academy Conference*. Berlin (CD-ROM). Berlin: Humboldt University.

LaBarbera, P., & Gurhan, Z. (1997) The role of materialism, religiosity, and demographics in subjective well-being. *Psychology & Marketing*, 14, 71–97.

Lee, S. L., Ibrahim, M. F., & Hsueh-Shan, C. (2005) Shopping-centre attributes affecting male shopping behaviour. *Journal of Retail and Leisure Property*, 4(4), 324–340.

Linn, S. (2004) *Consuming Kids: The Hostile Takeover of Childhood*. New York, NY: New Press.

MacInnis, D. J., Moorman, C., & Jaworski, B. J. (1991) Enhancing and measuring consumers' motivation, opportunity, and ability to process brand information from ads. *Journal of Marketing*, 55, 32–53.

Malhotra, N. K., Jain, A. K., & Lagakos, S. W. (1982) The information overload controversy: An alternative viewpoint. *Journal of Marketing*, 46, 27–37.

Melini, C. B. (1987, February) Learning disabilities—part 2. *N.J.S.S.N.A. Newsletter*, p. 3.

Mogilner, C., Kamvar, S. D., & Aaker, J. (2012) The shifting meaning of happiness. *Social Psychological and Personality Science*, 2(4), 395–402.

Moschis, G. P. (1991) Marketing to older adults: An overview and assessment of present knowledge and practice. *Journal of Consumer Marketing*, 8(4), 33–41.

Myers, H., & Lumbers, M. (2008) Understanding older shoppers: A phenomenological investigation. *Journal of Consumer Marketing*, 25, 294–301.

Nadeau, K., Littman, E., & Quinn, P. (1999) *Understanding Girls with ADHD*. Silver Spring, MD: Advantage Books.

Nairn, A., Griffin, C., & Gaya Wicks, P. (2008) Children and brand symbols: A consumer culture approach. *European Journal of Marketing*, 42, 627–640.

Nataraajan, R., & Goff, B. G. (1992) Manifestations of compulsiveness in the consumer marketplace domain. *Psychology & Marketing*, 9, 31–44.

Ofcom (2015) *Communications Market Report*. London, UK: Ofcom.

O'Guinn, T. C., & Faber, R. J. (1989) Compulsive buying: A phenomonlogical exploration. *Journal of Consumer Research*, 16(2), 147–157.

Palmer, S. (2006) *Toxic Childhood: How the Modern World Is Damaging Our Children and What We Can Do About It*. London, UK: Orion.

Prakash, V. (1986) Segmentation of women's market based on personal values and the means-end chain model: A framework for advertising strategy. In R. J. Lutz (Ed.) *Proceedings—Advances in Consumer Research*, Vol. 13, pp. 215–220. Provo, UT: Association for Consumer Research.

Reynolds, F. D., Crask, M. R., & Wells, W. D. (1977) The modern feminine life style. *Journal of Marketing*, 41, 38–45.

Richins, M. L. (1987) Media, materialism and human happiness. In M. Wallendorf & P. Anderson (Eds.) *Advances in Consumer Research*, Vol. 14, pp. 352–356. Provo, UT: Association for Consumer Research.

Richins, M. L. (2004) The material values scale: Measurement properties and development of a short form. *Journal of Consumer Research*, 31, 209–219.

Richins, M. L., & Dawson, S. (1992) A consumer values orientation for materialism and its measurement: Scale development and validation. *Journal of Consumer Research*, 19, 303–316.

Roberts, M. L., & Wortzel, L. H. (1979) New life style determinants of women's food shopping behaviour. *Journal of Marketing*, 43, 28–39.

Satow, K. L., & Johnson, D. K. (1977) Will the real working woman please stand up and approach the check-out counter? Paper presented at the Chicago Chapter, American Marketing Association Suburban meeting.

Schiffman, L. G., & Sherman, E. (1991) Values orientations of new-age elderly: The coming of an ageless market. *Journal of Business Research*, 22(2), 187–194.

Schor, J. B. (2004) *Born to Buy: The Commercialised Child and the New Consumer Culture*. New York, NY: Scribner.

Schroder, H. M., Driver, M. J., & Streufert, S. (1967) *Human Information Processing: Individuals and Groups Functioning in Complex Social Situations*. New York, NY: Rinehart & Winston.

Sherman, E. (1990) Aging, life cycle and the sociology of time. In M. E. Goldberg, G. Gorn, & R. W. Pollay (Eds.) *Advances in Consumer Research*, Vol. 17, pp. 902–904. Provo, UT: Association for Consumer Research.

Sherman, E., Schiffman, R. G., & Dillon, W. R. (1988) Age/gender judgements and quality of life differences. In S. Shapiro (Ed.) *Marketing: A Return to the Broader Dimensions*, pp. 319–320. Chicago: American Marketing Association.

Shim, S., & Kotsiopulos, A. (1992a) Patronage behaviour of apparel shopping: Part I. Shopping orientations, store attributes and information sources and personal characteristics. *Clothing and Textiles Research Journal*, 10(2), 48–57.

Shim, S., & Kotsiopulos, A. (1992b) Patronage behaviour of apparel shopping: Part II. Testing a patronage model of consumer behaviour. *Clothing and Textiles Research Journal*, 10(2), 58–64.

Shim, S., & Kotsiopulos, A. (1993) A typology of apparel shopping orientation segments among female consumers. *Clothing and Textiles Research Journal*, 12(1), 73–85.

Solden, S. (1995) *Women with Attention Deficit Disorder: Embracing Disorganization at Home and in the Workplace*. Grass Valley, CA: Underwood Books.

Sorce, P., Tyler, P. R., & Loomis, L. M. (1989) Lifestyles of older Americans. *Journal of Consumer Marketing*, 6, 53–63.

Steiner, G. A. (1963) *The People Look at Television: A Study of Audience Attitudes*. New York, NY: Alfred A. Knopf.

Stephens, N. (1982) The effectiveness of time-compressed television advertisements with older adults. *Journal of Advertising*, 4, 48–55.

Stephens, N. (1991) Cognitive age: A useful concept for advertising? *Journal of Advertising*, 20, 37–48.

Stoltman, J. J., Gentry, J. W., & Anglin, K. A. (1991) Shopping choices: The case of mall choice. *Advances in Consumer Research*, 18, 434–440.

Tifferet, S., & Herstein, R. (2012) Gender differences in brand commitment, impulse buying, and hedonic consumption. *Journal of Product and Brand Management*, 21(3), 176–182.

Underhill, L., & Cadwell, F. (1983) What age do you feel? Age perception study. *Journal of Consumer Marketing*, 1, 19–21.

Ying, B., & Yao, R. (2010) Self-perceived age and attitudes toward marketing of older consumers in China. *Journal of Family and Economic Issues*, 31, 318–327.

Yoon, C. (1997) Age differences in consumers' processing strategies: An investigation of moderating influences. *Journal of Consumer Research*, 24(3), 329–342.

Yoon, C., Laurent, G., Fung, H. R., Gonzalez, R., Gutchess, A. H., Heddon, T., Lambert-Pandraud, R., Mather, M., Park, D. C., & Peters, E. (2005) Cognition, persuasion and decision making in older consumers. *Marketing Letters*, 16, 429–441.

Ziff, R. (1971) Psychographics for market segmentation. *Journal of Advertising Research*, 11, 3–10.

6 Global Consumer Profiling

The emergence of global markets has already been noted. They have generated an important need for marketers to understand how to reach consumers who have been socialised within different socio-cultural settings and their incumbent values systems. The values given the greatest importance can vary greatly from one culture to another. This means that a brand marketing campaign developed in one culture that makes appeals to specific values that are central to that culture could strike entirely the wrong note in another culture (Kluckhohn & Strodbeck, 1961).

It is essential that global marketers are aware of these intercultural differences. In this context, even products defined by the specific demographic group at which they are targeted cannot be sold in the same way across all national markets. There are cultural values typologies that have been developed by social psychologists and marketing scholars that have attempted to define the dominant values that exist worldwide and to identify the different weightings each value type might carry in a specific culture (Kocak, Adimbola & Ozer, 2007).

Marketers can use this information to ensure that global campaigns have built-in variances in their messages to resonate effectively with the values that are held most dear by different national cultural groups (Koos, 2011). Thus, the way a brand is advertised in the United States or Europe might not work so well in the Far East, and vice versa. This chapter will examine the consumer profiling methods that have been developed and tested over the past 30 years and the extent to which different national markets can tolerate global campaigns.

Cultural Values and Consumerism

Marketers have used a number of different systems for profiling and segmenting consumers. This book is about the use of psychological dimensions to define consumers and differentiate between consumer communities and sub-groups in ways that might be relevant to marketing professionals in designing brand campaigns, developing media strategies to reach target consumers, and knowing how consumers are likely to respond to brands and their promotions. As the economies of nation-states have become increasingly intertwined and interdependent through international trade agreements and as communications technologies have evolved to enable marketing messages to be transmitted more quickly and effectively to mass and niche audiences, global markets have emerged.

Big corporations reach across national boundaries with their products and services and frequently employ international workforces. At this level, it is essential for businesses to understand not only the similarities that might exist across national borders, but also the idiosyncrasies of specific nation-states. As earlier chapters have shown, one system that has been developed for profiling consumers centres on their values. Values represent sets of conventions, principles and rules that govern behaviour. They embody expectancies concerning the appropriate ways to behave in different social settings (Crosby, Biner & Gill, 1990). Such values can be used to classify people living within specific societies in generic ways akin to demographics, but deeper in terms of their capacity not simply to describe behavioural differences associated with population sub-groups, but also to explain why those differences occur. Cultural values therefore represent variables not unlike personality attributes, except that they apply to collectives of people rather than to individuals.

These society level 'personality' types are helpful to marketers because they can provide guiding principles for the design and presentation of brands and brand marketing campaigns. They can signal warnings about whether certain symbolism associated with a brand projects the message its producers hope to achieve with consumers. In a cross-cultural context where a brand is being presented to a range of communities with different value systems, it can serve as a check on whether common symbolism will play out in the same way with these different groups of consumers. Thus, if a brand design uses a specific colour and that colour has significantly different meanings in two cultures—a positive meaning in one and a negative meaning in the other—it would be a mistake to utilise it in both markets because the outcomes would be different in terms of its acceptance.

Countries have been found to exhibit many differences associated with their cultural values systems. At the same time, some pairs of nations may display extensive value system overlaps. The populations of some countries display greater contentment with their lives than do those of other countries. Such differences can occur both between countries that differ in their economic performance as well as between those that are similar in terms of national wealth. Thus, while poverty is linked to life dissatisfaction in some parts of the world, the similar levels of relative affluence of two or more countries does not guarantee that their populations will always display similar levels of satisfaction with their lives. Lifestyle factors other than income can underpin happiness.

Within the context of values as a consumer profiling system, further conceptual distinctions need to be made between the ways people within a culture are expected to behave (that is, the behaviour that is desirable), the ways people themselves would like to behave (that is, behaviour that is desired), and the ways people actually behave. Society may set certain standards for its people. The people themselves may have specific objectives that might or might not match society-level expectations. Then, people display behaviour that might match or fall short of what society expects and what they would personally like or prefer (Hofstede, 2001).

These conceptual differences also provide important information for marketing professionals. It is not enough to look at what a society might expect of its people and set a brand image that is promoted in relation to an ideal, particularly if for most people in that market, the ideal is perceived as unattainable. It might be better to know what people want for themselves and what they may therefore believe is more realistic. Provided that lower goal is not offensive to the society and its authority institutions, a brand image and the way it is promoted should aim to include symbolism that focuses on the 'desired' (that is, attainable) rather than the 'desirable' (the unattainable).

Universal Values Versus Culture-Specific Values

There has been much debate within the social sciences, among anthropologists and sociologists as well as psychologists, about whether values can be identified that are universal across all cultures in the world. Then, are some values present only in some cultures and not in others? Or, are many values present across most cultures, but some values are more visible or powerful in some cultures than in others? Some researchers have attempted to define values that are present across all cultures (e.g., Murdock, 1945). It is important to distinguish between 'principles' that govern behaviour and 'needs' that drive or motivate propensities to engage in certain behaviours (Douglas & Craig, 2006). Thus, the need to consume food exists across all cultures because it is a basic human survival drive. It is determined by human biology rather than by social community structures and the rules associated with those social systems. The rules that relate to the ways food is consumed (while seated rather than standing, in a specific sequence for different food types) and which foods are consumed and how they are prepared for consumption are socially and culturally determined and follow prescribed rules and principles that are learned (Geertz, 1973).

Cross-cultural psychologists have discovered that there are classes of value dimensions that can be applied to all cultures. These dimensions can vary between cultures in their relative importance and the degree to which they set specific rules of conduct. The outcome is that they combine in different ways to give rise to different societal-level cultural values attribute profiles

(Schwartz, 2004). From a marketing perspective, it is feasible theoretically that these value dimensions can combine to yield different consumer profiles. These 'profiles' can in turn define orientations that will govern product and service usage patterns and variant or brand preferences. The trick for marketing professionals is to adopt appropriate brand symbolism in brand designs and related advertising campaigns. Message appeals and claims that would be acceptable and potentially persuadable in one national market might not work in another.

Recognising this phenomenon is only the start. What marketing professionals need next is a theoretical/explanatory model and associated empirical analysis model to define and quantify cultural value-profiles differences. Earlier attempts to achieve this outcome have produced mixed results in terms of how comprehensive, reliable, and robust specific classification systems turn out to be (e.g., Harris & Moran, 1987; Inkeles, 1997; Inglehart, Basanez & Moreno, 1998). These classification models have sometimes included variables such as language, living arrangements, feeding habits, and work-life balance. In addition, researchers have also developed distinctions between values associated with different needs, some of which are low-level basic survival needs and others that are higher-level aspirational needs (Inglehart et al., 1998).

Kluckhohn & Strodbeck (1961) outlined five value orientations following research carried out among small communities in the United States. These were concerned with general perceptions of human nature (that people are basically good or bad), people's relationships with the environment, their control over the environment, their concepts of time (whether a society lived in the present or dwelled upon the past), and the rules governing human relationships (hierarchical controlling regimes in which the individual is subjugated to the group or society or aspirational systems that enable people to achieve individual ambitions).

The fivefold typology outlined above has been conceptually influential in shaping later cultural values models. One example was a model devised by Trompenaars (1993), which outlined the following orientations: universalism-particularism, achievement-ascription, individualism-collectivism, emotional-neutral, specific-diffuse, time orientation, and orientation to nature. A further system that was informed by ethnographic observations differentiated four dimensions that included a marketing oriented attribute: communal sharing, authority ranking, equality matching, and market pricing (Fiske, 1992).

The most widely acknowledged cultural values models that provided measurement methodologies to not simply identifying but also quantifying differences between national cultures were those developed by Hofstede (2001) and Schwartz (1994; Schwartz & Bilsky, 1987, 1990). Hofstede presented a model with five dimensions that he labelled as: power distance, individualism/collectivism, masculinity/femininity, uncertainty avoidance, and long-term orientation.

Schwartz developed a different system of cultural values classification and measurement through his research with samples of teachers and students from 38 different countries. He and his colleagues were interested in discovering universal cultural values and began by investigating values adherence at the level of the individual before scaling up to the societal level. Initially, Schwartz & Bilsky (1987, 1990) reported 10 individual-level values, from which seven types were derived for application across different cultures. The seven culture-level values types were: embeddedness, intellectual and affective autonomy, hierarchy, mastery, egalitarianism, and harmony.

Two later cultural values models have emerged, both of which have some similarities with the Schwarz model and the Hofstede model. The first of these two models is called GLOBE (Global Leadership and Organisational Behaviour Effectiveness) and was developed at the Wharton School of Management by Robert House. This project was inspired by the work of Hofstede (1980), Schwartz (1994), Smith (1995), and Inglehart (1997).

This project examined cultural values associated with leadership across 62 different countries. The international sample comprised 17,300 middle managers from 951 organizations that operated in industries such as food processing, financial services, and telecommunications. It was launched in 1991. Nine cultural dimensions were distilled from this inquiry: uncertainty avoidance, power distance, two types of collectivism, gender egalitarianism, assertiveness, future orientation, performance orientation, and humane orientation (see Table 6.1 for further details). When surveyed, all respondents were asked about *values* and *practices*. Values represented principles concerning how people ought to behave, whereas practices represented reports concerning how they actually behaved (House et al., 2004).

The GLOBE study produced some interesting and at times unexpected results. One example of this was a frequent finding that values and practices were not always in tune with each other. A value might be strongly asserted by survey respondents, but not generally practiced. Further, the degree of harmony between specific values and their practice varied from country to country.

The second model derived from the World Values Survey and defined three cultural dimensions: Exclusionism versus Universalism, Indulgence versus Restraint, and Monumentalism versus Flexumility. The World Values Survey conducted five survey waves between 1981 and 2008 and obtained data from a total of 97 countries that represented 88 per cent of the world's population. The same countries did not participate in every wave, but the number of participants increased across successive waves from waves one to four (from 20 to 67 countries), before falling back (to 54 countries in wave five. Data have been made available as an open source resource for researchers to analyse. Data analysis by researchers associated with this project have uncovered many different cultural values, but found also that these can be largely aggregated into two major dimensions: (1) Traditional/Secular-Rational and (2) Survival/Self-Expression (World Values Survey, 2012).

Table 6.1 GLOBE Project: Summary of Values and Practices

Performance Orientation

"reflects the extent to which a community encourages and rewards innovation, high standards, excellence, and performance improvement" (pp. 30, 239)

Uncertainty Avoidance

"the extent to which leaders set ambitious goals, communicate high expectations for their subordinates, build their subordinates' self-confidence, and intellectually challenge them" (p. 277)

In-Group Collectivism

"the degree to which individuals express pride, loyalty, and cohesiveness in their organizations or families" (p. 30)

Power Distance

"the extent to which a community accepts and endorses authority, power differences, and status privilege" (p. 513)

Gender Egalitarianism

"the degree to which a collective minimizes gender inequality" (p. 30)

Humane Orientation

"the degree to which an organization or society encourages and rewards individuals for being fair, altruistic, friendly, generous, caring, and kind to others" (p. 569)

Institutional Collectivism

"the degree to which organizational and societal institutional practices encourage and reward collective distribution of resources and collective action" (p. 30)

Future Orientation

"the degree to which a collectivity encourages and rewards future-oriented behaviors such as planning and delaying gratification" (p. 282)

Assertiveness

"the degree to which individuals are assertive, confrontational, and aggressive in their relationships with others" (p. 30)

Source: Summary of House et al., 2004) by Grove, C.N. (n.d) Worldwide differences in business values and practices: overview of GLOBE research findings. Available at: http://www.grovewell.com/wp-content/uploads/pub-GLOBE-intro.pdf

The Traditional/Secular-Rational values dimension differentiates between societies where religion is important and those where it is not. Traditional societies place value on parent-child ties, traditional family values, and deference to authority. These societies tend tor reject divorce, abortion, euthanasia, and suicide. These societies are also frequently characterised by a sense of national pride. Secular-Rational societies tend to hold opposing views on all these issues.

Societies that placed emphasis on survival values are preoccupied with economic and physical security. These societies tend to have a nationalistic outlook and display low levels of trust and tolerance for alternative value systems. Societies defined by self-expression display more open-mindedness and tolerance for disparate viewpoints and world value orientations, display gender equality, more concern about the environment, and are more at ease with democratic political systems in which wider publics are encouraged to get involved in political processes. In countries with greater industrialisation and economic confidence, in which the physical security needs of most people have been satisfactorily addressed, there tend to be growing social pressures for movement away from authoritarian political systems and towards more open democracies. Trying to force democracy onto traditional and survival-oriented societies without first addressing economic inequalities will not usually meet with much success (World Values Survey, 2012).

The most widely adopted framework for global values assessments has been Hofstede's classification of cultural values. This framework has been critiqued for being supported by limited empirical evidence and for already being out of date. Yet, more recent models have not really provided significant advances on Hofstede's typology and the key dimensions he identified emerged again in later work, albeit with different names (Magnusson, Wilson, Zdravkovic, Zhou & Westjohn, 2008).

Magnusson et al., (2008) examined the values systems of Hofstede, Schwartz, Trompenaars, and GLOBE. They investigated how effectively each taxonomy clustered countries into values types. Cultural distance constructs based on Hofstede's and Trompenaars's models had strong convergent validity, whereas the same constructs from Schwartz and GLOBE had weaker validity. It was concluded from a close analysis of the values constructs derived from these different models that the Hofstede values types still performed well and that calls for this model to be abandoned could be premature.

High Context and Low Context Cultures

Cultures have been divided into high and low context types. This distinction is based on styles of communications that have been found to exist in different countries. Put simply, this difference is based on whether the preferred way of communicating is very literal and transparent in the meanings being expressed, or more symbolic and abstract. In the former instance, communications can be easily understood assuming the receiver is familiar with the language being used. In the latter case, even a good understanding of the natural language being used may not be sufficient to deconstruct subtle meanings that are conveyed by the use of symbolic references that are known only to those familiar with indigenous cultural values.

This distinction not only represents a device for classifying cultures, it also underpins the different styles of advertising that are preferred in different national markets. Thus, in so-called 'low context' cultures, great value is attached to clear verbal expression using everyday language that ordinary people can relate to and understand. Advertisements may contain images, but their core messages are delivered verbally using natural language terms familiar to anyone familiar with that language. In 'high context' cultures, advertising tends more often to be characterised by symbolic references that go beyond the words and pictures being presented. Interpretations of meanings from these surface features are not simply shaped by the receiver's knowledge of the language, but also by whether he or she has privileged knowledge of cultural references of specific words, expressions, phrases, terms, or images. Indeed, some words and images can have quite different meanings depending upon the cultural contexts in which they are being used (Ferraro, 2002).

Most Western cultures are low context and most Asian cultures are high context in their preferred styles of communication. This information is important to professional marketers in that it represents an important cultural backdrop to the kinds of persuasive communications likely to prove most effective when they try to reach local consumers in different national markets. The advertising messages that work well in countries such as France, Germany, Sweden, the United Kingdom, and the United States may not be so well received in places such as Chinas and Japan. In Western markets, consumers are mostly concerned about the performance of products as backed up by hard and clear statistical data. In Eastern markets, consumers may be more persuaded by whether the brand represents values that are important to the culture.

Hofstede's Classification of Cultural Values

Hofstede developed what has been the most widely utilised classification of national cultural values. The taxonomy outlined here comprises five key dimensions: power distance, individualism/collectivism, masculinity/femininity, uncertainty avoidance, and long/short-term orientation. A 100-point scale was established for measuring each of these dimensions, and a classification was produced covering 73 countries. Each country had its own idiosyncratic profile formed out of the score it received on these five dimensions (Hofstede, 2001; Hofstede & Hofstede, 2005).

The original data used to establish these cultural values types were obtained in the 1970s and 1980s. His key values types continued to receive support by later studies and even apparently new typologies based on more contemporary data confirmed the importance of at least some of Hofstede's dimensions. In China, the Chinese Cultural Connection (1987) produced a four-factor solution when searching for cultural values traits. Three of these factors—Integration, Human-Heartedness, and Moral Discipline—correlated with Hofstede's dimensions. A fourth dimension, which was called Confucian work dynamism, was distinctive and showed no conceptual or empirical links to any of Hofstede's values categories.

Power Distance

The power distance dimension defines a construct that measure the degree of tolerance within specific societies or cultures for social hierarchies in which some people have more power than others. In other words, the distance in terms of power and status can vary between the most and least powerful people in a society. Some cultures accept such divisions and recognise that a hierarchy can give structure and coherence to a society, which plays a critical part in maintaining social order. Thus, in some societies, social status is determined by the family or tribe a person is born into. That status is largely inherited and fixed and there may be limited tolerance, for example, for people from different social levels to intermingle and certainly to marry.

Societies that have strong power distance values will symbolise social status in terms of specific behavioural conventions. People of low status may not have the same rights and privileges as do people of high status. There may be expectations concerning how high- and low-status people should behave when in each other's company. There may be signals of respect a low-status person is expected to show towards a person of high status when they interact.

In the context of marketing, the association of brands with high social status signs can convey similar status to the brand. In doing so, however, that brand is then expected to observe the established cultural codes of high status sectors of that society in the way it is displayed and used, and in the kinds of actors seen on screen as demonstrators or endorsers of the brand.

If a high-status person is displayed in an advertisement using the brand, that person must be accorded due respect according to cultural conventions, for example, in the way they are dressed, the ways they behave, the settings in which they are shown, and the type of company they keep.

In low power distance cultures, hierarchies can still exist, but they are more porous and people can pass between them. Some individuals might be born into a privileged lifestyle, but even those who are not can still achieve it through their own efforts. The more important point in the context of the power distance construct, however, is that high social strata are not regarded as out of reach of people from lower social levels. Furthermore, people at the highest levels of society can be seen keeping the company of people from lower levels and even wearing fashions that symbolically are more usually associated with lower power levels without causing undue offence.

In markets characterised by large power distance cultures, such as in the Far East, respect is accorded to those who are older, and in positions of authority. Parents command the respect of their children. Teachers command the respect of their students. Subordinates show respect to their bosses. This is the order of things and this disposition is culturally imprinted upon the people who live in large power distance societies. In small power distance societies, in contrast, respect is not derived purely from the individual's position in a particular hierarchy. It is something that must be earned on the basis of behaviour and performance rather than position in a specific social structure.

Once again, these insights have importance for marketing professionals in determining the kinds of advertising campaigns to use in different cultural settings where power and status are used as selling propositions. It may be acceptable for an advertisement to show kids being cheeky to their parents in Western markets, but no so in Eastern markets, even when only in jest.

Individualism Versus Collectivism

This construct distinguishes cultures in terms of the orientations of the people who live in them to display selfishness versus community-centredness. In individualistic cultures, individuals are 'me' centred and seek to forge a self-identity based on their own needs, interests, and achievements. In collectivistic cultures, individuals are more concerned about their membership of and contribution to the group, organisation, or community to which they belong. In one case, the individual's identity is forged through experiences they have pursued out of personal interest, and in the other, it is defined by what they do for any social group they are members of. Put more succinctly, the difference is between an "I" culture and a "we" culture.

In a collectivistic culture, the central importance of the group or community to the individual's sense of self means that any actions of their part that bring shame on the group are frowned upon. It is critically important for members of collectivistic cultures not to lose face through failing to live up to the standards socially expected of them.

Collectivistic cultures require individuals to subjugate personal ambitions to the wider needs of the group. Their self-image is determined largely by the group to which they belong and an individual's social status is defined by this group. Distinctions are therefore made between those who are members of the group and those who are not. This perception can operate at the level of national identity, identity with one's company, and identity with one's family. Kinship ties are extremely important in collectivistic cultures and they will often determine decision-making across a range of settings. Knowing the right people, coming from specific families, and being members of other important social institutions can make all the difference to how much an individual can achieve.

In individualistic societies, the individual is regarded as more autonomous. This does not mean that all individuals are devoid of group membership. Families can be important to people in individualistic societies, as can other types of group membership, but individuals have the freedom to strike out on their own and achieve personal ambitions without recourse to reflecting on the relevance of their achievements to specific social groups they might belong to.

Individualism is associated with values that attach importance to making one's own way in the world and the acquisition of personal possession. Individual self-worth is more likely to be defined by material possessions and the ability to purchase premium brands. Premium brands can have great value also in collectivistic cultures, but such value is more often defined by how the brand might benefit the group or community rather than the individual user. Brand appeals in individualistic societies might therefore associate a brand with personal ambition and success, whereas in collectivistic cultures, marketers must be sure they make reference to the benefits for society or some other valued membership group with which the individual is connected.

People from individualistic cultures can often display different world orientations and social behaviour patterns from those in collectivistic cultures. Members of individualistic cultures are more likely to believe in a universal set of core values common to all cultures, whereas members of collectivistic cultures—which place emphasis on differences between in-groups and out-groups—more readily recognise that different cultures have different values.

There are differences between cultures in how people relate to brands. In collectivistic cultures, consumers are more likely to identify with corporate brands than individual product brands. This preference maps onto the value that is placed on the collective over the individual. This does not mean that corporate brands are not also valued in individualistic cultures or that product brands are not bought in collectivistic cultures. In terms of broader orientations, however, these differences exist and can influence consumers' choices and how well they respond to brand marketing campaigns.

For collectivistic cultures, product brands survive or fall on their perfor-mance attributes. They must bring value to the collective and to do that, they must deliver on functional performance features to benefit the group. For individualistic cultures, brand prominence and preference can be driven by whether the brand is believed to deliver image-enhancing features recog-nised by others and attached to the individual user rather than to any group to which he or she might belong (Shavitt, Lalwani, Zhang & Torelli, 2006).

Masculinity-Femininity

This dimension differentiates societies on the basis of whether the orienta-tions that are valued most are traditional 'masculine' ones, such as personal achievement and success, or traditional 'feminine', ones such as caring for others and living a good life. In a marketing context, this dimension can create a social climate that will accept or reject advertising in which brands are linked either to individual achievement or to being concerned primarily about the welfare of others. Masculine cultures promote ego consciousness that is then often reflected in consumption behaviours and the acquisition of brands that have been linked to being successful. Feminine cultures will respond better to brands associated with humility and selflessness.

Masculine cultures place emphasis on individual achievement and the divi-sion of roles in a stereotyped way between males and females. Feminine cultures place the cultivation of relationships with others above personal success and a social climate in which men and women's roles become more interchangeable.

Uncertainty Avoidance

National cultures can vary in their tolerance for uncertainty. Some cultures embrace unpredictable scenarios, value the stimulus they can bring to cre-ativity, and seek to learn new ways of coping with ambiguous situations and problems. Cultures that have low tolerance to uncertainty seek to create more rigid social structures accompanied by detailed and often conservative codes and rules to bring as much control into their social environments as possible. People who do not like uncertainty and who seek to avoid it tend to be less open to new ideas and new ways of behaving or doing things. They seek the certainty that comes from familiarity.

Uncertainty avoidance drives consumers to seek brands they feel confident about in terms of knowing what to expect. Consumers from these cultures respond best to brand promotions that confirm what the brand can do, that provide evidence that is scientifically verifiable or symbolic evidence that resonates with reassuring cultural codes. Uncertainty avoidance can interact with individualism/collectivism to determine how societies are structured and governed. In highly individualistic cultures with a high need to avoid uncertainty, explicit sets of rules and laws may be enacted to control and restrict behaviours within safe parameters. In highly collectivistic cultures with high uncertainty avoidance needs, cultural codes and tradition create deeply embedded conventions that are passed down the generations.

Long-Term Versus Short-Term Orientation

This dimension emerged from Eastern research and is shaped by Confucian philosophy concerning orientation to time. It was originally developed using the Chinese Values Survey, which was administered to samples of students in 23 countries (Chinese Culture Connection, 1987). A number of key values determined and defined this dimension: persistence, relationship status, thrift, and sense of shame on the positive poll and personal stability, protection of 'face', respect for tradition and reciprocation of favours and gifts on the negative pole (Minkov & Hofstede, 2012).

National markets can be distinguished in terms of the value they attach to short-term planning and objectives and longer-term aspirations. Some markets seek short-term results, whereas others are more willing to persevere when those outcomes are not forthcoming as soon as expected.

Long- versus short-term orientation can be combined with individualism/collectivism to produce further refinements to global market segmentation. Long-termism combined with collectivism embraces longer-term planning which will benefit the collective. Within this cultural environment, successful family businesses are developed over extended time periods and importance is attached to the creation of dynasties that will grow across generations. Each generation works not simply to benefit itself, but also to create healthy conditions for the next generation to take over and build upon. Collective long-termism can generate a pragmatic approach to doing business. This means that if one approach does not work, another will be embraced if it seems to offer better prospects.

Schwartz's Psychological Structure of Human Values

Shalom Schwartz conducted research to construct a theory of universal human values. Values were conceived to arise out of interactions between biological needs, social relationships, and societal demands. Values were believed to be underpinned by eight motivational needs: enjoyment, security, social power, achievement, self-direction, prosocial, restrictive conformity, and maturity. These needs were further mapped onto a structure that differentiated between the interests served they served—individualistic versus collectivistic—and the type of end goal to which they made reference—terminal or instrumental (Schwartz & Bilsky, 1987).

Following the work of Rokeach (1973), Schwartz believed that all human beings were driven to satisfy certain physical needs first of all and derived pleasure from doing so. Hence, the motivation to produce enjoyment in life was conceived to be a critical base drive. Following the conceptual lead of Maslow (1954), the need for humans to ensure their survival meant creating conditions under which they would be safe from threats to their existence. Hence, there was a fundamental need to ensure personal security.

Surviving through being safe represents a basic subsistence state, but if any organism is to flourish, it must learn how to live successfully within its immediate physical and social environment. This need was expressed as an achievement motive through which the individual gains skills and knowledge, enabling it to grow and develop within their environment.

Human beings were believed to be possessed by intrinsic needs to explore their environment and understand it better. Through this understanding, they might also learn to control outcomes. In this context, humans were therefore self-directed not simply to achieve, but to decide on the direction of that achievement.

As social beings, human must learn how to get along with others. Although they may initially be driven by selfish impulses, self-interest must be tempered with constraint and recognition of the needs of others. To ensure that everyone exhibits constraint, sets of rules must be established that lay down conventions and restrictions concerning how people may behave. These restrictive conformity needs motivate human beings in social settings to establish such parameters to underpin a civil or functional society.

Within a restrictive society with sets of rules, a further drive emerges to care for the welfare of others. As well as legal rules, moral codes emerge that place emphasis on values such as altruism and kindness. These codes are not restrictive practices, but instead promote the caring for others as a voluntary activity.

Within social settings, not all individuals are the same in nature or in their achievements. Inevitably, a status hierarchy will emerge representing power differentials between different individuals or groups within a society. At a community level, societies can differ in their tolerance for power differentials and in how firmly entrenched they become within social structures and systems.

Finally, there is the concept of the mature motive. Maslow referred to this drive as 'self-actualisation' and it represents the motive to attain a high level of excellence or competence in an activity or skill or simply in one's approach to understanding life. The main goal becomes to enhance personal understanding as an end in itself.

This motivational taxonomy was utilised to guide the development of a values instrument that was administered to samples of Israeli schoolteachers and German college students. The values instruments derived from an earlier instrument, the Rokeach Values Survey. Each value was verbally listed alongside a second value and a seven-point rating scale was used to enable respondents to indicate whether one value was of "identical importance" to the other (score = 1) or, at the other extreme, whether one value was "much more important" than the other (score = 7). After statistical analyses were used to confirm values clusters, these groupings of values items were then further categorised according to individualistic versus collectivistic orientations, instrumental versus terminal goals, and motivational domains. There was a great deal of consistency of outcomes between the two national samples used in this study.

Schwartz (1992) presented a modified theory of human values that contained four new motivational dimensions called 'Stimulation', 'Spirituality', 'Tradition', and 'Universalism'. Hence, eleven motivational types were conceived: (1) Self-Direction, (2) Stimulation, (3) Hedonism, (4) Achievement, (5) Power, (6) Security, (7) Conformity, (8) Tradition, (9) Spirituality, (10) Benevolence, and (11) Universalism. Benevolence replaced 'Prosocial' and Universalism replaced 'Maturity' from the initial typology. 'Stimulation' represented a drive to seek variety or novelty. It was conceived to be related to 'Self-Direction', but differed in the sense that the latter tended to be instrumental with goal direction and 'Stimulation' was really a drive for thrill seeking as an end in itself.

'Spirituality' was regarded as a universal type of motivation that represented a detachment from cares about the material world and a focus instead on reflection about the meaning of life and whether life as lived in the everyday sense is the only form of existence. 'Universalism' represented a high-order motivation that entailed individuals seeking to extend their knowledge—not necessarily to discover the meanings sought under 'Spirituality', but more to extend the limits of human capabilities (Schwartz, 1992).

As had been found earlier, orientations such as individualism/collectivism could mediate the manifestations of these motivations. Whereas motives such as 'Benevolence' and 'Universality' encouraged a focus on caring for others and seeking excellence in its own right as a means of extending human abilities for the benefit of all, they exhibited different forms of expression in individualistic and collectivistic cultures. Collectivist cultures place emphasis on the group over the individual, but there concerns were restricted to the specified in-group, whereas there was little concern about the needs and welfare of other out-groups. Individualist cultures many have placed more emphasis on the achievements of individuals, but they also differentiated in less clear-cut ways between in-groups and out-groups and could therefore be capable of displaying greater equity in their treatment of both (Triandis, 1990; Triandis, McCusker & Hui, 1990).

Schwartz conceived that Power, Achievement, Hedonism, Stimulation, and Self-Direction served mainly individual interests, and that benevolence, tradition, and conformity served mainly collectivist interests. Universalism and security served both individualistic and collectivistic interests. Spirituality was less easy to place and could switch back and forth between individualism and collectivism depending upon the way it was defined in a specific culture (Schwartz, 1992).

Schwartz (1992) further tested his values typology with 40 samples of respondents recruited across 20 countries, representing 13 different languages. The samples comprised mainly teachers and students, although general samples were also recruited in Australia, Israel, and Japan.

There were variances between cultures in the appearance of the motive types believed to underpin human values. Ten out of the 11 motive types were identified clearly in a majority of the 40 samples: Achievement (40), Power (37), Tradition (36), Self-Direction (36), Universalism (34), Hedonism (32), Stimulation (31), Conformity (29), and Benevolence (20). The criteria for confirming Spirituality were less clear in most samples (32 out of 40).

List of Values

The List of Values model has also been tested cross-culturally (Grunert, Brunso & Bisp, 1997). These values profiles were found to be linked across generations. Test that were run across the United States, Japan, New Zealand, France, West Germany, and Denmark found evidence for similar values being held by parents and their children, although more strongly so in some countries than in others (Grunert et al., 1997). Within cultures, some generational differences emerged. Parents placed more emphasis on accomplishment and security, whereas their children placed more value on hedonism (Grunert et al., 1997).

Comparisons of Values Models

Hofstede's (1980) original model outlined four values factors: Power Distance, Uncertainty Avoidance, Individualism/Collectivism, and Masculinity/Femininity. Schwartz (1992) found two principal dimensions: Self-Transcendence versus Self-Enhancement, and Conservation versus Openness to Change. The LOV model defined two core dimensions: Please Change versus Comfort Constancy, and Internal versus External (Kahle, 1983; Grunert & Scherhorn, 1990). The Chinese Cultural Connection (1987) reported four dimensions: Integration, Human Heartedness, Moral Discipline, and Confucian Work Dynamism.

Looking across these models, certain dimensions appear consistently even though they are called by different names. There is a stability dimension that is often tied to an orientation towards tradition. At the opposite poll is an openness to change. This dimension appears in Hofstede's model (uncertainty avoidance), the List of Values (pleasure/change versus comfort-constancy), and Schwartz (conservation versus openness to change).

There is a further dimension that contrasts 'self' and 'others'. For Hofstede, this was labelled as individualism versus collectivism. It is reflected in the internal/external dimension of LOV and in a subordinate individual/interpersonal factor in this model. Schwartz made reference to self-transcendence versus conservation. Finally, the Chinese Cultural Connection model identified relevant attributes in its human-heartedness and integration factors.

Cultural Traits and Advertising

Developing classification systems to distinguish cultural values has been a task undertaken by scholars intent on understanding more about the indigenous characteristics of people who live in different cultures. This work was conducted by cross-cultural psychologists and sociologists, with input also from anthropology, but was not always driven by the need to understand decision-making in consumer markets. It is clear from theoretical discussions of cultural value types that they are linked to different human needs and have a social purpose of creating parameters or sets of guidelines to restricted and control behaviour. It seems logical, therefore, that an understanding of cultural values ought to be relevant to planning marketing campaigns with the end goal of influencing the way people behave as consumers.

In the context of marketing research, cultural values have been investigated as mediators of consumers' responses to brand promotions, and especially to mainstream media advertisements. They have also been examined in terms of whether they are represented within advertising messages and brand symbolism. Although the study of the expression of values within advertisements does not represent evidence of their effects upon consumers, it does allow researchers to understand how different techniques are used in different cultures even when trying to promote the same brand. It can also indicate why some cross-cultural campaigns fail.

The standard methodology for the study of advertising copy and formats is content analysis. This methodology tries to break down the texts of scripts of communications, together with any visual or other physical features they have, into measurable units that can be classified and counted up. It is a formal technique that begins by defining its overall measurement objectives in terms of the entities that are to be identified and counted. If a study is interested, for example, in the way men and women are represented in advertisements, any appearance by a man or by a woman in a scene in an advertisement will be treated as a measurable unit to be catalogued. In addition, further details about each appearance might be noted down, such as what the man or woman was wearing, what was the physical setting in which they appeared, what types of behaviour did they display, and so on. In an advertising context, the nature of the advertising itself will be classified, such as the type of product or service being promoted.

With physical features, it is fairly straightforward to define what kinds of things are to be identified and counted. With abstract concepts such as values, this procedure is less straightforward. For instance, when deciding whether an advertisement displays an individualistic or masculine position, or portrays power distance or a particular conception of time or relationship to the environment, how is this to be done? What are the signifiers of these values within the actions and settings portrayed in an advertisement?

This issue was examined by Pollay (1983). He began with an anecdote about an advertisement for Kodak in which the company wished to get across the idea that consumers could trust its products. In one campaign, it ran an image of a farmer surrounded by small children with a simple strapline, "Trust Kodak". The image was designed to convey all that was needed about trust through the symbolism of small children who trusted and were in the care of the farmer. This anecdote does not provide scientific evidence of values, nor does it outline a methodology that could be used as a system for values identification and measurement. The simple informal analysis of that advertisement nonetheless provided a powerful indication of how this task might be approached.

Pollay went on to experiment with such a methodology. The first task was to decide which values should be measured. Was there a values classification system available that could be applied in this marketing context? There were a number of earlier lists of human needs and values. A list of 48 motives had been produced by Starch (1923). Another well-known list of needs was developed by Murray (1938), and was later developed further by Fowles (1976).

The most prominent values system of that time was one developed by Rokeach (1973). He had identified 18 'instrumental' values and 18 'terminal' values. Reference was made to this values model earlier in this chapter. Rokeach had developed and refined his values typology by reviewing other relevant research and conducting his only empirical research to validate specific values types and the measure used operationally to define them.

Rokeach developed a measurement method that allowed respondents to engage in self-evaluations using a list of adjectives. For example, listed under 'instrumental' values were descriptions such as: ambitious, broadminded, courageous, forgiving, independent, intellectual, responsible, and self-controlled, among others. Listed under 'terminal' values were: a comfortable life, a sense of accomplishment, a world of beauty, family security, freedom, happiness, self-respect, true friendship, wisdom, and a number of others.

Using these descriptors with survey respondents through which they could rate themselves by using a scale to indicate the personal importance or relevance of such sentiments is one thing. It is quite another to apply these descriptions to the content of advertisements. Pollay's approach was multistage and multifaceted. He collated samples of advertisements and studied their contents. He discussed the values with colleagues and experts from different social sciences and the marketing field to identify ways in which specific values could be fleshed out using other linguistic terms as well as how they might be represented in overt behaviours. He examined advertisements with other experts to identify the kinds of marketing objectives that defined specific messages and how those objectives might in turn be linked to specific values or human needs.

The end result was a coding system that identified a list of values accompanied by instructions concerning how these values might be further elaborated upon linguistically and identified through specific actions, events, portrayals, or character relationships in advertisements. This instrument was tested with a sample of magazine advertisements, and the reliability of individual measures was calculated across coders.

Each advertisement was evaluated in relation to a list of adjectives that represented specific values. Coders were asked to rate an advertisement in terms of the different ways the advertised product was 'good' in the context of its indigenous qualities, a feeling or sense it could create, and the type of outcome for consumers it would bring. Typical of adjectives concerning its specific qualities were: effective, durable, convenient, cheap, and traditional. Adjectives that created a certain sense or feeling included: affiliation, family, humility, modesty, relaxation, succorance, and wisdom. Finally, descriptions concerning how the advertised product could help consumers included: casual healthy, neat, and vain.

Pollay's system for measuring cultural values was not developed to classify consumers, but it could be used to classify advertisements and in that respect could be used alongside consumer research to find out whether advertisements make good cultural values matches in a specific national market.

Individualism, Collectivism, and Persuasion

Individualistic and collectivistic cultures differ in terms of how their members behave in different settings and in their sense of self. In collectivistic cultures, the self is defined more powerfully in terms of various in-group memberships such as family, tribe, and community than is true of individualistic cultures. Members of collectivistic cultures also tend to perceive greater similarities between themselves and other members of their group than is true of members of individualistic cultures. In individualistic cultures, the self is a more idiosyncratic concept that each individual holds about themselves that is defined through personal experiences and achievements more than by membership in specific social groups (Triandis, McCusker & Hui, 1990). Individualistic cultural patterns tend to dominate in the northern and western parts of Europe and in North America. Collectivistic patterns are more prevalent and prominent in Asia, Africa, Central and South America, and in Mediterranean Europe (Hofstede, 1980, 1983).

The different emphases on sources of personal identity between these cultural values systems are also relevant to the ways their members develop attitudes about the world and to the kinds of communications they are persuaded by. Persuasive communications work best when receivers perceive them as believable and trustworthy and these attributes are influenced by the nature of their source. The credibility of the source is a key factor here. Source credibility will depend upon the way the source is perceived by others and this perception will in turn be influenced by different source attributes and characteristics. This is the point at which cultural values can affect the outcome. In an individualistic society, consumers might be more persuaded by a source perceived to have specific attributes based on their individual qualities—achievements, abilities, experiences, and lifestyle. In a collectivistic society, source credibility may depend much more on whether the source is perceived to be a member of an in-group known to the recipient of the message that commands much social respect (Davidson et al., 1976; Triandis et al., 1986, 1988).

Han & Shavitt (1994) conducted a direct test of the mediating effects of culture type on how consumers from individualistic and collectivistic cultures reacted to advertisements. Their investigation had two parts. Initially, they compared magazine advertisements from Korea (collectivistic culture) and the United States (individualistic culture) for the expression of different types of values. Then they conducted research with samples of consumers from each country during which participants were exposed to magazine advertisements from each country and were asked about their attitudes towards and intentions to purchase specific brands afterwards.

A further distinction was made between product categories in terms of whether products were 'shared' products or 'personal' products. Shared products were ones for which the decision-making process was likely to involve more than one person, for example, members of the entire family for certain household acquisitions. Personal products were ones for which the decision to purchase was very much an individual one, with the consumer buying something for personal use, such as clothing, accessories, cosmetics, and so on.

The content analysis of magazine advertisements showed that overall individualism outweighed collectivism in terms of represented cultural values, but that collectivistic values were significantly more likely to be found in Korean advertisements than in American ones. There was also a difference in the use of values between 'shared' and 'personal' products. Personal products were much more likely to be promoted through individualistic than collectivistic values, whereas this position was reversed in advertisements for shared products.

In the follow-up consumer study, Han and Shavitt recruited 64 young people aged 18 to 27 from each country. Each participant was shown four pairs of magazine advertisements covering four product types. One advert in each pair contained an individualistic appeal, and the other contained a collectivistic appeal. For example, with two toothpaste adverts, the individualistic version told consumers: "Treat yourself to a breath freshening experience". The collectivistic version read: "Share the Freedent breath freshening experience". Thus, in one case, the sales pitch was centred on the individual receiving a personal benefit from the product. In the other, an emphasis was placed on sharing this experience with others. After exposure to each advertisement, participants gave their opinions about the product (e.g., whether they liked it or not) and the brand (e.g., whether it was desirable or not) and also indicated whether they were likely or not to buy it.

The results showed that overall American consumers were more persuaded by advertisements with individualistic appeals, whereas Korean consumers reacted similarly towards advertisements with collectivistic appeals. Individualistic appeals for American consumers were strongest for personal products and were somewhat weaker for shared products. Likewise among Korean consumers, collectivistic appeals were strongest for shared products, but had weaker effects on personal product choices. Indeed, Korean consumers reacted favourably to individualistic appeals for personal products. How involved consumers were with the product or advertisements did not make any difference to how they responded to different kinds of advertising appeal.

Although this research was carried out with small and unrepresentative samples of consumers, it nonetheless provided interesting findings that confirmed outcomes that were theoretically expected. The findings confirmed that cultural values can make a difference in persuasion through advertising and that there are cultural differences in how consumers will respond to the same advertisements. It is important that advertisers try to ensure that any cultural values references within their brand campaign represent the types of values consumers in specific markets hold most dear.

More generally, research has shown that cultural values dimensions can differentiate broad-based orientations towards innovation in different consumer markets. Yaveroglu & Donthu (2002) examined links between Hofstede's cultural values dimensions and the propensity for national markets to exhibit an orientation towards innovation versus imitation in relation to a number of product areas. Data from 19 countries showed that those high on individualism, low on uncertainty avoidance, and low in power distance displayed more innovative tendencies, whereas those low on individualism (and high on collectivism) and high on uncertainty avoidance were more likely to display product imitation.

In another investigation using Hofstede's cultural values dimensions, Yenihurt & Townsend (2003) found that greater uncertainty avoidance and power distance orientations tended to hinder new products becoming established in national markets, whereas individualism had a positive effect on acceptance of new products.

Values, Personality, and Consumerism

Several models have emerged that have influenced thinking about the definition and measurement of cultural values. These models have varied in their impact upon marketing activities in global settings. The most-cited models are the Hofstede model (Hofstede, 2001; Hofstede & Hofstede, 2005), the work of Trompenaars (1993), the framework established by Schwartz (1994; Schwartz & Bilsky, 1987), and the GLOBE study (House & Associates, 2004). These models have all attempted to define universal and normative values-based systems of population segmentation that can be applied to consumers. As this book has also shown, there are other models of psychographic segmentation in which typologies of consumers have been derived from models of psychological differences between people originally developed for non-consumer purposes. Is there any resonance between these approaches?

These models differ in the number of countries they studied, the samples on which values dimensions were established, and the conceptual structure of values typologies they produced. These differences mean that it can be difficult to make comparisons between these models (de Mooij & Hofstede, 2010). This point applies when considering how they might help marketing professionals design advertising campaigns that will be effective in culturally distinct national and regional markets. Interest here tends to centre on the ability of cultural values models to frame what consumers believe to be: (1) Desirable and (2) Desired. The former concept embraces the idea of how people think the world ought to be, and the latter is concerned with articulating what they desire for themselves.

Hofstede's model has proven to be very popular not just because it offers an elegant solution to framing cultural values in terms of broad types, but also because it has been developed from data collected from a large number of countries. Whereas its critics have observed that the research backing the Hofstede model is now dated, others have noted that more recent models, based on more recently collected consumer data, have not really advanced the modelling of cultural values in any significant ways as far as predicting consumer brand preferences and choices is concerned (Magnusson, Wilson, Zdravkovic, Zhou & Westjohn, 2008).

One of the problems facing the application of these cultural values models to the problem of consumer segmentation is that none of them was originally developed for that purpose. There are no obvious ways in which these models can be linked to relevant communications or marketing theories so as to create a conceptual framework in which culture models clearly have relevance to both the description of consumer populations and the prediction of how they might adopt specific brands or respond favourably to different kinds of brand promotions (Douglas & Craig, 2006).

The power distance dimension differentiates between cultures that accept social hierarchies that are largely fixed and where everyone knows their station in life and those in which there is greater fluidity of movement. Cultures and societies classed as high in power distance recognise that there are those with much power and those with little power, and the gap between them is great and usually cannot be traversed. In low power distance cultures, social hierarchies are flatter and individuals can change their power status by moving from low to high power through their own efforts.

Individualistic cultures have been described as being 'I' conscious and collectivistic cultures as 'we' conscious. In collectivistic cultures, people define themselves in relation to their existing social system. Consumers in individualistic cultures like to get straight to the point when seeking information and advice about brands. They expect advertisements to do the same. They want to know what is so special about the brand that they, as individuals, stand to benefit from using it? In collectivistic cultures, consumers need to know that a brand will not contravene values that are important to their community, group, or social system. Consumers in individualistic cultures are expected to make up their minds quite quickly about a brand once they have obtained information about it that confirms whether they personally stand to benefit from it. Their counterparts in collectivistic cultures may want to take more time finding out about a brand and getting to know its supplier before making a commitment (de Mooij & Hofstede, 2010).

The masculine/feminine dimension is also important in a number of potential respects to consumers' decision-making. In masculine-oriented societies, much weight is placed on achievement and success. In feminine-oriented societies, caring and support of others and overall quality of life that derives from social circumstances rather than material things are highly valued. Hence, consumers in masculine-oriented societies can be expected to respond favourably to brand images and promotions that associate achievement and dominance with its use. Brand status in such cultures is therefore determined by whether a brand's image resonates with these values. In feminine-oriented societies, status brands of this sort are less likely to be well received. Instead, it is important, at least hypothetically, that brands are associated with the promotion of positive and caring relationships with others (de Mooij, 2010).

The dimension of uncertainty avoidance defines the extent to which people in a society are not threatened by ambiguity and change or whether they generally feel more comfortable with a structured, well-ordered society that values tradition over social evolution. Such openness to change, which is not dissimilar to openness to new ideas in the Big Five Personality Inventory, is expected to be manifest in the degree to which a culture embraces innovations. Those cultures in which uncertainty avoidance is most valued will be slower than those in which uncertainty in the form of change is welcomed to adopt new products and services (Yaveroglu & Donthu, 2002; Yenihurt & Townsend, 2003; Tellis, Stremersch & Yin, 2003).

Finally, the Hofstede model identified a fifth dimension called long- versus short-term orientation. This dimension distinguishes between societies that have a future-oriented and longer-term perspective on life versus ones that take a more historical or conventional and short-term view. Societies with a long-term view value commitment and perseverance and attach weight to social status, which is a key structural factor ordering their communities. Such communities tend to be thrifty rather than profligate. It is important for such societies that everyone works to preserve the long-term interests of their community. Failing to do so can be a source of loss of face and shame that is to be avoided at all costs. In societies with a short-term view of life, there is respect for tradition, but at the same time, people pursue individual interests and personal happiness. Such societies are more focused on the present or near-term future and seek short-term gratifications that are designed to benefit the individual as much as society (de Mooij, 2010).

The Hofstede model goes beyond outlining key values dimensions that define cultures and considers also the orientations that specific social milieus create for the people living in those cultures especially in the way they define their personal identity or 'self'. The definition of the self in turn has implications for consumer activity because societies vary in the significance of consumerism as an aspect of self-concept.

Collectivism tends to promote the idea of the self as integrated with rather than separate from the social setting in which a person exists. Individualism is comfortable with the notion of a self-concept that is separate from the surrounding social context. Within an individualistic framework, the self has a distinct identity that is preserved even when the individual moves from one social setting to another (Markus & Kitayama, 1991). Whereas individuals in individualistic societies define their self-identity in terms of their personal characteristics and, through their extension into consumerism, through their possessions, in collectivistic societies, the individual's self-concept derives to a more significant extent from his or her relationships with other people in their group or community (Nezlek, Kafetsios & Smith, 2008; Tardiff et al., 2008).

The Eastern cultures tend to be collectivistic, and this means that they feel good about themselves when they are in situations in which they are with family and friends. Such relationships can take time to develop. It is important in consumer contexts, therefore, that collectivistic consumers are given time to get to know brands and their suppliers and that they receive positive recommendations about brands from people they know and trust. In individualistic Western societies, independence of identity from social circumstances is more highly prized. This means there is a constancy of 'self' from situation to situation. In a consumer context, therefore, commodities are valued if they can enhance the individual's self-identity in a desired way.

The masculine/feminine orientation has a further important role to play in self-identity, and this also in turn shapes consumer orientations. Feminine cultures value interpersonal relationships, being caring and supportive of others, and the display of humility. Masculine-oriented cultures are more focused on self-development and achievement, which feed self-esteem. The socially, economically, and professional successful person develops greater self-confidence and self-regard. When masculine/feminine orientation can interact with individualism/collectivism to influence how people conduct their lives and engage with consumerism. Feminine-oriented, individualistic cultures can display many of the qualities of a collectivistic society in valuing interpersonal relationships and caring for the group or community over self-promotion and enhancement (Watkins et al., 1998).

The cultural values dimensions outlined by Hofstede derive from societal-level rules and ideals about how people can or should live, but provide marketers with consumer segmentation criteria that can be applied at the level of the individual consumer. Given that they also link into specific psychological orientations of individuals, it is of interest to know whether they resonate with human personality dimensions that have been developed from the level of the individual and then subsequently applied at societal level in studies that have audited the prevalence of specific personality types.

The fixing of values types to personality types can prove challenging across cultures, however, because of the different cultural perspectives that exist on personality. In Western cultures, drive largely by individualism, the prevailing belief is that personality traits are fixed and permanent aspects of a person's character. In Eastern, collectivistic cultures, in contrast, human personality is regarded as more fluid and inclined to change across different social settings and circumstances (Norenzayan, Choi & Nisbett, 2002; Church et al., 2006). These differences can be seen also in the way people from these different cultures talk about themselves. When describing their own personality, for example, people from individualistic cultures will generally make reference to themselves in the first person: "I am like this" and "I am like that". People in collectivistic cultures will tend to use the third person and refer to how others perceive them as a person and individual differences are defined in terms of the behaviour that might be typical of a person in a specific social setting (Kashima, Kashima, Kim & Gelfand, 2005).

Despite these cultural differences, Hofstede (2007) has observed that there is some resonance between his cultural values dimensions and the Big Five personality factors outlined by McCrae (2002). Variations have been found in the prevalence and strength of these personality factors between cultures (Hofstede & McCrae, 2004). What is less clear, however, is whether these five personality dimensions really are universal across cultures or whether the same factors will emerge when the same statistical analyses are applied to data from similar sets of verbal questions when they are administered to samples from different cultures (Schmidt, Allik, McCrae, & Benet-Martinez, 2007). There is evidence that in collectivistic Eastern cultures, for instance, a sixth personality dimension can be found that has been termed 'dependence' (Hofstede, 2007). Furthermore, even the same personality dimension can be expressed through different components in different cultures (Cheung et al., 2008).

Extending this line of research, as well as commonalities in personality dimensions across cultures, culturally distinct personality factors have also been discovered in relation to brands. The concept of 'brand personality' was discussed earlier. This concept is built upon a collection of enduring

beliefs and perceptions about brands that consist of descriptors that effectively assign human-like personality attributes to specific variants of commodities and services. This phenomenon becomes manifest in the distinctive
brand personalities that are assigned to the same or similar product variants in different cultures (Aaker, Benet-Martinez & Garolera, 2001; Firscht,
Maloles, Swoboda, Morschett & Sinha, 2008).

These brand personality differences have been clearly identified when
consumers' perceptions of well-known brands have been compared in Western and Eastern cultures. In Korea, for example, consumer research revealed
brand personality attributes such as "Passive Likeableness" and "Ascendancy" that did not emerge among the same suite of well-known brands for
American consumers (Sung & Tinkham, 2005).

The potential of cultural values systems to mediate the impact of personality traits on human behaviour has been uncovered by studies of how
personality is expressed in different parts of the world. The core difference
between Western and Eastern cultures or between cultures defined predominantly by individualism or by collectivism can be found in relation to the
concept of identity. In individualistic cultures, emphasis is placed on self-
identity as a series of ideas a person has about their own being which singles
them out as unique. This does not mean that they cannot relate to other
people or perceive similarities between their own being and other people,
but over and above all this, a distinctive person emerge who is essentially a
one-off. The 'self' as a core aspect of individuality means that the individual
members of an individualistic society will seek to pursue courses of action
in their lives that are motivated by the need to enhance that self, strengthen
its individuality, and further its own interests.

In comparison, in collectivistic societies, although the individual exists
as a distinct being, his or her self-perceptions are strongly tied to a collective or group or community. In this context, activities are undertaken
to enhance the self, but the 'self' in this case is not focused on the idiosyncratic needs and interests of the individual, but on the establishment
of strong ties and positive relationships with others in the collective. In a
consumer context, therefore, the collectivist individual will acquire possessions and adopt brands that best represent the wider recognition of the
community. A person's own identity flows from their group memberships,
principally the family, school, neighbourhood, employer, and so on (de
Mooij, 2010).

Within an individualistic setting, materialism is geared very much to the
projection of an individual identity that stands apart from any group membership (Ger & Belk, 1996). Within collectivistic settings, although there are
words available to describe 'identity' in terms of the individual as an entity,
the ideas that underpin what it means to people in such cultures are defined
by the way the individual is connected to others. Social membership and
reference groups are the key to the self-concept and in the absence of such
references, the 'self' has little independent meaning.

Such cultural differences also influence the kinds of self-attributes that are assigned the greatest social and personal significance. In individualistic cultures, the emphasis on the individual as a stand-alone entity means that the significance of physical appearance to social status and self-regard is strengthened. Self-esteem in Western, individualistic societies is determined by social success and also by conforming to cultural standards of personal aesthetic beauty and attractiveness. Self-esteem is therefore closely interlinked with body self-esteem. There has been much debate about this issue, especially when it leads to extreme body shaping behaviours that pose health risks for the individual (Wykes & Gunter, 2005).

Further concerns associated with the emphasis of external appearance are that they somehow lack depth and promote superficiality in the way people are socially evaluated. In Eastern, collectivistic societies, such as China and Japan, cultural values place more emphasis on the internal attributes of the person than on how they appear outwardly. The body is less important to self-esteem than how one performs as functioning member of society (Kowner, 2002; Prendergast, Leung & West, 2002).

The focus on external appearance cuts across both genders, but in the West, it has had a greater and lasting impact on women and girls. The mass media and fashion industry, in particular, have emphasized the importance of a slender body shape, and this ideal has resonated with the way women have been presented in advertisements across many product and service categories. A dominant representation has been one that places women in certain social settings and presents them so as to emphasize their physical attributes. Although gender representation has evolved in Western advertising, the physical stereotyping of women has never fully disappeared. Women have to be slender or display an hourglass figure. Either way, the preferred representation of advertisers has tended not to match the normative reality of female body shapes in Western cultures where there have been growing concerns about people in general getting overweight. Even when women are not technically obese or overweight, they tend not normally to conform to the female body shape presented in mainstream brand advertising.

The propensity of women to question their body shape and in turn to experience negative self-esteem because of this has been associated with cultures that display specific patterns of values. This phenomenon is more prevalent in cultures that are mostly individualistic, exhibit low power distance, and low uncertainty avoidance. It is not surprising, therefore, that the biggest concerns among women about their body self-esteem occur in Western societies. This does not mean they are absent in Eastern cultures, but they are to some extent countered there by different values systems that encourage consumers to define themselves in terms that steer their attention away from their own characteristics and towards how they relate to others around them in their membership and reference groups (Etcoff, Orbach, Scott & D'Agostino, 2006).

Thus, when campaigns have been run that depart from this representational norm, they have attracted a great deal of attention. This out-of-the-ordinary phenomenon was illustrated by one of the world's biggest producers of fast-moving consumer goods, Unilever, with its campaign for the personal care brand *Dove*. Women who were fuller figured than the advertising norm, and who purportedly represented 'normal' women and body shapes, were featured with the message that beauty exists on the inside or is in the eye of the beholder. Even women who do not have the airbrushed body shapes on top fashion models or female celebrities can be deemed 'beautiful' in their own way (Etcoff et al., 2006).

In collectivistic cultures, brand personalities can emerge that are an important aspect of a brand's acceptance and success in their consumer markets. The nature of the 'personality' in this case is different from that found acceptable in Western, individualistic cultures. Comparisons of Eastern and Western consumer markets such as the United States, Germany, Japan, and Korea have found that a brand's personality is more likely to be accepted and rated positively in the East if it is demonstrably related to local social values. The reputation of the corporation behind the brand can be important in collectivistic cultures where consumers need to know what efforts companies have made to contribute to and become a functioning part of their society. A corporation's social reputation is therefore the key to a specific brand's standing rather than whether the brand is promoted on the basis of enhancing each individual consumer's own personal status (Souiden, Kassim & Hong, 2006).

These cultural differences in the way brands are defined and evaluated also have a bearing on the types of message appeals that work best in advertising campaigns. In Western societies, brand marketers can make appeals that are abstract in nature and make reference to personality and lifestyle enhancement. Such appeals might be conveyed through symbolic references to lifestyles that are associated with a specific brand. In collectivistic cultures, consumers are more likely to be persuaded by knowing in more concrete terms what a product or service will deliver and whether it is likely to be accepted by the wider community. If a brand is shown as being able to promote the quality of relationships with others in important membership and reference groups, it is more likely to be positively evaluated and purchased. In the East, therefore, celebrity endorsements from trusted local public figures can be influential where they help to quickly and unequivocally establish the social utility and relevance of a brand from the mouths of trusted sources (Praet, 2008). Although celebrity endorsements can be effective in Western consumer cultures as well, they are more extensively used in collectivistic Eastern markets.

The bottom line is that the value or equity attached to a brand is often defined differently in Western and Eastern cultures. There are many potential brand associations that can enhance a brand's personality and therefore its reputation among consumers in the West, but few of these same associations may have any real currency with consumers in the East (Hsieh, 2004; Kocak, Abimbola & Ozer, 2007).

There are yet more influences of cultural values types on the way products and services are categorised. There are differences between Eastern and Western epistemologies in the ideas they hold about objects and processes in the world. In Confucian thinking in China, the focus was placed on objects and their component parts and their place in the wider world in terms of a series of relationships between components whose behaviour was governed by specific rules.

In the West, where early thinking about objects derived from the Ancient Greeks, objects were classed as having specific properties which characterised all objects of their class and could be expected to occur regardless of the settings in which objects were found or used. In Western culture, therefore, objects were defined by the categories to which they were assigned, and the way they behaved was determined by how their constant properties interacted with the contexts and settings in which they were placed. While objects could interact with different forces in different settings to produce different outcomes, there was a degree of consistency in the properties of an object which ensured its independence from any environment in which it was placed (Nisbett, Peng, Choi & Norenzayan, 2001).

In the East, a different perspective existed in which objects were conceived in more fluid ways and could change in their nature as they moved from one setting to another. This was because the identity of an object was defined in terms of its relationships with other objects and with the characteristics of different events and settings. Consumers would regard themselves as embedded within a wider community and their identities are then defined in terms of their position in that setting and the ways they relate to other people and to objects they find there. There is no identity of self or of objects that is independent of their interrelationships with each other and with other features of a specific social setting (Markus & Kitayama, 1991).

The importance of this description of Eastern and collectivist ideas about objects is relevant to the consumer context because it can explain why consumers in such cultures differ in their reactions from their counterparts in Western, individualist cultures to new product lines or brand extensions. In the West, if a brand extension is created for a different product type from that for which a company is best known, consumers will regard this initiative as a fresh venture and might sometimes have difficulty recognising it as an extension of an existing brand. In the East, however, collectivists may find it easier to accept such a brand extension as being related to other manifestations of the brand when the parent company (and its corporate brand) is well known and has a good reputation (Monga & John, 2007).

Concluding Remarks

The behaviour of consumers is not only shaped by their individual personalities, but also by internalised societal standards that are expressed in terms of broad principles of conduct or values. As we saw in earlier chapters, values coupled with lifestyle characteristics have been used as defining attributes of consumers and used to develop normative consumer typologies. Quite independently of this empirical effort, psychologists have been engaged in research designed to classify cultural values and behavioural practices around the world. The aim of such enterprises has been to produce an all-embracing model of cultural values that has universal applicability around the globe. Although not developed with the intention of classifying people as consumers, these values models have in some instances been utilised within a marketing context.

As with the Big Five personality types applied at the level of individuals, a number of cultural value types have been reproduced across different theoretical models of societal-level values that can be embraced and internalised by individuals. They provide an alternative layer of consumer classification in addition to personality dimensions. Values are often deeply embedded with the society's cultural psyche and in turn become internalised by individual members of a society at a profound psychological levels, rendering them difficult to shift.

These principles that govern standards of behaviour within societies as well as defining the status of different societal sub-groups and expectations in terms of the ways societies are most effectively governed might not necessarily directly determine the consumer practices of individuals, but they might do so when brands offend core values. It is therefore important for brand marketers to understand cultural values in national markets to ensure that they do not cause such offence. It is critically important for brands that are marketed globally to devise promotional strategies that cater to variances in cultural values and ensure either that campaigns are sufficiently culture neutral to avoid causing offence or that they run different campaigns in different regions of the world that are designed to resonate with local values.

References

Aaker, J. L., Benet-Martinez, V., & Garoloera, J. (2001) Consumption symbols as carriers of culture: A study of Japanese and Spanish brand personality constructs. *Journal of Personality and Social Psychology*, 81, 492–508.

Cheung. F., Cheung, S. F., Zhang, J., Leung, K., Leong, F., & Yeh, K. H. (2008) Relevance for openness as a personality dimension in Chinese culture. *Journal of Cros-Cultural Psychology*, 39(1), 81–108.

Chinese Cultural Connection (1987) Chinese values and the search for culture-free dimensions of culture. *Journal of Cross-Cultural Psychology*, 18(2), 143–164.

Church, A. T., Willmore, S.L., Anderson, A. T., Ochiai, M., Porter, N., Del Mateo, N. J., Reyes, J. A. S., Ebanez-Reyes, J., Alvarez, J. M., Katigbat, M. S., & Ortiz, F. A. (2006) Implicit theories and self-perceptions of traitedness across cultures. *Journal of Cross-Cultural Psychology*, 37(6), 694–716.

Davidson, A. R., Jaccard, J. J., Triandis, H. C., Morales, M. L., & Diaz-Guerrero, R. (1976) Cross-cultural model testing: Toward a solution of the emic-etic dilemma. *International Journal of Psychology*, 11, 1–13.

De Mooij, M., & Hofstede, G. (2010) The Hofstede model: Applications to global branding and advertising strategy and research. *International Journal of Advertising*, 29(1), 85–110.

Douglas, S. P., & Craig, C. S. (2006) On improving the conceptual foundations of international marketing research. *Journal of International Marketing*, 14(1), 1–22.

Etcoff, N., Orbach, S., Scott, J., & D'Agostino, H. (2006) *Beyond stereotypes: Rebuilding the foundation of beauty beliefs*. Findings of the 2005 Dove Global Study.

Ferraro, G. (2002) *The Cultural Dimension of International Business*. Upper Saddle River, NJ: Prentice-Hall.

Fiske, A. P. (1992) The 4 elementary forms of sociality: Framework for a unified theory of social relations. *Psychological Review*, 99, 689–723.

Foscht, T., Maloles, C. III., Swoboda, B., Morschett, D., & Sinha, I. (2008) The impact of culture on brand perception: A six-month study. *Journal of Product and Brand Management*, 17(3), 131–142.

Fowles, J. (1976) *Mass Advertising as Social Forecast: A Method for Future Research*. Westport, CT: Greenwood Press.

Geertz, C. (1973) *The Interpretation of Cultures*. New York, NY: Basic Books.

Ger, G., & Belk, R. W. (1996) Cross-cultural differences in materialism. *Journal of Economic Psychology*, 17, 55–77.

Grunert, K. G., Brunso, K., & Bisp, S. (1997) Food-related lifestyle: Development of a cross-culturally valid instrument for market surveillance. In L. R. Kahle & L. Chiagouris (Eds.) *Values, Lifestyles and Psychographics*, pp. 161–182. Mahwah, NJ: Lawrence Erlbaum Associates, Ch. 18.

Grunert, S. C., & Scherhorn, G. (1990) Consumer values in West Germany: Underlying dimensions and cross-cultural comparison wit North America. *Journal of Business Research*, 20(2), 97–107.

Han, S-P., & Shavitt, S. (1994) Persuasion and culture: Advertising appeals in individualistic and collectivistic societies. *Journal of Experimental Social Psychology*, 30, 326–350.

Harris, P. R., & Moran, R. T. (1987) *Managing Cultural Differences*, pp. 190–195. Houston, TX: Gulf.

Hofstede, G. (1980) *Culture's Consequences: International Differences in Work-Related Values*. Beverly Hills, CA: Sage.

Hofstede, G. (1983) Dimensions of national cultures in fifty countries and three regions. In J. Deregowski, S. Dziurawiec, & R. C. Amis (Eds.) *Explications in Cross-Cultural Psychology*, pp. 335–355. Lisse, Netherlands: Swets and Zeitlinger.

Hofstede, G. (2001) *Culture's Consequences*, 2nd Ed. Thousand Oaks, CA: Sage.

Hofstede, G. (2007) A European in Asia. *Asian Journal of Social Psychology*, 10, 16–21.

Hofstede, G., & Hofstede, G. J. (2005) *Cultures and Organizations: Software of the Mind*. London, UK: McGraw-Hill.

Hofstede, G., & McCrae, R. R. (2004) Personality and culture revisited: Linking traits and dimensions of culture. *Cross-Cultural Research*, 38(1), 52–88.

House, R. J., & Associates (Eds.) (2004) *Culture, Leadership and Organisations: The GLOBE Study of 62 Societies*. Thousand Oaks, CA: Sage.

Hsieh, M. H. (2004) Measuring global brand equity using cross-national survey data. *Journal of International Marketing*, 12(2), 28–57.

Inglehart, R. (1997) *Modernization and Post-Modernization: Cultural, Economic, and Political Change in 43 Societies*. Princeton, NJ: Princeton University Press.

Inglehart, R., Basanez, M., & Moreno, A. (1998) *Human Values and Beliefs*. Ann Arbor, MI: University of Michigan Press.

Inkeles, A. (1997) *National Character*, pp. 45–50. New Brunswick, NJ: Transaction.

Kahle, L. R. (Ed.) (1983) *Social Values and Social Change: Adaptation to Life in America*. New York, NY: Praeger.

Kashima, Y., Kashima, E. S., Kim, U., & Gelfand, M. (2005) Describing the social world: How is person, a group, and a relationship described in the East and the West? *Journal of Experimental Social Psychology*, 42, 388–396.

Kluckhohn, C., & Strodbeck, F. (1961) *Variations in Value Orientations*. Evanston, IL: Row, Peterson.

Kocak, A., Abimbola, T., & Ozer, A. (2007) Consumer band equity in a cross-cultural replication: An evaluation of a scale. *Journal of Marketing Management*, 23(1–2), 157–173.

Kowner, R. (2002) Japanese body image: Structure and esteem scores in a cross-cultural perspective. *International Journal of Psychology*, 37, 149–159.

Magnusson, P., Wilson, R. T., Zdravkovic, S., Zhou, J. X., & Westjohn, S. A. (2008) Breaking through the cultural clutter: A comparative assessment of multiple cultural and institutional frameworks. *International Marketing Review*, 25(2), 183–201.

Markus, H. R., & Kitayama, S. (1991) Culture and the self: Implications for cognition, emotion and motivation. *Psychological Review*, 98(6), 224–253.

Maslow, A. H. (1954) *Motivation and Personality*. New York, NY: Harper & Row.

McCrae, R. R. (2002) NEO-PI-R data from 36 cultures. In A. J. Marsella & R. R. McCrae (Eds.) *The Fiove-Factor Model of Personality across Cultures*. Dordrecht, The Netherlands: Kluwer.

Minkov, M., & Hofstede, G. (2012) Hofstede's fifth dimension: New evidence from the World Values Survey. *Journal of Cross-Cultural Psychology*, 43(1), 3–14.

Monga, A. B., & John, D. R. (2007) Cultural differences in brand extension evaluation: The influence of analytic versus holistic thinking. *Journal of Consumer Research*, 33, 529–536.

Murdock, G. P. (1945) The common denominator of culture. In R. Linton (Ed.) *The Science of Man in the World Crisis*, pp. 123–144. New York, NY: Columbia University Press.

Murray, H. (1938) *Explorations in Personality*. New York, NY: Oxford University Press.

Nezlek, J. B., Kafetsios, K., & Smith, V. (2008) Emotions in everyday social encounters. *Journal of Cross-Cultural Psychology*, 39(4), 366–372.

Nisbett, R. E., Peng, K., Choi, I., Norenzayan, A. (2001) Culture and systems of thought: Holistic versus analytic cognition. *Psychological Review*, 108(2), 291–310.

Norenzayan, A., Choi, I., & Nisbett, R. E. (2002) Cultural similarities and differences in social inference: Evidence from behavioural predictions and lay theories of behaviour. *Personality and Social Psychology Bulletin*, 39(4), 366–372.

Pollay, R. W. (1983) Measuring the cultural values manifest in advertising. *Current Issues and Research in Advertising*, 6(1), 71–92.

Praet, C. L. C. (2008) The influence of national culture on the use of celebrity endorsement in television advertising: A multi-country study. In *Proceedings of the 7th International Conference on Research in Advertising (ICORIA)*, Antwerp, Belgium.

Prendergast, G., Leung, K. Y., & West, D. C. (2002) Role portrayal in advertising and editorial content, and eating disorders: An Asian perspective. *International Journal of Advertising*, 21, 237–258.

Rokeach, M. (1973) *The Open and Closed Mind*. New York, NY: Basic Books.

Schmitt, D. P., Allik, J. A., McCrae, R. R., & Benet-Martinez, V. (2007) The geographic distribution of Big Five personality traits: patterns and profiles of human self-description across 56 nations. *Journal of Cross-Cultural Psychology*, 38, 173–212.

Schwartz, S. H. (1992) Universals in the structure and content or values: Theoretical advances and empirical tests in 20 countries. M. P. Zanna (Ed.) *Advances in Experimental Social Psychology*, 25, 1–65.

Schwartz, S. H. (1994) Beyond individualism/collectivism. In U. Kim, H. Triandis & Kagiticibasi, C., Choi, S-C., & Yoon, G. (Eds.) *Individualism and Collectivism: Theory, Method and Applications, Vol. 18: Cross-cultural Research and Methodology*. Thousand Oaks, CA: Sage.

Schwartz, S. H. (2004) Mapping and interpreting cultural differences. In H. Vinken, J. Soeters & P. Ester (Eds.) *Comparing Cultures: Dimensions of Culture in a Comparative Perspective*, pp. 43–73. Leiden, Netherlands: Brill.

Schwartz, S. H., & Bilsky, W. (1987) Toward a universal psychological structure of human values. *Journal of Personality and Social Psychology*, 53, 550–562.

Schwartz, S. H., & Bilsky, W. (1990) Toward a theory of the universal content and structure of values: Extensions and cross-cultural replications. *Journal of Personality and Social Psychology*, 58, 878–891.

Shavitt, S., Lalwani, A. K., Zhang, J., & Torelli, C. J. (2006) The horizontal/vertical distinction in cross-cultural consumer research. *Journal of Consumer Psychology*, 16(4), 325–356.

Smith, S. N. (1995) Marketing strategies for the ethics era. *Sloan Management Review*, 36, 85–97.

Souiden N., Kassim, N. M., Hong, H. J. (2006) The effect of corporate branding dimensions on consumers' product evaluation, a cross-cultural analysis. *European Journal of Marketing*, 40(7/8), 825–845.

Starch, D. (1923) *Principles of Advertising*. New York, NY: A. W. Shaw.

Sung, Y., & Tinkham, S. F. (2005) Brand personality structures in the United States and Korea: Common and culture-specific factors. *Journal of Consumer Psychology*, 15(4), 334–350.

Tardiff, T., Fletcher, P., Liang, W., Zhang, Z., Kaciroti, N., & Marchman, V. A. (2008) Baby's first ten words. *Development Psychology*, 44(4), 929–938.

Tellis, G. J., Stremersch, S., & Yin, E. (2003) The international take-off of new products: The role of economics, culture and country innovativeness. *Marketing Science*, 22(2), 188–208.

Triandis, H. C. (1990) Cross-cultural studies of individualism and collectivism. In J. Berman (Ed.) *Nebraska Symposium on Motivation, 1989*, pp. 41–133. Lincoln, NE: University of Nebraska press.

Triandis, H. C., Bontempo, R., Betancourt, H., Bond, M., Leung, K., Brenes, A., Georgas, J., Hui, C. H., Marin, G., Setiadi, B., Sinha, J. B., Verma, J., Spangenberg,

J., Touzard, H. M., & de Montmollin, G. (1986) The measurement of etic aspects of individualism and collectivism across cultures. *Australian Journal of Psychology*, 38(3), 257–267.

Triandis, H. C., Brislin, R., & Hui, C. H. (1988) Cross-cultural training across the individualism-collectivism divide. *International Journal of Intercultural Relations*, 12, 269–289.

Triandis, H. C., McCusker, C., & Hui, C. H. (1990) Multimethod probes of individualism and collectivism. *Journal of Personality and Social Psychology*, 59, 1006–1020.

Trompenaars, F. (1993) *Riding the Waves of Culture: Understanding Cultural Diversity in Business*. London, UK: Nicholas Brealy.

Watkins, D., Akande, A., Fleming, J., Ismail, M., Lefner, K., Regmi, M., Watson, M., lYu, J., Adair, J., Cheng, C., Gerong, A., McInerny, D., Mpofu, E., Singh-Sengupta, S., & Wondimu, H. (1998) Cultural dimensions, gender, and the nature of self-concept: A fourteen country study. *International Journal of Psychology*, 33, 17–31.

World Values Survey (2012) *Values Change the World*. Available at: http://www.worldvaluessurvey.org/WVSContents.jsp. Accessed 9th December 2015.

Wykes, M., & Gunter, B. (2005) *The Media and Body Image*. London, UK: Sage.

Yaveroglu, I. S., & Donthu, N. (2002) Cultural influences on the diffusion of new products. *Journal of International Consumer Marketing*, 14(4), 49–63.

Yeniurt, S., & Townsend, J. D. (2003) Does culture explain acceptance of new products in country? *International Marketing Review*, 20(4), 377–396.

7 Profiling Consumers for Old and New Media Markets

Media markets around the world have expanded immensely in the 21st century. The major changes in consumer markets have been driven by the emergence of digital communications technologies. These developments comprise those that have changed the face of established communications technologies, such as television and the telephone, and introduced the major new platforms of the Internet and related World Wide Web. With the older media such as newspapers, magazines, radio, and television, consumer segmentation was applied to the users of these media to produce profiles of consumers of their contents. These profiles in turn would be matched with the target consumer types of specific products and services to guide decisions about the placement of advertising messages. All the 'old' media have experienced market expansion as more operators have entered their markets. In addition, they have migrated into the new environment of the Internet with virtually all established newspapers and magazines, radio stations, and TV channels having a Web presence regardless of the size and scope of their offline markets.

Digital technology developments have expanded the options available to marketers to reach consumers and also changed the nature of consumer behaviour. The online world has become a major site of consumer activity, with consumers not just being exposed to advertising and other marketing messages in this environment, but also using it increasingly for product and service purchase transactions. These new technologies have also spawned new methods for tracking consumer activity. The emergence of 'big data' has enabled marketers to accumulate massive amounts of information about consumer behaviours and can be used to segment consumers on the basis of their online activity.

Online sites have also been used to obtain ad hoc data based on their attitudes, beliefs, and intentions, likes and dislikes, and other psychological responses associated with brands and product ranges and their responses to advertising and other marketing messages. In addition, the popularity of online social media sites has led marketers to engage more directly with consumers and to commission them as brand champions, significantly expanding the range and speed of impact of 'word-of-mouth' recommendations. Thus, psychological profiling of consumers has expanded beyond the traditional media and become more closely integrated with consumer behaviour. Have these developments rendered old media typologies redundant, and are they effective as predictors of consumer tastes and choices? This chapter will examine these developments and the latest evidence concerning their impact upon consumer profiling methods and the continuing role and relevance specifically of psychological profiling techniques.

Psychological Types and Media Choices

The media choices made by consumers are important to media businesses themselves and also to marketers in general in other business sectors that depend upon the mass media as platforms for brand promotion. Thus, in marketing, it is crucial to know how consumers use different media and whether certain categories of consumer congregate around specific media. Knowing which media outlets command mass audiences and which others rely upon niche users is essential to decision-making about the positioning on marketing campaigns. In a more academic setting, the interest in the segmentation of media markets has been an aspect of understanding the extent to which media use is largely passive or active.

If determining the degree of 'activity' that characterises media use was a focus of attention in an era when the number of media platforms and outlets was limited, then it is even more so in the complex and disaggregated media environment of the digitised 21st century. This concern centres of the analysis of what are mostly psychological variables. 'Activity' in media use includes both overt behaviours and internal cognitive processes. Questions are asked about the extent to which media users switch between different media platforms (e.g., print versus broadcasting versus online) or different media operators on the same platform (e.g., different print magazines, different radio stations, different TV channels, different websites). Do consumers that use one medium have a greater or lesser likelihood of using another medium? Or are patterns of use of different media unrelated to each other? Do people who like TV drama also like magazines about fishing? Are heavier viewers of the new on the BBC's TV services also more likely than average to get their online news from the BBC's news website?

These questions concern behavioural and therefore psychological processes and an understanding of their causes or of the ways consumers are motivated must include some analysis of audience psychology.

The mass media are also vehicles for marketers working across many other business sectors. Manufacturers and service suppliers utilise different media in their marketing campaigns. They seek out consumers of their brands through the audiences for different media outlets. Consequently, it is essential for marketers, regardless of their business sector, to have an understanding of the psychology of media audiences if they are going to utilise those media to reach potential customers. It is not surprising, therefore, that marketing researchers have explored the use of psychographics in the study of media markets. Media consumers were differentiated in terms of personality factors in order to understand more about their choices of media, genres, and specific units of media outputs. Psychographics and personality variables were perhaps most sensitive in relation to predicting content type (or genre) choices and reactions to specific types of content (e.g., sexual and violent content).

Psychological types were developed in the early years of psychographics research for magazine readership (Roper, 1970; Tigert, 1969; Tigert et al., 1971). Television audience researchers have also examined different psychology-based typologies to classify viewers (Feost, 1969; Green, Maheshwari & Rao, 1969). In the scholarly literature about media such as television, communications researchers have focused primarily on the passivity/activity debate. This meant considering internal processes that underpinned audiences' motives to using specific media (Katz, Blumler & Gurevitch, 1974; Palmer & Rayburn, 1982; Rubin, 1979, 1981, 1983). Marketing-oriented researchers tended to give the greatest attention to overt behaviour patterns (Barwise & Ehrenberg, 1987, 1988).

The idea that media consumers are selective in their media habits intrigued media and communications scholars seeking an alternative to psychological models of media use based on behaviourism. As Barwise and Ehrenberg, along with others working with large-scale audience datasets, explained, specific patterns could be discovered in the way people, for example, watched television. There was a growing interest in this phenomenon at a time when the numbers of television channels expanded.

During the 1970s and 1980s, in North America and across Europe, new broadcast and cable services were launched that significantly expanded people's viewing choices. The big question was whether there was really room for all these channels. Would television audiences display increasingly fragmented patterns of viewing as they attempted to distribute their viewing time budgets across more channels? Or would some channels dominate the market while others would be squeezed and command only tiny audiences? Would viewers extend their viewing time budget to accommodate more channels?

Early research indicated that when increasing the total number of available TV channels, viewers did not increase their overall amount of viewing time. Instead, most of their viewing time budget would be devoted to a small number of channels (usually not more than four or five) even when they had 30 or more to choose from. Most of the other channels they would dip into from time to time (Heeter & Greenberg, 1985; Gunter, 1989).

Growing evidence emerged that selectivity in relation to television viewing was not apparent simply through analyses of overt patterns of behaviour, but also in relation to expressed needs of viewers and the content they would subsequently seek out to gratify those needs. Viewers would seek out programmes for specific types of information (Mendelsohn, 1983). People who adhered to specific social beliefs and who displayed personality profiles associated with being risk averse would seek out certain kinds of entertainment content (Gunter & Wober, 1983). Individuals who experienced unpleasant mood states would seek consumer-specific types of entertainment thought best able to help them cope with or alleviate those feelings (Boyanowsky, 1977; Zillmann & Bryant, 1985).

In the context, some communications researchers have identified collections of motivations that purportedly drive media and media content choices (Rubin, 1979, 1981, 1983). These motives were usually measured through levels of agreement or disagreement with statements that described reasons for using different media. For example, "I watch TV to relax" or "TV is an important source of information about the world". Endorsements of these statements were then in turn statistically related to self-reported media usage patterns or content preferences. These 'gratifications' were often conceptually ill founded, however. Their predictive validity in relation to media consumption patterns was also frequently weak or imprecise.

Some theorists argued that media-related motives could only be fully understood when related back to individuals' personality profiles. These motives per se did not exist at the core of a media consumer's being, but were instead verbalised manifestations of deeper-seated orientations underpinned by personality traits. These traits were in part determined by genetics and in part by early life experiences. As with psychographics in general, some of the psychology-based typologies of media consumers tried to provide generic profiles and others produced profiles associated with preferences for specific types of media content. One of the most poignant examples of a content-specific typing of media consumers derived from research showing that personality traits were linked to preferences for violent entertainment (Gunter, 1985). In particular, viewers with aggressive predispositions were found to seek out and consume more violent entertainment that did those who had non-aggressive personalities (Atkin, Greenberg, Korzenny & McDermott, 1979; Lynn, Hampson & Agahi, 1989; Aluja-Fabregat & Torrubia-Beltri, 1998).

Selectivity of media use was also explained in terms of the degree of cognitive involvement generated by specific types of content (Biocca, 1988; Gunter, 1988). Audience activity was conceived to include the selection of content to consume, the evaluation of content in terms of its potential utility, the nature of motives underpinning content choices, the degree of involvement with content that has been selected, and the susceptibility to influence by content that has been consumed (Biocca, 1988). While 'activity' was conceived here largely as a psychological process, differences in the propensities to engage in these processes could also be considered as a structural typological feature of media audiences.

Conceptualising Media Markets

As the media industries have grown and diversified with the evolution of new communications technologies, media markets have become more fragmented. This process had got underway at least two decades before the onset of the modern digital era. Media industries have become more competitive as more suppliers have entered their markets. Following the emergence of digital communications networks, formerly discrete media systems that operated on different platforms have entered direct competition on the same platforms. The rapid adoption of the Internet by consumers around the world has facilitated the latter development more than anything else.

Media markets have been differentiated by media platforms and suppliers and also by indigenous media consumer characteristics. One approach to the concept of the fragmented audience therefore is to compare users with non-users of specific media. Readers and non-readers of magazines can be compared in this way. So too can viewers and non-viewers of television or users and non-users of the Internet. Taking this approach further, audience differences can be examined for those who report regularly using a specific media outlet (e.g., TV channel, magazine publication, website, etc) and those who claim to be non-users.

Another approach is to take a market for a specific medium and then to differentiate among users in terms of their psychological characteristics. Thus, within a specific geographical market, media consumers might be distinguished in terms of how many exhibit specific demographic, life stage, lifestyle, or personality attributes. The latter discriminating factors can also be cross related with the use of different media and media suppliers.

Through these approaches, therefore, it is possible to segment media consumers in terms of their media behaviours, their media-related motives, and their indigenous personality characteristics or lifestyle traits. When further breaking down an overall geographical market area by media use patterns, do heavy and light users of different media exhibit different lifestyles and psychological profiles? Do these profiles for specific media differ from the profile distributions for all consumers in that market area?

One early study found that relationships could be found between magazine readership, consumption patterns for other products, life stage, and lifestyle variables. Lifestyle variables were found to have the capability of accounting for up to 30 per cent of the variance in product consumption patterns and almost 25 per cent of the variance in magazine readership levels (Bass, Pessemeier, & Tigert, 1969).

General Media Types

Numerous researchers have used psychological dimensions to classify media consumers. Research on this topic has a history going back several decades. These audience segmentation studies were in part driven by theoretical needs to understand how people used the mass media. They also often had more practical applications in providing guidance to advertisers who used mass media to carry their brand promotions. Audience segmentation studies were utilised to produce profiles of the typical users of specific media and to facilitate comparisons between media in terms of the types of consumers from which they attracted patronage (Furse & Greenberg, 1975; Teel, Bearden & Durand, 1979).

Researchers explored generic audience types across different media and for specific media, such as magazines, newspapers, and television. Peterson (1972) found that there were different audience profiles associated with television, radio, newspapers, and magazines. These types could be differentiated by demographic and psychographic profiles. In this specific study, demographic profiles proved to be the most effective variables for discriminating between audiences for different media. Psychographic profiles derived from a single personality instrument—the Edwards Personal Preference Schedule—that had not originally been developed for the classification of media consumers. As it turned out, this schedule proved to be ill suited to this job.

Other researchers examined audiences across broadcast media—radio and television. A sample of 750 people was interviewed to obtain data about their demographic details and psychographic attributes (Teel et al., 1979). Psychographics were measured using AIO (activities, interests, and opinions) statements, with each statement endorsed along a linear scale. These data were appropriate for entry into factor analysis, which revealed clusters of responses that defined different psychographic types. Five psychographic types were identified here: Old-Fashioned, Outgoing/Individualist, Service/Quality Conscious, Fashion Conscious, and Other-Directed.

It is clear that these 'types' comprised a mixture of generic VALS-type factors and service-specific factors. The researchers found that users differed from non-users for both radio and television in terms of their psychographic attributes. Television viewers were more individualistic and outgoing than were non-viewers. Daytime TV viewers were more old-fashioned than other viewers. The latter finding, however, might also have been explained in part by the greater availability of older viewers to watch during the day. Viewers who stayed up late to watch tended to be less old-fashioned, and more outgoing and individualistic.

In contrast to TV, daytime radio listeners were *less* old-fashioned and more outgoing, more individualistic, and more fashion conscious. The differences between daytime viewers and listeners are undoubtedly underpinned by demographics. As noted above, daytime TV viewers will tend to have an older profile than TV audiences during peak viewing times. In contrast, daytime radio listeners will include young listeners who tuned into the radio while driving to work.

Television Viewer Types

Television has been a primary source of attention for consumer profilers. For many decades from the middle of the 20th century, television was the dominant medium for media consumers and for advertisers. As the numbers of TV channels grew, there was also more interest in knowing how this might impact upon viewing behaviour. Would new TV channels cannibalise the audiences for older channels? Would some channels in a multi-channel setting attract very few viewers ever? Could distinctions be made between viewers who devoted most of their viewing time to one channel and others who grazed liberally across many channels? As channel and genre choices further expanded, researchers also started asking questions about whether programme selections were driven by the psychological makeup of viewers, that is, by their personality profiles.

The emergence of many TV channels following the establishment of TV markets populated for many years by only two or three channels was greeted enthusiastically by those who believed that viewers had reached a stage where they sought more choice. The choices made by viewers in a setting in which their TV menus had expanded would not be the same for all members of the TV audience. These choices might result in audience segments emerging that were defined by the types of programmes some viewers watched most or by the clustering of genres such that viewers who watched a lot of genre A also watched a lot of genre B but not of genres C and D (Kirsch & Banks, 1962; Frost, 1969; Bowman & Farley, 1972; Watt & Krull, 1974; Goodhart, Ehrenberg & Collins, 1975).

As well as these behaviour-based typologies, there were need-based typologies that depended upon the self-reports of respondents of the reasons why they watched television. Researchers that used this perspective focused a lot on the need gratifications achieved through watching specific programmes or genres (Glick & Levy, 1962; Greenberg, Dervin & Dominick, 1968; Frost, 1969; Bower, 1973; Katz et al., 1974; Frank & Greenberg, 1980; Rubin, 1981).

It emerged fairly early on that typologies based on needs did not correspond to or map directly on to demographic divisions. Hence, men and women could share the same needs, as could people from different age groups. Frank & Greenberg (1980, 1984) discovered as many as 14 'interest segments' that defined the TV audience in America. These segments derived from factor and cluster analyses of data obtained from respondents' ratings of different activities and interests, TV-related needs, and evaluations of TV programmes. The authors produced further data revealing the distribution of these categories of viewers across the viewing population. They found also different audience types, defined by psychographics and demographics, exhibited different viewing patterns. Some types were more likely than others to watch TV news or TV entertainment shows and so on (Frank & Greenberg, 1984).

In the 1960s, Glick & Levy (1962) had differentiated between three types of TV viewers: those who accepted the medium and were enthusiastic users, those who protested against it and were concerned about its possible effects on them, and those who accepted there were good and bad points about the medium and tried to watch a range of programmes to balance out different potential effects. Later research was conceptually and methodologically inspired by this study and generated a long list of items designed to measure people's reasons for watching TV, their perceptions and evaluations of different programmes, and a range of other opinions (Domzal & Kernan, 1983).

This newer research largely confirmed the audience types previously identified by Glick and Levy, with three types: Television Embracers, Television Accommodators, and Television Protesters. Television Embracers not only watched and enjoyed TV, they were avid radio listeners and general news consumers, with interests also in cooking, entertainment, gardening, sports, and travel. Television Accommodators also enjoyed TV and had eclectic tastes covering many forms of news, drama, and entertainment. They had a rage of high-brow and low-brow interests, enjoyed reading and going to the movies, and consumed a range of genres through these media. Finally, Television Protesters watched news and high-brow drama and comedy but regarded much of what they saw on TV as being poor quality and dull. They pursued high-brow activities and both in their leisure and TV watching tended to seek out what they classed as worthwhile experiences. This group tended to have the highest incomes.

Research using the Big Five Personality questionnaire found that both children's viewing patterns and their reactions to certain kinds of television scene were linked to their personality scores. Heavier TV viewers tended to display higher scores on emotional instability, and lower scores on agreeableness, openness to experience, and conscientiousness. Children with higher scores on extraversion, agreeableness, and emotional instability were also more likely to be upset by disturbing scenes in programmes (Persegani, Russo, Carucci, Nicolini, Papeschi & Trimarchi, 2002).

Home Video Use

The introduction of home video in the 1980s changed the complexion of TV viewing. Audiences in the 21st century are accustomed to watching pre-recorded rather than live video content that is available from a wide range of sources. This non-linear viewing has become increasingly prevalent and has eroded the proportion of time viewers devote to watching live broadcasts on standard linearly organised TV channels (Gunter, 2010).

Contemporary viewing of pre-recorded video content has been facilitated by technology advances that have not only underpinned the expansion of sources of this content, but also the ease with which it can be captured by viewers and the amount of content that can be stored in the home. Thirty years earlier, home video recording was a much more cumbersome procedure, and only limited amounts of video content could be stored at any one time.

Research was conducted into the psychographics of early videorecorder users. Initially, questions were asked about whether users differed from non-users. At first, video recorder (VCR) users were undifferentiated in research. As the market grew, however, the idea that VCR owners were a single, homogenous mass became increasingly unsustainable.

Potter, Forrest, Sapolsky, & Ware (1988) used value measures from Rokeach's (1973) inventory and a battery of AIO statements that respondents endorsed along five-point agree-disagree scales. Five VCR segments emerged from claims about VCR use: Time Shifter, Source Shifter, Videophile, Low User, and Regular User. The Time-Shifter type, for example, was derived from responses to two specific measures: the frequency of recording programmes while watching TV and the frequency of recording programmes using a timer. The Source-Shift type was measured by responses to questions about how often respondents either bought or rented pre-recorded videotapes. Time Shifters were high on the time-shifting index and low on the Source-Shifting index. Source Shifters were high on the source-shifting index and low on the time-shifting index. Videophiles were high on both of these indices. Low Users were low on both indices. Regular users were those not included in any of the above categories.

These VCR types differed in their amount of use of the VCR and the nature of their use of it. Time Shifters, as expected, engaged in far more viewing of video content they had self-recorded than did the other types (except for Videophiles). Source shifters reported far more viewing of pre-recorded video content from other sources than did the other VCR types (except for Videophiles). Psychologically, Time Shifters liked to be in control more than did Source Shifters and other types. Time Shifters were also high on seeking personal happiness, valuing novelty in their lives, and being free to choose to do whatever they want. Source Shifters liked to solve complex puzzles, sought inner harmony, and were positively disposed towards wider use of computers. Videophiles were more upwardly mobile than were Low Users. That is, they were more ambitious and adventurous and had more clearly developed opinions than did Low Users.

In sum, this investigation showed that psychographics provided valuable insights into differences between VCR user groups that went beyond their demographic profiles.

The Digital Era

The final years of the 20th century marked the beginning of a period during which information and communications technologies have evolved at a dramatic pace. The switch from analogue to digital transmission systems, whether wireless or wired, greatly expanded the capacity to communicate huge amounts of data and information both local and globally. Increased computer power also meant that information-processing systems were able to handle much larger quantities of data. Not only did the information holding capacity of information and communication technologies grow exponentially, but so too did the speed with which data and information could be transmitted and processed.

This technological revolution had effects that impacted upon all aspects of people's lives around the world. The emergence of the Internet and the development of mobile communications have probably had the most profound effects of all. Citizens and consumers can and do engage in information searching and a wide range of transactions 'online'. In doing so, they create massive amounts of data that are logged automatically by computer systems following their online activities. Where these activities occur in a consumer context, they can generate data that are potentially of great value to brand marketers and producers. The online world also provides an extensive range of new platforms on which brands can be promoted. In this digital world, brands can engage with consumers more interactively and therefore seek to forge relationships with past, present, and potential future customers that are more dynamic than any that went before (Wallace, 1995).

The digital world has not been embraced by everyone to the same extent or at the same pace. In general, the young generations have been more enthusiastic early adopters of new computer and communications technologies and the many applications they provide. Market segmentation distinctions have been identified that define consumers in terms of whether they were brought up in eras that provided different levels of technological sophistication and in particular whether they were brought up with or before the Internet was fully established as a public platform.

One distinction that has been made here is between Generation X and Generation Y. Generation X consists of people born between 1965 and 1976, and Generation Y is those who were born between 1977 and 1995. The latter consists of individuals who became familiar with online communications systems during their childhood, and the former of those whose childhood years pre-dated this digital era (Wolburg & Pokrywczyski, 2001; Bartlett, 2004; Huntley, 2006).

Their different childhood experiences have generally meant that Generation Y have been classed as more practical, tech savvy, and better at multitasking than Generation X. Generation Y's have also been observed to display stronger achievement orientation, are more goal directed and more team oriented than Generation X's (Busch, Venkitachalam & Richards, 2008; Griffin, Jones & Spann, 2008). Generation Y, perhaps because of their involvement with the online world, tend to be better informed as consumers than are Generation X, but they also tend to show less brand loyalty. Generation Y are fashion conscious, but as fashion and trends change, so do their tastes and choices (Heaney, 2007).

Some evidence has emerged that Generation X and Generation Y members display different psychographic profiles. This was confirmed by an Australian study with business students that examined the cultural values traits to which each generation adhered, using the four values types from

Hofstede (2001)—individualism-collectivism, uncertainty avoidance, power distance, and masculinity (Mitsis & Foley, 2012).

Generation Y displayed high collectivism, high uncertainty avoidance, high power distance, and high masculinity. Generation X was high on three out four of these dimensions, the one exception being masculinity. Among Generation Y, participants that scored highest on collectivism, uncertainty avoidance, and power distance were also more likely to say they would spread positive verbal recommendations about their university course to others.

Among Generation X, only high collectivism predicted an intention to pass on positive word-of-mouth recommendations. Findings of this sort have indicated that different marketing strategies are probably needed to reach and persuade Generation X and Y consumers. Furthermore, psychographic variances within as well as between these two groups indicate the need to employ additional classifications based upon psychological profiling exercises (Heaney & Gleason, 2008).

New Media Markets

The emergence of the digital communications technologies and networks has created a vast new world for business and consumer activity in which marketing professionals and researchers can ply their trades. Although not all consumers have embraced the digital world, there are many that have. The advantage of online consumerism for marketers and business in general is that consumer behaviour is often tracked automatically. Each transaction leaves behind an electronic record together with additional information about the purchaser and the nature of the product or service that was bought. In addition, there is a huge amount of information about products and services available via the Internet. Some of this information is generated by the manufacturers and suppliers of products and services, and other information derives from other sources, including consumers themselves. All this activity—both purchase transactions and reactions to products and services—has resulted in the accumulation of vast quantities of data. These online data can be differentiated between structured data in numerical form and less structured or unstructured data that might be in part numeric, but are mostly verbal or pictorial in nature.

Thus, online data linked to consumerism may comprise records of transactions, search data derived from online inquiries made by consumers about products/services and brands, website traffic, and comments made about product ranges, service types, and/or specific branded variants of products/ services. Whereas in the offline world, marketers have been accustomed to commissioning market research from agency sources on an ad hoc basis or from periodically or regularly refreshed consumer monitors, in the online world, a lot of data emerges naturally. The challenge for businesses and, in particular, for marketing professionals is to make sense of all this data.

The concept of 'big data' has emerged to describe the availability of this vast universe of commodity and service-related material (Bollier, 2009). Data in numerical formats can be entered into computer data files for statistical analysis and patterns of consumer behaviour can often be detected that provide insights into how consumers behave online. If offline data are digitally integrated with these online data, it is possible to bring together consumers' behaviours in both worlds. The power of 'big data' derives from the sheer size of the databases and often also their continuity in that data are being collected all the time. Relationships between different classes of behaviour, such as online brand search volumes and subsequent brand purchase levels, can mean that marketers can utilise continuously update online search data to predict future market movements in relation to specific brands and product ranges.

The online world is not simply a vast repository of quantitative data representing different types of consumer-related behaviour: it also is the site of much qualitative data. The emergence of social network sites has been especially significant in this context. Some of these sites, most especially MySpace, and then Facebook, Twitter, and YouTube but also Instagram, Snapchat, and What's App, have evolved as important platforms for brand-related conversations among consumers. These conversations can also be triggered by product manufacturers and service suppliers, some of whom have created their own online social networks. These sites represent massive-scale repositories of qualitative consumer data that was traditionally collected on a much smaller scale in the offline world, for example, through focus group research.

Social networking sites generate huge amounts of commentary about products and services that take the form of largely unstructured attitudes, beliefs, and opinions, likes and dislikes, impressions, and accounts of personal user experiences. Such 'textual data' is often supported by pictures. It can be uploaded as documents, included in emails, and presented as brief posts on micro-blogging or social media sites. Much of this textual commentary is produced by consumers themselves and provides marketers with a ready-made source of brand-related evaluations. The problem for the end users of such data is how to handle such massive amounts of content and more importantly, how to lend structure to largely unstructured content.

Computer science has been a key source of support for marketing and social researchers interested in making use of the vast quantities of unstructured data being constantly generated on the Internet. This digital environment has become a site of online focus—group like data only produced on the sample scales normally associated with offline consumer surveys. While the business world might in principle welcome having access to rich qualitative data for the first time on a massive sample scale, the data being generated have little information value unless they can be analysed in ways that are relevant to solving business problems.

Fortunately, computer scientists have developed various analytical software tools that can both handle large quantities of data and turn unstructured textual or picture data into more structured, numerically coded data. This means that online qualitative data can be expressed in more quantitative forms, and this can make their interpretation more straightforward. In addition, once transformed in this way, structured qualitative data can often be integrated with quantitative data to undertake complex and inclusive data analyses. The broad label that can be used to describe these analytical techniques is text mining. This term, however, represents more than one type of analytical procedure. It also covers tools that operate on different kinds of textual or image-based data.

There are two aspects of consumer segmentation grounded in psychological variables that will be considered in the context of the digital media, which for the purposes of this analysis includes the Internet and World Wide Web, with the various types of websites and online communities to which the Internet gives people access. The first of these comprises a form of 'behavioural segmentation' based on the online behavioural activities of consumers. The second category entails the use of psychographic measures, including personality traits originally developed outside consumer contexts, to explain online behaviour. The behavioural activities can in turn be differentiated into overt (non-verbal) behaviour, such as online information searches and online transactions, and verbal behaviour, such as conversations, comments, and information exchanges.

Online Behaviour and Segmentation: Text Mining

Text or data mining originally emerged within the academic community to enable scientists to derive more value from the rapidly growing volume of scientific studies being published across many disciplines. As many publications became digitised, journals and other repositories of scientific research findings migrated onto the online world. This meant that they could potentially be scanned electronically by computer software written to 'read' natural language. Early forms of this software were crude in their applications and could identify specific linguistic terms that had been coded into their digital lexicon. Thus, any documents that contained text with those terms could be identified. To narrow down search options, computer tools would enable users to combine sets of terms, for example, the themes covered by a publication and the names of the authors of specific articles. In time, these techniques evolved further and their application spread from specialised online publications to the World Wide Web (Korgaonkar & Wolin, 1999; Arusu & Garcia-Molina, 2003).

Initially, text mining focused on the identification of thematic words as physical entities without much sensitivity to their meaning. Over time, not only were the lexicons of online search systems extended, but so too were their grammatical skills and ability to read 'meanings'. The latter function meant that computer linguistic processing tools were developed that 'knew' when two differently formed words shared the same meaning. Moving beyond this development, a further level of depth to text mining occurred when the 'thinking' or 'feeling' behind the word could also be interpreted. In this instance, comments about topics by social networking site users might represent opinions which in turn represent feelings or emotionally toned evaluations. While a simple text mining system might know how to identify a word such as 'truthful' and then be coded so as to know that it means the same as 'honest', could it also use this information as a measure of 'positive' (as opposed to 'negative') public opinion about a brand when social networking site users make reference to it as 'honest'?

The emergence of 'sentiment analysis' represented a step forward in text mining whereby the words or phrases used by online commentators about specific entities such as celebrities, politicians, or brands could be interpreted as intended 'opinions' by those individuals. Assuming this exercise could be carried out reliably and that the linguistic coding enabled valid interpretations of semantic and affective meanings, it could provide a new form of public opinion polling methodology (Balasubramanyan, Cohen, Pierce, & Redlawsk, 2011; Bollen, 2011). Research evidence has emerged to show that news content on broadcast, print, and online news media can be subjected to sentiment analysis to measure the emotional tone of the language used by journalists to describe social action movements and political uprisings (Leetaru, 2011). Similar techniques can be used to measure the nature of customer feedback about products and services provided on the Internet (Lee, Dongjoo, Ok-Ran & Lee, 2008; Pang & Lee, 2008). It has also been found that sentiments expressed on open-ended comments about movies on blog sites can predict their future box-office performance (Mishne & Glance, 2006). Similar findings emerged from big data research combining online restructured qualitative product evaluations data on websites with sales data (Ghose, Ipeirotis & Sundararajan, 2007).

Further data has emerged about using online sentiments expressed about brands and corporations and subsequent stock market movements. Thus, online 'opinion' as measured using sentiment analysis tools in real time can provide sensitive indicators of feelings about specific businesses that might reflect current market sentiments—including market confidence in specific corporations. That confidence in turn can be reflected in the valuations given to the stocks of those companies (Gilbert & Karahalios, 2010; Bollen, 2011).

There has been growing recognition and use of these computer software tools in market research. A number of online applications have been developed and are being applied in the commercial sector (Hamilton et al., 2007; Reinhold & Bhutaia, 2007; Casteleyn et al., 2009). Early forms of these tools were used to examine textual content in Usenet news groups and discussion forums in which users posted comments about specific themes and topics. Further software applications emerged to examine the more open texts generated on later social networking sites such as Facebook and micro-blogging sites such as Twitter. These tools have been used to investigate comments posted about brands by consumers and how these commercial products fit into their lives (Schillewaert, De Ruyck & Verhaeghe, 2009).

These new linguistic analysis methods have certainly extended the toolkits of market researchers. Despite the commercial sector's enthusiasm for new techniques that might also save them money, some writers have nevertheless urged caution against rushing into acceptance of tools such as sentiment analysis as a substitute for regular opinion polls (Hardey, 2011a). Even so, online discussions can provide indications of people's feelings about brands. In addition, they might also yield insights into the thought processes that underpin those opinions.

Consumer review websites represent one source of unstructured data about brand-related opinions to which tools such as sentiment analysis can be applied. Another important group of sources is social media sites that were originally established for purely social connection purposes but have evolved over time to become platforms for the discussion of many objects and issues. From a marketing-relevance perspective, the verbal exchanges that take place on these websites often take the form of word-of-mouth recommendations of brands between consumers. As a mechanism for the promotion of brands, word-of-mouth pre-dates the Internet era (Arndt, 1967). In the offline world, word-of-mouth comments tend to be ephemeral and once they are spoken, they are lost (Stern, 1994). In the online world, however, where they are written down and posted on a site where they enter an archive, they can persist and more significantly are quickly spread across social networks to large numbers of consumers (Breazdale, 2009). This 'electronic' word of mouth can represent a powerful instrument in the making (and breaking) of brand reputations. It has become an especially important mechanism for obtaining and spreading brand-related opinions among younger consumers who have grown up only knowing a world with the Internet (Hardey, 2011b).

One of the concerns about public opinions being given online is that the anonymous nature of the setting can encourage the articulation of extreme views, and sometimes even offensive comments. Research with consumers who use online review sites has indicated, though, that most seek to provide and obtain genuine opinions based on real brand experiences. Within that environment, although there may be some extreme opinions, review sites exhibit a self-correcting nature with other comments being posted that challenge or critique extreme views and bring more balance to the overall body of opinion that develops (Hardey, 2011b). Increasingly, psychological profiling has been applied to online content. This has taken two principal forms: the study of the relationships between psychographics and personality measures and online behaviour and the use of text mining tools to identify clues to the personalities of authors on online posts. This chapter will review some early findings from this relatively new field, and in the last chapter, a final look will be taken at the pros and cons of analysing consumers profiles unobtrusively through online activity patterns and styles of language use.

Online Behaviour and Psychographics

Marketing and social researchers have explored how variances in online behaviour can be explained by the psychological characteristics of Internet users (Wallace, 1995). As with other applications of psychographics, some researchers have developed custom-built measures of Internet users' motives and gratifications associated with the use of digital media. Another approach has been to apply established measures of human personality and to relate scores on these dimensions to digital media usage patterns.

The emergence of the Internet brought with it a new form of advertising that was more interactive and customised to the interests of specific consumers (Hoffman & Novak, 1996; Quinn, 1999; Hofacker & Murphy, 2000). Websites also introduced other new facilities that could help marketers. Among these were tracking devices that could not only log visits to a site by identifiable users, but could continue to track the online behaviour of those consumers subsequently. This meant that data could be compiled that was not just linked to an advertiser's own site, but also about the more generic behaviour of consumers (Maes, 2000).

Researchers did not stop here. If Internet users' online behaviours could be tracked, it might also be possible to incorporate additional information about the character of individual consumers so as to build a more detailed psychological profile about them. This profile could include indicators that classified a consumer's personality. While many consumers might be unwilling to verbally disclose information about their personal character, a picture could be built up of the type of person they were simply by monitoring the kinds of websites they visited or transaction in which they engaged. In other words, an 'intelligent' psychographic profiler could be developed to build up a 'personality profile' of consumers without their conscious awareness (LaBarbera, 1999). It would even be possible to manipulate the content and design of websites and monitor how different consumers reacted to this in terms of their behaviour on those sites.

Among the established personality measures that have been used to differentiate between how Internet users engage with we sites, sensation seeking and the need for cognition have been explored and found to provide useful insights. Sensation seeking is a personality dimension associated with the Openness to Experience dimension in the Big Five model and is also known to have links to Extraversion. High scorers on this scale exhibit preferences for more complex and stronger levels of external stimulation of their senses (Raju, 1980; Zuckerman, 1983, 1994). High sensation seekers, for instance, enjoy more complex visual scenes and works of art (Furnham & Bunyan, 1988; Zuckerman, Ulrich & McLaughlin, 1993).

Need for cognition measures the propensity of people to seek out experiences or settings that require them to think a lot (Cacioppo & Petty, 1982). With high scorers on this scale, attitude change is best achieved by messages that present complex arguments that require effortful cognitive processing (Cacioppo, Petty, & Kao, 1984). In contrast, individuals scoring low on this scale prefer simpler messages without complex arguments and will tend to process such messages in a more superficial fashion, often being influenced by the appearance of the messages rather than its substantive content (Cacioppo, Petty, Kao & Rodriguez, 1986; Cacioppo, Petty, Feinstein, & Jarvis, 1996).

Martin, Sherrard, & Wentzel (2005) found that personality factors were related to how young people—in this case, university students—evaluated a commercial website for a fictitious soft drinks brand. The researchers manipulated the verbal and visual complexity of the website and randomly assigned the students to different web conditions. In these tests, the students browsed the site on a computer screen and then answered a series of evaluative questions about it. A number of weeks earlier, they had completed personality tests to measure need for cognition and sensation seeking.

Overall, there was a preference for websites with a moderate amount of content complexity, but personality factors interacted with these preferences. High sensation seekers, people who seek out new experiences and enjoy high levels of stimulation, preferred websites with complex visual content, whereas for low sensation seekers, the opposite was true. When high sensation seekers were presented with a website that had high visual complexity combined with low verbal complexity, their attitudes towards the brand being advertised on that site became more positive. For low sensation seekers, however, their brand attitudes were more likely to be improved by a site that had low visual complexity combine with high verbal complexity. For participants with high need for cognition scores, there was a preference for websites characterised by high verbal complexity. This type of website also enhanced the brand-related attitudes of those high in need for cognition.

Non-Interventionist Digital Market Segmentation

Social media sites provide ready-made samples of people that can be fed information, asked questions, engaged in activities, and orchestrated within campaigns. For professional applications such as social and market research, they have spawned new methodologies. Commercial polling agencies have adapted social media memberships for regular research exercises to a point where online research has now achieved parity with more conventional offline research methods.

Understanding who you are dealing with in social media sites, however, presents a challenge to researchers, regardless of whether their research has academic or commercial objectives, because researchers do not always know what types of people they are studying. In offline survey research, respondents provide identifying information that enables researchers to classify them according to different demographic variables such as age, gender, socio-economic class, ethnicity, and so on. The growth in use of 'psychographics', that is, measures of the psychological characteristics of research study participants, means that even more detailed classifiers can be deployed to predict and explain the attitudes and behaviour patterns of those being investigated.

In the offline world, research participants can be administered questionnaires that present questions and scales designed to measure these different personal attributes. In online surveys that mimic self-completion offline surveys in terms of format and other methodological features, these instruments can also be circulated. Social media sites, however, present a different kind of opportunity. On these sites, their users already disclose information about themselves. This information is often regularly updated. These sites therefore present researchers with a wealth of data about people that simply needs to be structured.

What is also not always so clear with social media users is who they are as people. Some demographic details might have been submitted on enrolment, and some of these details might be posted for public consumption. Psychologically, however, it may not always be apparent who these people are. Getting them to complete personality tests is often not feasible, although some research studies have been carried out with volunteer samples of social media site users in which they have responded to requests to provide data on their psychological profiles. What if the personalities of social media users could be effectively measured from the materials users post about themselves? What if it wasn't necessary to upload special tests for them to complete in order to measure the type of person they are?

The text mining methods used to read and lend structure to the unstructured data contained in open texts online have been combined with psychological measures by researchers seeking to develop personality-typing tools based on feature and linguistic analysis. This research has focused predominantly on social media sites where users can post vast quantities of information about themselves. Some of this information in presented within in predetermined structural frameworks imposed by the sites themselves, while much occurs in open-text form.

Computerised analysis tools have been developed that can extract and codify specific site features and meanings contained within texts posted by social media site users. Site profile attributes can be related to personality traits measured by standard psychological tests. Linguistic analysis can be deployed to classify texts in terms of linguistic nuances that can serve as 'giveaways' or 'insights' into the user's personality profile. Through validation methods in which personality test scores are statistically related to the language styles of the user in their social media posts, it is possible to identify specific recurring linguistic styles that signal a particular type of personality. Linguistic profiles can also be used to produce measures of positive and negative feeling states of social media users that can be related in turn to specific behavioural or lifestyle outcomes.

A body of research has evolved during the era of social media that has experimented with language interrogation tools to classify open texts on social media sites and lend them structure so that they can be entered into mathematical models with standard quantitative data. These text-typing tools can be instructed to identify and quantify linguistic terms that could be indicative of the personality profile of the producer. Validation of these hypothesized indicators can be obtained by systematically relating text profiles to scores of self-completion psychological tests clinically tested to measure different personality traits. Much of this research has used the Big Five Personality Inventory as the core psychological framework.

Personality and Social Media Disclosures

There is no doubt that social media sites have evolved into massive data repositories. Much of the data uploaded onto these sites, however, lacks structure. It is therefore necessary to develop methods that can create structure where there was none. A further feature of social media in terms of the way they are used is that users can vary greatly in the detail of their personal disclosures and the types of information about themselves that they decide to make public or keep private. Thus, one clue to the type of person using a social media site lies in the nature of their personal disclosures. On Facebook, for instance, there is evidence that users vary in their selectiveness about the personal details they will publicly disclose (Back et al., 2010). Often, the extent to which users will play around with different privacy settings depends upon their overall level of computer literacy. Those with greater confidence in these settings display more complexity in the patterns of disclosures that characterise their social media sites (Papacharissi, 2010).

There is a growing body of research that has linked personality traits to social media use. Much of this evidence indicates that the way users behave on their social media sites can reveal clues to their psychological makeup (Gosling, Augustine, Vazire, Holtzman & Gaddis, 2011). The personality traits of people online can sometimes take the form of impressions formed by others who visit their websites (Vazire & Gosling, 2004). As we will see, however, there is also a firmer scientific basis on which personality can be reliably indicated by the way individuals use social media sites and the styles with which they express themselves on those sites (Golbeck, Robles, Edmondson & Turner, 2011b; Quercia, Kosinski, Stillwell, & Crowcroft, 2011). When studies have revealed only weak or non-existent links between personality and social media site features, this outcome could have arisen from design limitations whereby usage motives and patterns were insufficiently defined (Schrammel, Koffel & Tscheligi, 2009).

From a marketing perspective, being able to measure the personality characteristics of consumers on a large scale and in an unobtrusive fashion could have substantial benefits in terms of understanding how consumers make purchase decisions, how they react to commercial campaigns and promotions, and their perceptions of brands. There is evidence, for example, that in commodity ratings tasks, high scorers in Conscientiousness will take the trouble to rate the required number of items, but high scorers on Openness will rate far more than required, and high scorers on Agreeableness with give many more positive product/service evaluations (Hu & Pu, 2013). Such insights into how specific consumer groups are likely to give product and service reviews and the types of reviews specific kinds of personality types might be expected to provide can be important to planning of review gathering, especially in the face of evidence that such online consumer reviews can have a profound influence on other consumers' perceptions of commodities and brands (Lee & Ma, 2012).

Research studies that utilised the Big Five Personality Factor model have discovered significant statistical relationships between the nature of users' disclosures on Facebook and specific personality factors. Higher scorers on Extraversion tended to use more terms linked to being physically and socially active and seeking out excitement. They tended to be very active offline but also established extensive social networks online (Ross et al., 2009; Amichai-Hamburger & Vinitzky, 2010). Whereas individuals high in neuroticism (who tend to be more impulsive) are more likely to post lots of personal information and especially photos of themselves, those high in conscientiousness (who like to plan ahead, think carefully before acting, and not take undue risks) are less likely to do so. Individuals high in openness, who tend to be imaginative and spontaneous in their thinking, liked to experiment with new methods of communicating via social media and use a greater number of features (Ross et al., 2009; Amichai-Hamburger & Vinitzky, 2010)

Quercia et al. (2011) carried out a study to develop a text reading methodology for identifying the personality characteristics of Twitter users. The same authors had previously studied relationships between personality and numbers of contacts among Facebook users. Data had been collected from Facebook users who were invited to complete an application called *myPersonality*. This instrument provided data based on the Big Five personality traits.

In this study, 335 Twitter users who were also visible on Facebook were identified from their Facebook profiles and approached to take part. Of these participants, 171 were women. Personality data were derived from their *myPersonality* data they had supplied via Facebook. The researchers used publicly available Twitter data on 'following' (how many people the participant followed on Twitter), 'followers' (how many other Twitter users followed the participant's tweets), and listed count, which shows the number of Twitter users whose reading lists contain the participant's tweets.

These data were used to define a number of Twitter types: *listeners* (who followed many users), *popular* (who were followed by many users), *highly read* (who were often listed in other's reading lists), and finally *influential* users based on *Klout* and TIME measures. The *Klout* score is based on data concerning how often a user's tweets were clicked, repeated, and retweeted.[1]

The TIME measure indicated a person's popularity on both Twitter and Facebook, and takes their number of Twitter followers multiplied by two and adds to this their number of Facebook contacts, and then divides that outcome by two. (See: http://content.time.com/time/specials/packages/article/0,28804,1984685_1984713_1984669,00.html).

These four Twitter profile scores were then statistically related to the participants' personality scores on the Big Five personality factors. Higher scorers on *Listener* and *Popular* Twitter dimensions were significantly higher scorers on Extraversion and lower scorers in Neuroticism. These findings made sense in light of other evidence showing that people who are more outgoing and less anxious tend to be more sociable and have more friends in the offline world as well as on Facebook. Twitter users who were *Highly Read* were much higher in Openness. This was also logical given that people high in Openness are more open to new ideas and seek out new knowledge from different sources. *Influentials* who were determined by the *Klout* and TIME scores were significantly higher in Extraversion and Conscientiousness. Thus, people who could be judged as more 'influential' on Twitter because others paid close attention to their tweets and would repeat them to others also tended to be much more outgoing personalities who were also ambitious and persistent in achieving their aims.

This study represents but a single investigation of how Twitter profiles are related to users' personality attributes. The sample of participants were not representative of any broader population, so we cannot draw normative conclusions from the findings. Nonetheless, this research indicates that it might be possible to estimate a Twitter user's personality profile from publicly available indicators of their Twitter profile.

Golbeck, Robles & Turner (2011b) developed a method to detecting a Facebook user's personality profile from their Facebook user profile. They administered a sample of Facebook users with a short-form version of the Big Five personality Inventory. This inventory measured the five personality traits of Openness, Conscientiousness, Agreeableness, Extraversion, and Neuroticism (sometimes shortened to the acronym of OCEAN). Openness measures how imaginative and creative people are. Conscientiousness identifies how ambitious, resourceful, and organised people are. Agreeableness indicates people's character in terms of whether they are friendly, thoughtful, and kind-hearted. Extraversion defines people in terms of their need for stimulation of any kind, whether physical, mental, or social. Neuroticism characterises people in terms of their emotional stability.

Next, the researchers compiled data about the density of the user's Facebook network, personal information they posted on their site, their listed activity and interest preferences, and linguistic features of the open text they wrote about themselves. The final sample was 167 people for whom the researchers collected personality data and who had also produced sufficient open text about themselves to enable a meaningful linguistic analysis to be computed.

The linguistic analysis examined the texts produced by Facebook users in terms of references to things they had experienced, work-related words, references of money, social activities they had taken part in, use of swear words, and expressions of emotion. These linguistic features were combined with structural site attributes such as number of friends and density of their friendship network online, preferred activities, favourite books, and relationship status (single versus not single) for entry into statistical analyses designed to reveal relationships between these Facebook profile measures and scores on the Big Five personality attributes.

Extraversion was significantly related to six Facebook profile variables, with extraverts being less likely to reflect on specific perceptual experiences, more likely to use work-related words, and also to have a greater number of Facebook friends but less intense links with many of them, and also reporting many more activity preferences than did introverts.

Conscientiousness exhibited significant statistical relationships with five Facebook profile variables, with those participants who scored high on this attribute being less likely to use swear words, and more likely to talk about their perceptual and social experiences. This finding was consistent with what is known about people who score high on Conscientiousness who tend to think carefully and reflect on their real-world experiences.

Those Facebook users who scored higher on Openness were less likely to make reference to money issues, had less dense friendship networks (indicating looser links between the people they knew), and provided more information about their favourite books. Higher scorers on Agreeableness were more likely to express their emotions online, indicating their sensitive side. They also made more references to biological references to physically pleasurable or painful conditions. Finally, high Neuroticism scorers expressed more anxiety-related words and more words related to food consumption.

These findings provide interesting indications of the possibilities for using content regularly posted on Facebook sites to determine the personality profiles of users. Assuming these Facebook indicators of personality can be reliably validated, they could provide ways for social and market researchers to generate population or market segmentation data based on human personality measures without the need for further research interventions in the form of the administration of personality instruments.

Golbeck and her colleagues carried out further research on personality profiling with Twitter users (Golbeck, Robles, Edmondson & Turner, 2011a). A sample of 50 Twitter users was recruited to take part. The most recent 2,000 tweets produced by each of these individuals were collected (or all their tweets, if they had produced fewer than 2,000). Basic descriptive statistics were then collected about each person, including their number of followers, the number of people following them, the density of their social network, the number of times another Twitter user mentioned them with an '@ mention', the number of replies they received to their tweets, the number of applications of hashtags, the number of links to other sites, and the words used an average per tweet.

Tweets were collated into continuous texts and linguistic analyses were then applied to assess the use of different types of words and expressions, as well as the classification of words used in terms of their perceptual, social, work-related, and emotional references. As with their Facebook study, a short-form of the Big Five Personality Inventory was used to measure the OCEAN personality traits.

High Openness scorers used more articles (a, an, the), more quantifiers (few, many), more references to causation (because, effect), more certainty terms (always, never), and more references to human beings, and made more work references. They were less likely to make references to biological functions and human body parts, were less likely to use exclamation marks and parentheses, and less likely to use hashtags.

High Conscientiousness was related to greater use of the word 'you', less use of auxiliary verbs (am, will, have), of future tense words, emotional words, and words describing cognitive mechanisms (cause, known, ought) and of discrepancy terms (should, would, could). They were more likely to make work references and were more precise in their use of grammatical features such as commas, colons, and exclamation marks.

Extraverts were more likely than introverts to refer to family members and social activities and relationships, and were more likely to use question marks and had more words per tweet. Extraverts were less likely than Introverts to make health (especially ill-health) references. Those Twitter users high on Agreeableness were also more likely to use the term 'you' and to make references to eating, but were less likely to use causation terms (because, effect), and achievement or money references.

Finally, high scorers on Neuroticism were more likely to make perceptual experiences references and religious references and were more likely to use exclamation marks. Unlike the earlier work with Facebook users, there were no indications here that high scorers on this dimension used more emotional language.

While there is a growing body of research about relationships between the Big Five Personality Traits and the use of social media, some researchers have focused specifically on whether it is possible to determine specifically antisocial traits from textual data such as that posted on Twitter. Byers and her colleagues focused on the so-called 'Dark Triad' of personality traits: narcissism, Machiavellianism, and psychopathy (Sumner, Byers, Boochever & Park, 2012). They obtained data from nearly 3,000 Twitter users from 89 countries, with the great majority living in the United Kingdom or United States. Each participant completed a test designed to measure each of the traits of the 'Dark Triad' together with short-form tests of the Big Five Personality Traits. Samples of tweets, replies, and retweets for each participant were linguistically analysed to identify a number of content and stylistic features.

Personality traits measures were found to be related to the use of specific features within tweets. Narcissism was statistically positively related to the use of @ and #, which are designed to draw attention to one's messages. Twitter users who were high scorers on narcissism were also more likely to make sexual references in their posts. Those high in Machiavellianism displayed more positive emotion than others and made more references to 'we'. Psychopathic high scorers were more likely to use swear words, display anger, refer to death, and post tweets with generally negative emotional tones. Although the match between linguistic styles and references and conventionally tested personality traits was not perfect, the findings showed that linguistic features can provide indicators of the type of person behind specific messages.

Concluding Remarks

Media markets have expanded dramatically from the final years of the 20th century. This phenomenon has been global. The emergence of digital communications technologies have played a major role in driving forward these developments by increasing media production and distribution capacities and speeds. 'Old' media such as newspapers, magazines, radio, and TV stations operate both in the offline and online worlds. They are also confronted by many new competitors that operate exclusively in the online world. These changes have created new challenges for marketing professionals. As media choices have grown, so media markets have segmented. This outcome has important implications for marketers who use these media as platforms to carry brand promotion campaigns. The rapid spread of the Internet and World Wide Web has also meant that new platforms have opened up. At the same time, media reception technologies have evolved with the greater prevalence and significance of mobile communications technologies not simply as communications devices, but also as receptacles of content. This technology revolution has changed the nature of consumers' behaviour in relation to their media habits, the way they obtain information about brands, and the locations of their buying transactions.

For professional marketers to keep on top of technological changes and their effects on consumer markets, they need to have an understanding of how consumers now behave in this new world and how their behaviours are underpinned by their personal characteristics. The expansion of the mainstream media and the entry of many new players into their markets is a phenomenon that has created new niche consumer markets, the needs of which must be understood by brand marketers. This means that psychographics has an important a role as ever in consumer marketing practice.

The emergence of the Internet, however, has scaled up immensely the quantity of content for media consumers to access and process. This includes a massive increase in marketing-related material. At the same time, the migration of shopping expeditions and consumer transactions into the online world has also generated a massive database that is continually refreshed about consumer activity. Electronic records of such online activity have created a huge database for tracking consumer activity and potentially for segmenting and classifying it. The sheer volume of content means, however, that standard marketing research techniques cannot cope or ever hope to produce usable and timely business models to map and predict consumer choices. Hence, new digital toolkits have emerged that are capable of aggregating and processing huge quantities of data very quickly.

The online world is also a repository of huge amounts of unstructured data. Computer software tools now exist that can make sense of such data by lending them structure. Such digital tools have enthused many marketing professionals, but their efficacy in terms of delivering valid representations of consumers' brand-related attitudes and behaviour choices or responses to brand promotions that can be converted into usable business models to predict consumer choices in the future remains open to question. 'Big data' can potentially yield a lot of potentially valuable marketing intelligence, but the quality of these databases and the value of the methods of data analysis used to interrogate them and give them structure are factors that marketing and social researchers are still working on. Early studies have begun to provide evidence of links between consumer profiles defined by personality tests and online activity profiles and styles of language use. We will return to this subject in Chapter 9 when considering the strengths and weaknesses associated with this approach.

Note

1 See: https://klout.com/corp/about.

References

Aluja-Fabregat, A., & Torrubia-Beltri, R. (1998) Viewing of mass media violence, perception of violence, personality and academic achievement. *Personality and Individual Differences*, 25, 973–989.

Amichai-Hamburger, Y., & Vinitzky, G. (2010) Social network use and personality. *Computers in Human Behavior*, 26, 1289–1295.

Arndt, J. (1967) The role of product-related conversations in the diffusion of a new product. *Journal of Marketing Research*, 4(3), 291–295.

Arusu, A., & Garcia-Molina, H. (2003) Extracting structured data from web pages. In *Proceedings of the 2003 ACM SIGMOD International Conference on Management of Data*, New York: ACM, pp.337–348. Available at: www.dl.acm.org/citation/cfm?doid=872757.872799. Accessed 24th January 2014.

Atkin, C., Greenberg, B., Korzenny, F., & McDermott, S. (1979) Selective exposure to televised violence. *Journal of Broadcasting*, 23, 5–13.

Back, M. D., Stopfer, J. M., Vazire, S., Gaddis, S., Schmukle, S. C., Egloff, B., & Gosling, S. D. (2010) Facebook profiles reflect actual personality, not self-idealization. *Psychological Science*, 21(3), 372–374.

Bartlett, M. (2004) Analyst: Understanding what shapes generation can help . . . *Credit Union Journal*, 8(21), 14–17.

Barwise, P., & Ehrenberg, A. S. C. (1987) The liking and viewing of regular TV series. *Journal of Consumer Research*, 14(1), 63–70.

Barwise, P., & Ehrenberg, A. S. C. (1988) *Television and Its Audience*. London, UK: Sage.

Bass, F. M., Pessemeier, E. A., & Tigert, D. J. (1969) A taxonomy of magazine readership applied to problems in marketing strategy and media selection. *Journal of Business*, 42, 337–363.

Biocca, F. A. (1988) Opposing conceptions of the audience: The active and passive hemispheres of mass communication theory. In J. A. Anderson (Ed.) *Communication Yearbook*, Vol. 11, pp. 51–80. Beverly Hills, CA: Sage.

Bollen, J. (2011) Computational economic and finance gauges: Polls, search & Twitter. Paper presented at the Behavioural Economics Working Group, Behavioural Finance Meeting, Palo Alto, CA. Available at: www.nber.org/~confer/2011/BEf11.BEf11prg.html. Accessed 3rd March 2013.

Bollier, D. (2009) The promise and peril of big data. Paper presented at Extreme Inference: Implications of Data Intensive Advanced Correlation Techniques. The Eighteenth Annual Aspen Institute Roundtable on Information Technology, Aspen, Colorado, The aspen Institute. Available at: www.bollier.org/sites/default/files/aspen_reports/InfoTech09_0. Accessed 15th April 2012.

Bower, R. T. (1973) *Television and the Public*. New York, NY: Holt, Rinehart & Winston.

Bowman, G. W., & Farley, J. (1972) TV viewing: Application of a formal choice model. *Applied Economics*, 4, 245–259.

Boyanowsky, E. O. (1977) Film preferences under condition of threat: Whetting the appetite for violence, information or excitement? *Communication Research*, 1, 32–43.

Breazdale, M. (2009) Word of mouse: An assessment of electronic word-of-mouth research. *International Journal of Market Research*, 51(3), 297–318.

Busch, P., Venkitachalam, K., Richards, D. (2008) Generational differences in soft knowledge situations: Status, need for recognition, workplace commitment and idealism. *Knowledge and Process Management*, 15(1), 45–58.

Cacioppo, J. T., & Petty, R. E. (1982) The need for cognition. *Journal of Personality and Social Psychology*, 42, 116–131.

Cacioppo, J. T., Petty, R. E., Fenistein, J. A., & Jarvis, W. B. G. (1996) Dispositional differences in cognitive motivation: The life and times of individuals varying in need for cognition. *Psychological Bulletin*, 119, 197–253.

Cacioppo, J. T., Petty, R. E., & Kao, C. F. (1984) The efficient assessment of need for cognition. *Journal of Personality Assessment*, 48, 306–307.

Cacioppo, J. T., Petty, R. E., Kao, C. F., & Rodriguez, R. (1986) Central and peripheral routes to persuasion: An individual difference perspective. *Journal of Personality and Social Psychology*, 51, 1032–1043.

Casteleyn, J., Motart, A., & Rutten, K. (2009) How to use Facebook in your market research. *International Journal of Market Research*, 51(4), 439–447.

Domzal, T. J., & Kernan, J. B. (1983) Television audience segmentation according to need gratification. *Journal of Advertising Research*, 10, 37–49.

Frank, R. E., & Greenberg, M. G. (1980) *The Public's Use of Television*. Beverly Hills, CA: Sage.

Frank, R. E., & Greenberg, M. G. (1984) Interest-based segment of TV audiences. *Journal of Advertising Research*, 11, 45–54.

Frost, W. A. K. (1969) The development of a technique for TV programme assessment. *Journal of the Market Research Society*, 11, 25–44.

Furnham, A., & Bunyan, M. (1988) Personality and art preferences. *European Journal of Personality*, 2, 67–74.

Furse, D. H., & Greenberg, B. A. (1975) Cognitive style and attitude as a market segmentation variable: A comparison. *Journal of Advertising*, 4, 39–44.

Ghose, A., Ipeirotis, P. G., & Sundararajan, A. (2007) Opinion mining using econometrics: A case study on reputation systems. Paper presented at the 45th Annual Meeting of the Association of Computational Linguistics, Prague, Czech republic, Association for Computational Linguistics. Available at: www.pages.stern.nyu.edu/~aghose/acl2007. Accessed 8th May 2012.

Gilbert & Karaholios (2010). Widespead worry and the stock market. Fourth International AAAIO Conference on Weblogs and Social Media held at Washington, DC: Association for the Advancement of Artificial Intelligence, 23rd May. Menlo Park, CA: AAAI.

Glick, I. O., & Levy, S. J. (1962) *Living with Television*. Chicago: Aldine Publishing Co.

Golbeck, J., Robles, C., Edmondson, M., & Turner, K. (2011a) Predicting Personality from Twitter.*IEEE International Conference on Privacy, Security, Risk and Trust*. Available at: http://www.demenzemedicinagenerale.net/pdf/2011%20-%20Predicting%20Personality%20from%20Twitter.pdf

Golbeck, J., Robles, C., Edmondson, M., & Turner, K. (2011b) Predicting personality with social media, *CHI 2011*, May 7–12. Vancouver, BC, Canada. ACM 987–1–4503–0268–5/11/05

Goodhart, G. J., Ehrenberg, A. S. C., & Collins, M. (1975) *The Television Audience: Patterns of Viewing*. Aldershot, Hampshire: Gower.

Gosling, S. D., Augustine, A. A., Vazire, S., Holtzman, N., & Gaddis, S. (2011) Manifestations of personality in online social networks: Self-reported Facebook-related behaviors and observable profile information. *Cyberpsychology, Behavior and Social Networking*, 14(9), 483–488.

Greenberg, B., Dervin, B., & Dominick, J. (1968) Do people watch "television" or "programmes"? *Journal of Broadcasting*, 12, 367–376.

Griffin, M. D., Jones, B. A. P., & Spann, M. S. (2008) Knowledge versus certification: Which is the premier emphasis for Gen Y business students? *International Journal of Business Research*, 8(4), 61–69.

Gunter, B. (1985) *Dimensions of Television Violence*. Aldershot, Hampshire: Gower.

Gunter, B. (1988) The perceptive audience. In J. A. Anderson (Ed.) *Communication Yearbook*, Vol. 11, pp. 22–50. Beverly Hills, CA: Sage.

Gunter, B. (1989) The UK: Measured expansion on a variety of fronts. In L. B. Becker & K. Schoenbach (Eds.) *Audience Responses to Media Diversification: Coping with Plenty*, pp. 71–89. Hillsdale, NJ: Lawrence Erlbaum Associates.

Gunter, B. (2010) *Television Versus the Internet: Will TV Prosper of Perish as the World Moves Online?* Oxford, UK: Chandos.

Gunter, B., & Wober, J. M. (1983) Television viewing and public trust. *British Journal of Social Psychology*, 22, 174–176.

Hamilton, J., Eyre, L., Tramp, M., Virens, M., & Galarerneau, L. (2007) Why do some online communities work? In *Proceedings of the ESOMAR Qualitative Research Annual Conference*, 12–14 November, pp. 8–27. Paris. Amsterdam, The Netherlands: ESOMAR.

Hardey, M. (2011a) To spin straw into gold? New lessons from consumer-generated content. *International Journal of Market Research*, 53(1), 13–15.

Hardey, M. (2011b) Generation C: Content, creation connections and choice. *International Journal of Market Research*, 53(6), 749–770.

Heaney, J-G., & Gleason, D. J. (2008) Corporate social responsibility in business courses: How can Generation Y learn? Paper presented at the Academy of World Business, Marketing and Management Development, Rio de Janeiro, Brazil.

Heaney, R. A. (2006) An empirical analysis of commodity pricing. *Journal of Futures Markets*, 26(4), 391–415.

Heeter, C., & Greenberg, B. S. (1985) Cable and programme choice. In D. Zillmann & J. Bryant (Eds.) *Selective Exposure to Communication*, pp. 203–224. Hillsdale, NJ: Lawrence Erlbaum Associates.

Hofacker, C. F., & Murphy, J. (2000) Clickable World Wide Web banner ads and content sites. *Journal of Interactive Marketing*, 14, 49–59.

Hoffman, D. L., & Novak, T. P. (1996) Marketing in hypermedia computer-mediated environments: Conceptual foundations. *Journal of Marketing*, 60, 50–68.

Hofstede, G. (2001) *Culture's Consequences*, 2nd Ed. Thousand Oaks, CA: Sage.

Hu, R., & Pu, P. (2013) Exploring relations between personality and user rating behaviors. In *Proceedings of the 1st Workshop on Emotions and Personality in Personalized Services (EMPIRE 13)* in conjunction with the 21st Conference on User Modelling, Adaptation and Personalization (UMAP '13), Rome, Italy, 10th June. Available at: http://citeseerx.ist.psu.edu/viewdoc/summary?doi=10.1.1.366.870

Huntley, R. (2006) *The World According to Y: Inside the New Adult Generation*. Mayborough, Victoria: Allen & Unwin.

Katz, E., Blumler, J. G., & Gurevitch, M. (1974) Utilization of mass communication by the individual. In J. G. Blumler & E. Katz (Eds.) *The Uses of Mass Communications*, pp. 19–34. Beverly Hills, CA: Sage.

Kirsch, A. D., & Banks, S. (1962) Programme types defined by factor analysis. *Journal of Advertising Research*, 2, 29–31.

LaBarbera, P., & Gurhan, Z. (1997) The role of materialism, religiosity, and demographics in subjective well-being. *Psychology & Marketing*, 14, 71–97.

LaBarbera, P. A. (1999) Marketing on the internet: The role of cognitive style in user attitudes and behavior. *28th Annual Conference of the European Marketing Academy*, May, Berlin, Germany.

Lee, D., Ok-Ran, J., & Lee, S. (2008) Opinion mining of customer feedback data on the web. *2nd International Conference on Ubiquitous Information Management and Communication*, New York, USA. Available at: www.ids.snu.ac.kr/w/images/7/7e/IC-2008–01. Accessed 8th May 2012.

Lee, H-H., & Ma, Y. J. (2012) Consumer perceptions of online consumer product and service reviews: Focusing on information processing confidence and susceptibility to peer influence. *Journal of Research in Interactive Marketing*, 6(2), 110–132.

Leetaru, K. H. (2011) Culturonomics 2.0: Forecasting large-scale human behaviour using global news media tone in time and space. *First Monday*, 16(9), Available at: www.firstmonday.org/htbin/cgiwrap/bin/ojs/index.php/fm/article/viewArticle/3663/3040. Accessed 5th May 2012.

Lynn, R., Hampson, S., & Agahi, E. (1989) Television violence and aggression: A genotype-environment, correlation and interaction theory. *Social Behaviour and Personality*, 17, 143–164.

Maes, P. (2000) Smart commerce: The future of intelligent agents in cyberspace. *Journal of Interactive Marketing*, 13, 66–76.

Martin, B. A. S., Sherrard, M. J., & Wentzel, D. (2005) The role of sensation seeking and need for cognition on web-site evaluations: A resource-matching perspective. *Psychology & Marketing*, 22(2), 109–126.

Mendelsohn, H. (1983) Using the mass media for crime prevention. Paper presented at the Annual Convention of the American Association for Public Opinion Research, Buck Hill Falls, PA, May.

Mishne, G., & Glance, N. (2006) Predicting movie sales from blogger sentiment. Paper presented at the Spring Symposium on Computational Approaches to Analysing Weblogs AAAI. Accessed 3rd April 2012.

Mitsis, A., & Foley, P. (2012) Do generational membership and psychographic characteristics influence positive word of mouth in a university context. *Asian Academy of Management Journal*, 17(1), 1–12.

Palmgreen, P., & Rayburn, J. (1982) Gratifications sought and media exposure: An expectancy value model. *Communication Research*, 9, 561–580.

Pang, B., & Lee, L. (2008) Opinion mining and sentiment analysis. *Foundations and Trends in Information Retrieval*, 2(1–2), 1–135.

Papacharissi, Z. (2010) Privacy as a luxury commodity. *First Monday*, 15(8). Available at: http://firstmonday.org/ojs/index.php/fm/article/view/3075/2581

Persegani, C., Russo, P., Carucci, C., Nicolini, M., Papeschi, L. L., & Trimarchi, M. (2002) Television viewing and personality structure in children. *Personality and Individual Differences*, 32(6), 977–990.

Peterson, R. A. (1972) Psychographics and media exposure. *Journal of Advertising Research*, 12, 17–20.

Potter, W. J., Forrest, E., Sapolsky, B. S., & Ware, W. (1988) Segmenting VCR owners. *Journal of Advertising Research*, 28, 29–37.

Quercia, D., Kosinski, M., Stillwell, D., & Crowcroft, J. (2011) Our Twitter profiles, our selves: Predicting personality with Twitter. *IEEE Social Com*. http://www.cl.cam.ac.uk/~dq209/publications/quercia11twitter.pdf

Quinn, C. (1999) How leading edge companies are marketing, selling, and fulfilling over the internet. *Journal of Interactive Marketing*, 13, 39–50.

Raju, P. S. (1980) Optimum stimulation level: Its relationship to personality, demographies, and exploratory behaviour. *Journal of Consumer Research*, 7, 272–282.

Reinhold, N., & Bhutaia, K. L. (2007) The virtual home visit. In *Proceedings of the ESOMAR Qualitative Research Annual Conference*, Paris, 12–14 November, pp. 28–41.

Rokeach, M. (1973) *The Open and Closed Mind*. New York, NY: Basic Books.

Roper, E. (1970) *Movers and Shakers*. New York, NY: Harper-Atlantic Sales.

Ross, C., Orr, E. S., Sisic, M., Arseneault, J. M., Simmering, M. G., & Orr, R. R. (2009) Personality and motivations associated with Facebook use. *Computers in Human Behavior*, 25(2), 578–586.

Rubin, A. (1979) Television use by children and adolescents. *Human Communication Research*, 5, 109–120.

Rubin, A. (1981) An examination of television viewing motivations. *Communication Research*, 8, 141–165.

Rubin, A. (1983) Television uses and gratifications: The interactions of viewing patterns and motivations. *Journal of Broadcasting*, 27, 37–51.

Schrammel, J., Koffel, C., & Tscheligi, M. (2009) Personality traits, usage patterns and information disclosure in online communities. HCI 2009 —people and Computers XXIII—celebrating people and technology. Available at: http://www.bcs.org/upload/pdf/ewic_hci09_paper20.pdf

Schwillewaert, N., De Ruyck, T., & Verhaeghe, A. (2009) 'Connected research': How market research can get the most out of semantic web waves. *International Journal of Market Research*, 51(1), 11–27.

Stern, B. (1994) A revised model for advertising: multiple dimensions of the source, the message, and the recipient. *Journal of Advertising*, 23(2), 5–16.

Sumner, C., Byers, A., Boochever, R., & Park, G. J. (2012) Predicting dark triad personality traits from Twitter usage and a linguistic analysis of tweets. *Conference Proceedings* at the IEEE 11th International Conference on Machine Learning and Applications ICMLA.

Teel, J. E., Bearden, W. O., & Durand, R. M. (1979) Psychographics of radio and television audiences. *Journal of Advertising Research*, 19, 53–56.

Tigert, D. J., Lathrope, R., & Bleeg, M. (1971) The fast food franchise: Psychographic and demographic segmentation analyses. *Journal of Retailing*, 47, 81–90.

Vazire, S., & Gosling, S. D. (2004) E-perceptions: Personality impressions based on personal websites. *Journal of Personality and Social Psychology*, 87, 123–132.

Watt, J. H., & Krull, R. (1974) An information theory measure of television programming. *Communication Research*, 1, 44–68.

Wolburg, J. M., & Pokrywczyski, J. (2001) A psychographic analysis of Generation Y college students. *Journal of Advertising Research*, 41(5), 33–53.

Zillmann, D., & Bryant, J. (1985) *Selective Exposure to Communication*. Hillsdale, NJ: Lawrence Erlbaum Associates.

Zuckerman, M. (1983) Sensation seeking: The initial motive for drug abuse. In E. H. Gotttheil, K. A. Druley, T. E. Skoloda, & H. M. Waxman (Eds.) *Etiological Aspects of Alcohol and Drug Abuse*, pp. 202–220. Springfield, IL: Charles C. Thomas.

Zuckerman, M. (1994) *Behavioural Expressions and Biosocial Bases of Sensation Seeking*. New York, NY: Cambridge University Press.

Zuckerman, M., Ulrich, R. S., & McLaughlin, J. (1993) Sensation seeking and reactions to nature paintings. *Personality & Individual Differences*, 15, 563–576.

8 Psychological Profiling and Consumers' Reactions to Marketing Campaigns

Knowing about the psychological characteristics of consumers can provide valuable information to guide the development of marketing campaigns. The psychological makeup of consumers is not simply a device that can be used to classify them in descriptive terms. It provides a consumer taxonomy in which different consumer types are distinguished in terms of the way they process information they receive from around them. This information processing orientation is critical in relation to the way consumers respond to messages presented to them in brand marketing campaigns. If consumers in a target market are defined by the values they hold most dear and these values in turn underpin specific motivations that drive the consumer's brand choices, it is essential that brand advertisements contain appeals that resonate with the reasons why a consumer is in the market for that brand to begin with.

An understanding of consumer psychology is vitally important to the design of persuasive messages. This chapter will review evidence concerning the efficacy of different psychographics typologies in predicting consumer reactions to brand marketing messages and in comparing personality typologies originally developed outside the consumer context, generic lifestyle trait systems designed for the consumer world, and custom-built psychographic typologies linked to specific product/service ranges and types.

Involvement as a Market Segmentation Variable

The concept of 'involvement' has featured prominently within theories about and explanations of marketing effects for many years. It embraces the idea that consumers forge a psychological relationship with products/services or with brands and with their promotional campaigns. Involvement has often been conceived as a 'process' variable that can influence decision-making about purchase decisions and that also plays a part in the nature and amount of information consumers take away with them from advertising campaigns or from specific advertising messages (Antil, 1984). As the consumer's involvement with an advertisement gets 'deeper', by which is usually meant, their attention is more acute or sharply focused on the message being presented, the more information they take away (Krugman, 1967; Andrews, Srinivas & Akhter, 1990).

The notion that involvement is important to the ways consumers react to marketing messages derives from social psychological theory and research about attitude change. Social psychologists, working outside the context of marketing, found that persuasive messages could influence the attitudes of people who received them under certain conditions. In particular, it was necessary for the message receiver to feel that the message was relevant and important to them. There had to be a degree of what was termed 'ego involvement'. This might occur, for instance, if the issue being discussed was something that was close to the person's own interests or concerns. If the positions adopted on that issue represented a belief set that was central to the individual's own identity, then he or she would be particularly interested to find out more (Sherif, Sherif & Nebergall, 1965). In a highly ego-involved scenario, the individual might be motivated to take an extreme position and their reaction to a persuasive message might therefore be to accept it without question (where it confirms or supports a pre-existing position) or to reject it without reservation (where it runs counter to the individual's existing beliefs) (Laaksonen, 1994).

Level of involvement as a process is therefore linked to what psychologists have called 'depth of processing'. The nature of the involvement phenomenon, however, can vary and its relationship to brand decision-making and even to the absorption of information from marketing messages can get quite complex. It is not simply the case that a consumer with more involvement processes advertisements more 'deeply'. The actual nature of the information processing can vary and the aspects of an advertisement to which most attention is paid by a consumer can change as involvement deepens (Krugman, 1967; Greenwald & Leavitt, 1984).

According to some theorists, deeper processing of an advertisement results in the consumer focusing more intently on the central message about the brand being promoted (Petty & Cacioppo, 1981; Cacioppo, Petty, Kao & Rodriguez, 1996). The core arguments that concern why the promoted brand is high performing, better than its competitors, or has special attributes that make it a good value are the most important elements of a promotion for involved and committed consumers. Their attention focuses specifically on these aspects of the message. With advertisements that command less involvement, perhaps because the product being marketed itself does not require much thought before purchase, core arguments tend to be less closely monitored and the impact of the advertisement is more likely to be mediated by peripheral features such as visual effects, music, the use of attention-grabbing colours or sound effects, or possibly humour or the presence of an attractive endorser.

A typology of involvement can be established from the different entities and processes that represent the target of the consumer's attention.

Involvement as a psychological process can relate to a product or service, a brand, an advertisement or other promotional message, a decision-making process that might entail internal cognitive deliberations, or externally vocalised discussions with other consumers (Michaelidou & Dibb, 2008).

Typologies of involvement have also distinguished between enduring, situational, and response (Houston & Rothschild, 1978; Rothschild, 1979, 1984). This classification system has a temporal dimension. Involvement with products/services or brands can endure over long periods of time or can be temporary and transient, being situation specific (Richins & Bloch, 1986). An example might be that a consumer need arises based on a special set of circumstances. Let us suppose that the consumer's dishwasher has broken down. At that moment, the consumer is in the market for a new device and will engage in an information search about this product type and take advice from different sources about the best brands.

Price comparisons might also be undertaken and cost could also be an important deciding factor. Once a purchase has been made, the need subsides and the consumer is no longer 'involved' with that market or the product ranges in it. In contrast, fashion purchases that are important to personal image will need to be constantly refreshed and established brands may therefore command longer-term loyalty from the consumer. Although this may not be true of all consumers, clothing purchases represent a domain of consumerism in which either situational or enduring involvement could occur.

Thus, there is a distinction between involvement in a product range that is situation specific versus involvement that endures over time and might include products that are perhaps ego-related or have personal relevance in terms of their importance to personal identity (Bloch, 1981; Celsi & Evans, 1988). There are products to which a consumer might therefore form a psychological attachment. In the case of situational involvement, by the nature of the products usually being sought here, this psychological attachment is much less likely to occur (Laaksonen, 1994).

Some scholars in this field have identified a middle way between enduring and situational involvement that conceives of the two processes working together. Involvement is regarded as ultimately linked to an end goal on the part of the consumer. There are cognitive and affective (or emotional) aspects to the processes that underpin this goal orientation. At a cognitive level, consumers make judgements about the functionality and performance of products and services as well as whether they offer good value for money. On the affective side, consumers also make more symbolic assessments of brands to determine whether they will bring certain psychological or social benefits, and especially enhanced self-esteem and social status. Brands and their promotions must arouse consumers' interest and deliver what is expected. They must do this consistently across a range of consumer purchase and usage settings to command enduring outcomes such as customer or user loyalty and establish a positive brand image (Park & Mittal, 1985; Laaksonen, 1994).

Marketing scholars have also identified 'response involvement', which focuses predominantly on behavioural activity surrounding products and services. Although this type of involvement was originally conceived as a mental state, in this context it is also defined in terms of the overt display of behaviour linked to use of a product or service (Stone, 1984). This behaviour goes beyond the actual use of a commodity. It also includes pre-purchase behaviour such as the level of information searching activity in which the consumer engages before deciding to make a purchase. It also includes the amount of effort a consumer is willing to make to find the commodity once information about it has been studied. The greater the degree of involvement between consumers and branded items, the more energy and time they will be willing to expend finding out about them and locating where they are sold (Dholakia, 1997, 2001; Kinley, Conrad & Brown, 1999).

It is clear from this review that 'involvement' is not a single type of phenomenon or a concept that can be defined in terms of a single dimension. It embraces a number of psychological processes, both internal and external to the consumer as an organism. Some marketing researchers have tried to devise verbal and numerical scales to provide operational measures of involvement. Many of these scales have tried to represent both situational and enduring involvement (although the latter has received closest attention) and involvement that is behavioural and cognitive in nature (Lastovicka & Gardner, 1979; Jensen, Carlson & Tripp, 1989; Mittal, 1989). A great deal of effort has been expended on refining methodologies for the measurement of involvement (Celuch & Evans, 1989; McQuarrie & Munson, 1990; Zaichkowsky, 1994; Mittal, 1995). Measures have examined consumers' interest in different products and services, the specific motives that underpin their purchase decisions, including its relevance to them in different ways, and the different ways that consumer expend effort finding out about what it is they want to buy (Slama & Tashchian, 1985; Mittal, 1989).

The research into consumer involvement as a classification variable has also recognised that consumers can and do distinguish between high and low involvement scenarios and perceptually differentiate between commodities usually associated with those scenarios. Such distinctions are also frequently associated with the price status of products and services. Expensive products and services are distinguished from inexpensive items. These distinctions can apply between different categories of a product as well as between variants within the same product range.

Thus, a car is an expensive product and a container of soap powder is a cheap product. The consumer may therefore display a great deal more psychological involvement—cognitively, affectively, and behaviourally—in a car than in soap powder. With a car, much more time may be spent seeking advance information about purchase options, talking to others about it, seeking expert advice, and finding the right supplier than would ever be the case with buying a fast-moving consumer product such as soap powder (Mittal & Lee, 1989).

Within another consumer context, such as purchases of clothes, accessories, cosmetics and jewellery, for example, there may be considerable price variances within the same product range and differences in the status of specific brands. Some brands may be unbranded and cheap to buy, others known cheap brands, and yet others well-known expensive brands. In each case, levels of psychological involvement will vary. Each type of product will invoke different amounts of effort on the part of the consumer thinking about purchases beforehand, getting comparative information, and wrestling with issues about value for money and symbolic as well as functional value. Situational factors might come into play, such as whether this is a routine or spontaneous purchase or a planned purchase (e.g., a gift for someone to celebrate a special occasion). These differences can be used by consumers as psychological signifiers of the nature of the purchased item, with some brands finding themselves more often in one involvement category than the other (Mittal, 1989).

Consumer Purchasing Styles

The rise of a consumer culture during the 20th century led to an expansion of purchase choices across a wide range of product and service categories. Not only did those categories expand in number, but also the variety of choices within product or service categories, that is, the number of variants or brands, also increased. This consumer culture infiltrated all aspects of people's lives and created a growing consciousness about consumerism not simply as an activity designed to furnish people with the basic essentials of everyday living, but choices that went much further and enabled those who were so motivated to consume as a form of self-expression. This behaviour could vary between individual consumers. Some consumers were more preoccupied by consumerism than were others (LaBarbera, 1999; Mogilner, Kamvar, & Aaker, 2011; Mogilner, Aaker, & Kamvar, 2012).

Such individual differences were associated with factors such as age, gender, and socio-economic circumstances. The latter were especially important in that they were usually closed tied to an individual's personal income and wealth. The amount of disposable income a consumer had in their possession on a regular basis underpinned their ability to engage in choosy consumerism. The emergence of a certain level of consumer consciousness was also linked to indigenous, societal-level values linked to the concept of materialism. In other words, the acquisition and possession of specific types of material commodities became central to the definition of a person's social status. At the same time, the propensity to engage in this cultural mindset and to be influenced by it also depended upon the internal wiring of the individual. Such internal dispositions that shaped how the individual responded across a range of social situations were linked to his or her personality (LaBarbera & Gurhan, 1997).

Compulsive buying has been defined as a tendency for individuals to buy products beyond their personal needs Mittal, Holbrook, Beatty, Raghubir & Woodside, 2008). Researchers have striven to develop psychometric tests to measure this syndrome (Faber & O'Guinn, 1992; Edwards, 1993; Roberts, Manolis & Tanner, 2003; Manolis & Roberts, 2008). Compulsive buying has been found to display different psychometric properties in different studies, with some researchers producing single-dimension solutions and other finding that it took on a multidimensional psychological structure (Manolis & Roberts, 2008).

Most of the psychometric development work has been conducted with university student populations in different parts of the world. Thus, even though the literature has an international spread, the nature of the samples has typically been limited and non-representative of the general consumer population in the country of origin of each study. In a comparison of two of the most widely used psychometric scales, developed respectively by Faber and O'Guinn and by Edwards, it emerged that the former was unidimensional, whereas the latter had four distinct dimensions. These different measures of compulsive buying behaviour also yielded different predictions of credit card use (Manolis & Roberts, 2008).

Compulsive buying has been associated with anxiety, depression, and low self-esteem, but whether it is caused by or causes these psychological conditions is less clearly established. If these psychological reactions represent emotional states that arise from compulsive buying, this would not be surprising, given that this behaviour often leads to bad debt and bankruptcy, resulting in serious negative impacts upon family and home life (McGregor, Klingander & Lown, 2001).

The reverse causation, whereby negative mood states create a psychological condition that increases the chances that consumers will engage in compulsive buying, has been examined by psychologists (Dittmar, 2004, 2005a). The acquisition of consumer goods can provide compensation for perceived gaps and shortfalls elsewhere in the individual's life (Richins, 2004). The persistence of compulsive buying in the face of mounting debts has been classified as a clinical disorder (American Psychiatric Association, 2000).

Demographically, evidence emerged from different non-representative samples in Britain that compulsive buying behaviour was more prevalent among women and young people. Compulsive buying behaviour was also linked to materialistic values, and many individuals who display a strong psychological disposition towards materialism have also been found to exhibit poor self-confidence and esteem, poor adjustment to the challenges that life can throw at them, and general life dissatisfaction (Dittmar, 2005b).

Measurement Issues

Psychographics has been presented as a parallel strand of measurement and classification of consumer types to run alongside geographical and demographic variables. The latter variables have been used as stand-alone consumer classifiers and have been combined to give rise to compound geo-demographic classification measures such as 'life stage'. These variables are mainly descriptive in nature, although they can be linked to clear differences in patterns of consumer behaviour, brand attitudes, and brand preferences. Psychographics have brought the added benefit of being able to add explanation to description. Not only can psychological variables be used to classify consumers in a descriptive sense, but those descriptions embrace concepts about consumers that can be used to explain the nature of their attitudes, beliefs, motives, and behaviours.

Psychological variables can be particularly useful—or at least in theory, they ought to be—in relation to explaining why consumers react to brand marketing messages the way they do. These messages are designed with one ultimate purpose in mind, and that is to persuade consumers that the brand being promoted is desirable and better than its rivals. This persuasion process has the objective of influencing consumer behaviour, but it does so through a stage-like set of processes that include first of all working on consumers' perceptions, beliefs, and attitudes relating to specific variants of a product or service.

Research with consumers has been theoretically influenced by a broader social psychological literature that has attempted to create explanatory models to show how and to what degree internal cognitive variables such as beliefs and attitudes, and other internalised cultural rules and standards of conduct—or values—can shape the overt behaviours that people display in different social settings. In addition, there are personality factors that represent more enduring dispositions that are defined and developed by a combination of genetic characteristics operating at a biological level and environmental experiences (or learning).

In the study of the effects of advertising campaigns, therefore, these campaigns have been treated as persuasion exercises and research interest has centred not simply on the eventual effects they might have on consumers' behaviours, but also prior to that, the effects they might have on consumers' beliefs and attitudes, and the way that value systems that often underpin the kinds of beliefs and attitudes consumers might display that also play an active role in mediating consumer's responses to brand promotions. As we have seen already, values can influence consumers' preferences and choices in a number of product categories (Pitts & Woodside, 1983; Homer & Kahle, 1988). Critics have observed that while values research does provide interesting descriptions of consumer types and further insights into how values embrace codes that could affect how consumers respond to marketing campaigns, they often fail to explain in precise terms how these influences come about (Shrum & McCarty, 1997).

More also needs to be established empirically about the strengths of any relationships between values and consumer behaviour. Marketers use values to generate typologies of consumers, but these typologies frequently fail to pinpoint quantitative differences between types in their product preferences or reactions to advertising promotions for specific brands. There is a further issue that is related to these observations, and this concerns the way values are measured. Similar issues have been observed with social psychological studies of attitude formation and change.

Social psychologists have struggled for many years to establish whether attitudes shape behaviours in a direct causal way that can be effectively measured (Krugman, 1967; Wicker, 1971; Abelson, 1972). Refined measures of attitudes, beliefs, and intentions resulted in models of attitude-behaviour links that were able to demonstrate that causal connections did exist between these variables, although their appearance and strength could vary between different population samples and social settings (Fishbein & Ajzen, 1974; Fazio, 1986, 1989). Furthermore, different orientations could occur towards persuasive communications, often defined by how involved or focused on their attention receivers were, that could also mediate receivers' responses to those messages (Petty & Cacioppo, 1986). Personality factors could also come into play in these circumstances to present a further set of variables that could mediate receivers' reactions of persuasive messages (Fenigstein, Scheier & Buss, 1975).

The way core variables such as values are measured can make a lot of difference to research outcomes. The Rokeach Values Survey, for example, used an ordinal method that invited respondents to rank order values items in terms of their importance. These measures do not permit complex statistical tests to be run of the kind needed to explore cause-effect relationships among variables. Values researchers did switch to ratings systems that use linear scales that enabled respondents not only to identify the relative importance of one value compared to another, but also how much difference they perceived to exist between them (Bond, 1988; Crosby, Bitner & Gill, 1990; Horton & Horton, 1990; Shrum, McCarty & Loeffler, 1990; Shrum & McCarty, 1992; McCarty & Shrum, 1993a, 1993b).

Even linear ratings methods are not without their limitations. The absence of a significant correlation between a value item and product purchase frequency does not mean that the value is unimportant as a consumer behaviour predictor. It might simply mean that the value item is relatively unimportant compared with other values in the context of consumer decision-making about that particular product type. To tackle this problem, some researchers developed measurement systems that combined ranking and rating methods. Thus, values items in a list are first ranked by respondents and then each item in turn is given its own linear score (see Munson, 1984; Crosby et al., 1990). This system has been called the 'rank and then rate' method. Another approach has been to ask respondents to select the value item from a list that is most important to them and then the one that is least important. Following these twos selections, each item is independently evaluated on a linear scale. This 'least-most' procedure resolves problems that can occur when respondents are invited to rank long lists of items.

Methodological tests have been run to compare these different approaches. One set of studies reported by Shrum & McCarty (1997) used rank-then-rate, least-most, and rate-only techniques. These techniques were applied to the Rokeach Values Scale and Kahle's List of Values scale. Results showed that the rank-then-rate and least-most methods yielded lower mean scores than did the rate-only method (McCarty & Shrum, 1997). When these different measures were subsequently tested further for the relationships they displayed with other variables, such as measures of TV viewing and materialism, the least-most method produced the strongest statistical associations, followed by rank-then-rate and finally by rate-only. These findings indicated that previous studies that reported apparently weak statistically relationships between values and other criterion variables might have resulted at least in part out of a measurement artefact (Shrum & McCarty, 1997).

Further research indicated that individual differences, as measured by personality, represent a further set of factors that can affect relationships between value measures and some consumer choices. One variable believed to be sensitive to relevant psychological differences was the private self-consciousness (PSC) dimension. This differentiated people in terms of their degree of consciousness of their innermost feelings, attitudes, motives, and behavioural intentions (Fenigstein et al., 1975). The PSC dimension was found to mediate consumers' sensitivities to persuasive messages. Those individuals who scored high on this dimension and who therefore exhibited greater awareness of the internal cognitive dispositions were more resistant to persuasive messages that touched on issues about which message recipients already had much confidence about. Individual who scored lower on this dimension and who therefore seldom reflected on their internal thoughts and feelings were more susceptible to the persuasive influences of the message (Shrum & McCarty, 1992).

The best results for values as predictors of behaviour have come from studies of social issues campaigns. These include issues such as the consumption of healthy foods, taking part in civil rights activities, organ donation, political behaviour, and other health-related behaviour such as smoking (Grube, Weir, Getzlaf & Rokeach, 1984; Homer & Kahle, 1988; Horton & Horton, 1990). Even with social issues, where there is no commercial-consumer aspect, however, value measures do not always prove effective as predictors of behavioural outcomes (McCarty & Shrum, 1993b, 1994).

The Emergence of Cognitive Neuroscience

Marketing researchers have long been dependent upon what consumers can tell them verbally about their brand preferences, product, and services choices and buying activities. Social surveys have been characterised by these verbal self-reports in which data about consumer behaviour derive from the memories of consumers of past brand choice and buying episodes and consumption experiences. Although consumers' recollections of specific brand experiences or reception of knowledge they have gained about products and services in terms of their functionality and brands in terms of their reputations linked to their abilities to deliver what they promised have genuine currency in many marketing research contexts, it is important to recognise that memory records can be incomplete, irretrievable, or inaccurate.

In the context of direct tests of consumers' attitudes towards marketing campaigns and brand promotions, memory can be set to one side as marketing professionals seek to measure consumers' immediate reactions to advertisements, product displays, packaging, symbolic logos, and general chatter about brands. These measures are used to represent cognitive and emotional responses to brands as well as consumers' motivations to use specific products and services and variants of them. Consumers' reactions here can be measured here both verbally and non-verbally.

Verbal responses tend to be underpinned by conscious thoughts about products and services and their different variants. Verbal responses are measured using questionnaires. Survey respondents provide answers to questions in verbal form. They are sometimes invited to generate their own answers in their own words. More often, the researcher provides a choice of answers for survey respondents to select one from that most closely matches their own thoughts or feelings. The latter forced-choice responses are numerically coded to convert them into quantitative data that can be entered into statistical analyses.

Non-verbal responses more often represent unconscious or autonomic reactions to commodities and their promotional campaigns. Non-verbal measures include physiological responses such as changes in electrical conductance of the skin, facial reactions, heart rate, pupil dilation, and changes in brain wave patterns (Costa, Rognoni & Galati, 2006; Knutson, Rick, Wimmer, Prelec & Loewenstein, 2007).

Verbal responses might sometimes not represent the whole truth about the nature of consumers' thoughts and feelings when under research conditions they decide not to disclose the way they really think or feel. Non-verbal responses are more difficult to disguise or to withhold. At the same time, the meanings of these responses are not always clearly discernible. One example of this might be when a physical response to a product is the same whether the nature of an experienced emotion for the consumer is positive or negative.

Marketing researchers have increasingly tested the efficacy of non-verbal measures of consumer responses to commodities that can also be interpreted in more verbal forms. These tend to take the form of brain wave measures and have been underpinned by the emergence in the mainstream of cognitive neuroscience as an important discipline that has sought to define thought patterns, emotional responses, and behavioural motivations in terms of quantitatively measurable electrical activity in the brain. The merger of neuroscience and marketing has added to the toolkit of marketing researchers in a field that has become commonly labelled as 'neuromarketing' (Fugate, 2007; 2008). Other widely used terms to label this new research perspective include 'neuroeconomics' and 'consumer neuroscience' (Hubert & Kenning, 2008; Kenning & Plassmann, 2005).

Economists were among the quickest in the social sciences to explore the utility of brain imaging methods to supplement the more traditional mathematical models of behaviour and verbal response data used to analyse and explain purchase and other business activities (Camerer, Loewenstein & Prelec, 2004; Glimcher & Rustichini, 2004; Braetigam, 2005; Kenning & Plassmann, 2005). This early work triggered further work in the consumer marketing field (Reimann, Schilke, Weber, Neuhaus & Zaichkowsky, 2011). The use of neuroimaging methods spread to the commercial marketing research sector and many new agencies were identified that provided specialist neuromarketing services to clients (Fisher, Chin & Klitzman, 2010; Plassmann, Zoega Ramsoy & Milosavljevic, 2012).

In choosing to study brain activity, marketers can adopt a different perspective that combines disciplines such as clinical and cognitive psychology and brain physiology and neuroscience to analyse how consumers react to different variants of products and services, how they make choices between brands, and how they respond to brand marketing campaigns. Psychological perspectives on consumer profiling have been underpinned to a significant extent by personality psychology. Human personality attributes are known to be founded in turn upon specific types of brain physiology and patterns of neurological activity in response to external stimuli. It makes sense therefore to dig deeper into that neurological activity to understand how it works and to relate specific brain activity measures to brand perceptions and consumer behaviour.

The founding father of neuromarketing is widely recognised as being Martin Linstrom, who conducted extensive neuroscience research with large numbers of consumers at the University of Oxford. His work culminated in a book (*Buyology: How Everything We Believe About Why We Buy Is Wrong*), in which he argued that an overwhelming majority of consumers make buying decisions at a subconscious level (Lindstrom, 2009).

In neuromarketing, marketing researchers work with cognitive neuroscience specialists to deploy tools such as electroencephalography, magnetoencephalography, transcranial magnetic stimulation, and most popularly, functional magnetic resonance imaging (fMRI). These tools enable researchers to identify changes in electrical activity in the human brain in response to controlled exposure to different stimuli and often to represent these changes not just as line charts that trace activity profiles, but also as colour images which identify areas of the brain that were activated when different stimuli appeared. The latter neuroimaging techniques have experienced growing popularity in consumer marketing research because they yield quantitative data that reveal the nature and strength of responding to specific marketing stimuli and also provide visual displays of patterns of brain arousal (Braetigam, 2005; Butler, 2008; Fisher et al., 2010).

Can Neuroscience Predict Consumer Choice?

There has been an optimistic assumption on the part of its proponents that neuromarketing represents a valuable and informative new perspective for understanding consumer behaviour. It provides a distinctive perspective for analysing consumers' decisions about brands and purchases that can offer explanatory insights standard social research methods are unable to produce. One reason why neuromarketing has specific value is that conventional market research is dependent upon consumers consciously articulating their reasons for the brand choices they make, whereas analysis of brain activity can reveal subconscious processes that come into play of which consumers are not aware (Lindstrom, 2009; Ariely & Bems, 2010). This observation is more than hopeful conjecture, but tallies well with evidence from other social research fields that human behaviour can be driven by cognitive processes that research participants are not consciously attuned to (Calvert & Brammer, 2012).

Neuromarketing has generated a lot of debate about whether it represents a genuinely new theoretically underpinned discipline or simply a business activity. The term itself originated in the commercial environment and not in an academic setting (Fisher et al., 2010). To be received as a *bona fide* academic discipline, neuromarketing must demonstrate its ability to generate a new model for analysing and predicting consumer behaviour (Fugate, 2007). In this respect, there must be greater clarity over the meanings of specific neurological measures and their links to consumers' psychological responses to commodities they might purchase (Renvoise & Morin, 2007). Part of this process also involves producing reliable and interpretable data concerning the psychological processes that are controlled by different parts of the brain and then providing consistent empirical demonstrations of the activation of these brain centres to different commodity and brand marketing stimuli.

In this context, a body of research evidence has started to accumulate in which distinctive visual neuroimaging display patterns generated by fMRI scans of consumers' brains have been linked to verbalised responses and behavioural choices linked to brands. These responses include preferring one brand over a rival, subjective value for money judgements, and intentions to purchase (Chib, Rangel, Shimojo & O'Doherty, 2009; Plassmann, O'Doherty & Rangel, 2007; Fitzgerald, Seymour, & Dolan, 2009; Venkatraman, Clithero, Fitzsimons & Huettel, 2012).

One study examined brain activity in relation to preferences for car brands. Some parts of the brain were found to be activated in response to specific design features of well-known brands. Consumers who attached great value to high-performance and premium brands such as BMW and Ferrari displayed activity in brain centres known to be relevant to judgements about wealth and social status (Hunt, 2008).

Sometimes, brain activity can reveal consumer reactions that differ from conscious verbal responses. This is where such unconscious responses to commodities might reveal characteristics of consumers' allegiance to brands of specific types or to lifestyle aspirations they may be unable or unwilling verbally to articulate. Thus, brain activity heightened in centres known to be associated with feelings of pleasantness when tasting wine revealed to be very expensive, even though consciously, taste testers claimed there was little difference between it and less expensive wines (Garcia & Saad, 2008).

Functional magnetic resonance imaging has been used by the Hollywood film industry when conducting pre-release audience tests. In one example of this application, fMRI results were found to differentiate between viewers' experiences of watching conventional versus 3D versions of the same movie (Randal, 2011). Differential emotional responses to film sequences register in the brain as activity levels change in different locations, for example, in the case of happy versus unhappy incidents (Costa, Rognoni & Galati, 2006).

Further consumer neuroscience research has shown variances in the activation of the frontal cortex and occipital regions of the brain when making judgements about most and least liked food items (crackers with different toppings). This kind of research reveals that consumers' sensitivities to stimuli believed to bring greater or lesser pleasure can trigger different patterns of brain activation that appropriate technology can render as visibly manifest (Khushaba, Wise, Kodagoda, Louviere, Kahn & Townsend, 2013).

A further body of evidence has accumulated that when viewers watch TV advertisements, changes in their levels of cortical and parietal lobe activity in the brain can be detected. This activity is also correlated with performance on psychological tests that test conscious memories of commercials to which viewers were exposed (Astolfi et al., 2008; Ohme et al., 2010; Vecchiato, Kong, Maglione & Wei, 2012).

Issues Associated With Neuromarketing

It is premature to believe that neuromarketing represents some kind of "Holy Grail" for consumer profilers. There are logistical and ethical issues that characterise the field and which, for many practitioners and theorists, still need to be resolved. Measuring brain activity is an exciting development because at first brush, it appears to represent genuine and ungarnished reactions of consumers to products and services and their variants and promotions. Yet, when exploring more deeply what these reactions really mean, their validity as indicators that can generate useful business data is not something that can be automatically accepted.

Neuromarketing must meet the quality standards of any other form of market research. We have already seen that this point applies to other new areas of consumer profiling involving the use of 'big data' and computer-driven data trawling, classification, and analysis systems that have emerged as increasingly popular alternatives to standard social surveys as more and more consumer and brand marketing activity takes place online. Just as the 'public opinions' revealed by sentiment analysis must be validated against more conventional verbal response measures, so too brain activity must be set alongside verbally articulated thoughts and feelings of consumers when confronted with specific commodities or brand marketing campaigns.

Neuromarketing research is usually conducted under controlled laboratory conditions. This setting tends to be far removed from the natural environments in which consumer activity normally occurs. Controlled conditions are necessary because measuring brain waves accurately requires special equipment that is not readily portable. Precision measurements also usually require participants in such experiments to keep still while their brains' responses to commodities are gauged (Kenning, Plassmann & Ahlert, 2007; Riedl, Hubert & Kenning, 2010).

There are ethical questions about the use of cognitive neuroscience in marketing research settings. Codes of professional research practice generally require that participants in social research are able to provide informed consent before they take part. This means they must understand what they are being required to do and what kinds of data are being collected about them. Although it should generally be possible to provide this information, the fact that non-conscious reactions of consumers are being measured to specific stimuli could equip commercial marketers with data that would enable them to use marketing techniques that are designed to re-activate those neurological responses without consumers' awareness (Lovell, 2008). It will be important, therefore, that participants in experiments understand the full implications of the research being carried out before they decide to cooperate (Fleming, 2006; Kenning et al., 2007; Ariely & Bems, 2010).

The ethical cause of neuromarketing has not been helped by problematic journalistic coverage that has classed this new approach to marketing as a mysterious science designed to help marketers deceive consumers. Reports about neuroscience developments in the marketing context have been linked to subliminal advertising whereby marketers learn how to influence consumers' brains without their conscious awareness and in turn manipulate their buying behaviours (Pratkanis & Greenwald, 1988; Fullerton, 2010). What has also not helped with the establishment of neuroscience as a respectable discipline when used in the marketing sphere is the enthusiasm with which it has been adopted by commercial market research agencies. It was therefore labelled as a commercial service driven by financial imperatives rather than a genuine desire to discover new knowledge about consumer behaviour (Lee, Broderick & Chamberlain, 2007).

It will be important for the value of neuromarketing to be underpinned by establishing its credibility and trustworthiness through references to neuroscience conducted under commercially independent scientific conditions in which the primary goal is to understand how the brain works in different behavioural settings (Javor, Koller, Lee, Chamberlain & Ransmayr, 2013). Much neuroscience has targeted our understanding of reward systems within the brain that become activated when we are confronted with pleasurable stimuli, regardless of the social context. Where these emotional reactions attach to specific commodities and they can be identified through patterns of brain activity, there are opportunities to develop a deeper understanding of the choices consumers make (Miller & Cohen, 2001).

This scientific discipline has many positive applications for understanding how some people engage in various social activities and how specific patterns of neurological activation are associated with specific behavioural choices (Ballard et al., 2011). There is also a research orientation designed to understand how to trigger feelings of positivity and well-being among those who have experienced depression that could also have implications for the comprehension of some forms of consumer decision-making (Gray, 1987).

Pleasure and reward might, for some people, derive from the consumption of certain foods, propensities to take drugs, and ownership of premium brands of cars, cosmetics, clothes, and accessories. Neuroscience has revealed that consumers' purchase decisions are frequently related to the activation of specific areas of the brain that are known to underpin our reactions to experiences of pleasure and pain (McClure et al., 2004; Knutson et al., 2007). Such responses are linked in particular to product-related choices driven by price. A high price (or one which seems to represent poor value for money) can produce 'painful' reactions in consumers that mirror in brain wave terms the responses that might be exhibited to physically or emotionally painful experiences. At the same time, brands that are most liked deliver brain activation patterns that bear striking resemblances to those elicited by physically and socially rewarding experiences (Schaefer & Rotte, 2007; Plassmann, O'Doherty, Shiv & Rangel, 2008).

This type of science has a degree of respectability about it. Its utility in consumer profiling applications is likely to gain acceptance as it becomes more widely used and therefore more 'normative'. To give further reassurance to consumers and marketing regulators, there will need to be transparent, publicly released disclosures about the latest research findings and how they are being used, if at all, in practical marketing scenarios. Neuroscience research that is sponsored by commercial interests must be signalled and evidence provided that its findings have been independently verified in the same way as academic literature (Bekelman & Gross, 2003; Farah, 2005; Madan, 2010).

Personalised Persuasion

In Chapter 7, we saw that the emergence of new marketing approaches associated with the online world, and especially with social media, has spawned new methodologies for analysing vast quantities of unstructured data produced every day by consumers about their product and service habits, brand preferences, and consumption activities. Non-interventionist techniques have been developed by computer scientists working in partnership with social and market research specialists to scan, read, and interpret unstructured online texts and elicit patterns of meaning that can ultimately be represented in a more structured and numerical language available to statistical modelling. These techniques can not only be used to identify and measure attitude and behaviour profiles of consumers in the online world, but also to provide insights into the nature and character of consumers in ways that can in turn be applied to define consumer segments. Thus, it may be possible to identify a consumer's personality type from the remarks he or she writes on a social media site and the style of language used to express thoughts and feelings. This can be done without any need to interact directly with consumers by administering personality test questionnaires to them.

As well as providing a new methodological approach to define consumer segmentation, these techniques might also have further value in guiding the way marketers promote their brands to consumers. One variable of special significance in this context is 'brand personality'.

The concept of brand personality is important in marketing because it distinguishes specific product or service variants from competitors. Apart from this descriptive function, however, it also serves to assign human-like attributes to commodities that enable consumers to make psychological judgements about whether specific brands make a good image fit for them. A brand that has a 'personality' that has similarities to the consumer's perceptions of his or her own personality might stand more chance of being chosen over a brand that has no such personal resemblances (Aaker, 1997). Thus, when consumers invest in brands with personality attributes like their own, those brands can be rendered by appealing (Hawkins, Best & Coney, 2001).

To assess brand 'personality', Aaker (1997) developed a verbal test that measured five dimensions (Sincerity, Excitement, Competence, Sophistication, and Ruggedness). Each of these dimensions was further elaborated in terms of other descriptive characteristics that respondents could endorse as being attributable to a specific brand. For example, Sincerity was defined in terms of such attributes as 'down to earth', 'family-oriented', 'honest', and 'wholesome'.

The importance of brand personality derives also in part from its relationship to consumers' perceptions of brand 'quality'. Brands with stronger identities tend also to be rated higher in terms of quality (Richardson, Dick & Jain, 1994). When a brand has a more distinctive and strongly defined 'personality', this contributes to that perception of quality (Beldona & Wysong, 2007). In a global context, the character of brands can also be defined in terms of cultural values, and the same principles apply in regard to the importance of finding a profile match between the brand and the dominant symbols of specific cultures (Aaker & Benet-Martinez, 2001).

Taking this notion of 'brand personality' a step further, it is also fundamentally important for guiding the nature of any persuasive messages produced to promote it to consumers. There is growing evidence that persuasive messages that have been custom-built to fit the interests, needs, and dispositions of receives will prove to be more effective. Compelling evidence of this phenomenon has emerged from research in the field of health communication.

Products with health-giving properties, such as toothpaste, can be rendered more attractive to consumers when promotional messages are framed to reflect reasons that might be important to consumers for making these purchases. Thus, if it is important for specific consumers to maintain a high standard of oral hygiene and having healthy teeth and gums is regarded as a critical aspect of this objective, brands that can present convincing appeals that represent those outcomes might stand out as the ones to buy. The health-giving properties of such products can be framed in different ways, however. They can be presented as 'giving' health (by strengthening teeth) or as preventing losses (by reducing the probability of cavities) (Cesario, Grant & Higgins, 2004; Cesario, Higgins & Scholer, 2008). Such appeals might resonate differently with consumers defined by different personality profiles (Dijkstra, 2008). What we also need to know is whether there are systematic relationships between consumer personality types and the reception of differently framed persuasive messages.

One hypothetical possibility is that if an advertisement for a product highlighted features of the brand that were likely to resonate strongly with the kinds of experiences known to appeal to a particular personality type, then it would make sense to construct such a message when the primary target market for that type of product is known to comprises a large proportion of consumers of that character type.

Empirical evidence has emerged that advertising appeals written to reflect to key motivational interests of a specific personality tended to be classed as more persuasive by consumers of that personality type. One study that adopted an experimental intervention examined the mediating influence of scripting adverts in ways that match consumers' self-constructs. This investigation grew out of a body of work that had indicated that people store knowledge about themselves as 'self-schemata' (Markus, 1977). Taking up this idea, some social psychologists interested in attitude change discovered that when a persuasive message contains ingredients that resonate with the receiver's existing attitudes or beliefs, any related object (e.g., a brand being promoted in the case of an advertisement) is likely to be rated more favourably (Snyder & DeBono, 1985; Edwards, 1990).

In further research on the effects of advertising, it emerged that brand preferences can be strengthened when the messages associated with them reflect the self-schemata held by consumers. Alternatively, brand promotions must demonstrate that the character of a brand makes a good fit with a specific social occasion in terms of the way it is understood by the consumer (Aaker, 1999).

Some researchers have gone further to test to importance of matching the advertising descriptions of a brand with consumers' personality profiles. Wheeler, Petty & Bizer (2005) reported two experiments that provided evidence that a brand was significantly better liked and that consumers displayed significantly stronger intentions to purchase when the advertising message was framed to provide a close match with their own personality type. This outcome emerged from two separate experiments that matched advertising messages to extraverts/introverts or on the basis of the strength of the need for cognition.

Extraverts tend to be more outgoing and socially confident than introverts. Hence, the target product—a videocassette recorder—was advertised either with an extravert frame or an introvert frame that reflected these differences. In the extravert frame, participants in the experiment were told, "With the Mannux VCR, you'll be the life of the party, whether the party's in your home or out of it". In the introvert frame, they were told, "With the Mannux VCR, you can have all of the luxuries of a movie theatre without having to deal with the crowds".

One of the reasons why matching the advertising message to the consumer's personality seemed to work so well was that in the presence of such matching, the quality of the argument being made was rated as much higher as compared to a mismatch between the ad message and a consumer's personality. The findings for extraversion/introversion were largely replicated in a second study that examined need for cognition.

In the second study, high scorers on the need for cognition were expected to think carefully about the outcomes before making a decision and to appreciate having a choice between different complex and detailed arguments in favour of different courses of action. Different advertising messages were created for a brand of toothpaste that contained either powerful or weak arguments for purchase. High scorers preferred the strong argument, and low scorers preferred the weak argument, and each reacted accordingly in terms of their brand liking and intention to purchase. These responses were strengthened whenever the nature of the advertising message matched the personality of the consumer.

In a further study in this same vein, Hirsch, Kang & Bodenhausen (2012) constructed five advertisements for a cell phone, each of which had few lines of text that outlined a specific quality of the brand. Each of these brand descriptions was manipulated to appeal to each of the Big Five Personality Types (Extraversion, Agreeableness, Conscientiousness, Neuroticism, and Openness). One example of this procedure given by the authors, in the case of extraverts, was "With XPhone, you'll always be where the excitement is", and for Neuroticism, "Stay safe and secure with XPhone". The participants rated the effectiveness of each advertisement using a five-point scale. They were asked to say how much they liked each advertisement, whether they thought it was effective, whether it made them more interested in the product, and whether they were more likely to buy it.

The findings showed that consumer-advertisement personality congruence was important to the perceived effectiveness of the advert. Thus, extraverts rated an "extravert" promotional message as more appealing than they did other ad messages and more than did other consumer personality types. The only personality dimension where this outcome failed to reach statistical significance was neuroticism, although relationships between key variables were in the right direction.

Summing up, there was evidence produced from this study that the appeal of brand promotions to consumers can be enhanced when the message resonates with the personality type of the consumer. Extraverts seek rewarding social experiences. Agreeable types are attracted by appeals to family and friendship. Conscientious types are goal directed and react well to adverts promising the achievement of desired social or professional objectives. Open types respond well to creativity and fresh ideas and will be better persuaded by brand promotions that present a new way of looking at things. Neurotic types seek reassurance and security. The important lesson to be learned from tailored persuasion research is that, when affordable and logistically feasible, customising brand promotions is generally more effective that trying a one-size-fits-all approach (Noar, Benac & Harris, 2007).

Concluding Remarks

The use of psychological measures to profile consumers is applied not only in relation to product and service variant choices and preferences, but also in the context of providing a deeper understanding of how consumers react to specific band promotions. The way consumers process advertisements, for example, depends upon their level of psychological involvement with the commercial message. For some products and services, consumers are extremely involved, whereas with others, they are not. In this context, 'involvement' refers to the importance of a specific commodity or brand to the consumer and therefore to the significance of the decision he or she might take about whether to purchase it or not. Such involvement is a psychological aspect of the way consumers weigh up products/services and branded variants of them.

In effect, 'involvement' means that when a commodity has great personal significance to the consumer—either because of its cost or because of what it signals about their taste or social status—they will tend to pay greater attention to promotional claims that are made about a variant of it by marketing professionals. Expensive products such as cars will tend to command more careful thought by consumers than do everyday goods such as soap powder. What this means is that for goods that have great monetary or social value, consumers will weigh up information about different brands and especially about the brand they are leaning towards before committing to a purchase. With goods that have limited social significance and are inexpensive to buy, consumers give much less thought to their purchases.

Whether involvement is strong or weak has been found by researchers to make a difference in the way that consumers process information from brand advertisements. For highly involving products, consumers seek detailed information about their social value, functionality, and performance. For products that command little consumer attention of this kind, potential buyers are more likely to be affected by cosmetic features that make the commercial message more of a stand out, such as the use of a famous celebrity endorser, special production effects, background music, and humour. The aim here is to make consumers enjoy the advertisement with the intention that this pleasant experience will transfer to their impression of the advertised brand.

As marketing practices have grown in sophistication, so too marketing professionals and social researchers specialising in the study of the field have sought stronger scientific evidence to understand how consumers react cognitively and emotionally to brands and their promotions. In this context, marketing researchers have followed economists in adopting cognitive neuroscientific perspectives to analyse consumers' responses to brands and brand advertisements at the level of brain functioning. This approach has been used on its own and in combination with traditional market research methods. It can generate new forms of consumer profiling that combine measures of human personality, verbalised cognitive and emotional responding, and neuro-physiological measures of brain activity that can locate which parts of the brain are engaged by specific marketing stimuli.

So far, this field of neuromarketing has shown some early promise. There is scope for much more research to be done to establish the validity and reliability of specific physiological methods and the meanings of different kinds of brain activation patterns in terms of how they can be re-interpreted at the level of consumer psychology.

References

Aaker, J. L. (1997) Dimensions of brand personality. *Journal of Marketing Research*, 34(3), 347–356.

Aaker, J. L. (1999) The malleable self: The role of self-expression in persuasion. *Journal of Marketing Research*, 36(1), 45–57.

Aaker, J. L., Benet-Martinez, V., & Garoloera, J. (2001) Consumption symbols as carriers of culture: A study of Japanese and Spanish brand personality constructs. *Journal of Personality and Social Psychology*, 81, 492–508.

Abelson, R. (1972) Are attitudes necessary? In B. T. King & E. McGinnies (Eds.) *Attitudes, Conflict and Social Change*, pp. 19–32. New York, NY: Academic Press.

American Psychiatric Association (2000) *Practice Guidelines*. Available at: www.psychiatryonline.org/guidelines

Andrews, J., Srinivas, D., & Akhter, S. H. (1990) A framework for conceptualizing and measuring the involvement construct in advertising research. *Journal of Advertising Research*, 19(4), 27–40.

Antil, J. H. (1984) Conceptualization and operationalization of involvement. In T. C. Kinnear (Ed.) *Advances in Consumer Research,* Vol. 11, pp. 203–209. Provo, UT: Association for Consumer Research.

Ariely, D., & Bems, G. (2010) Neuromarketing: The hope and hype of neuroimaging in business. *Nature Reviews Neuroscience,* 11, 284–292.

Astolfi, L., Fallani, F. D. V., Cincotti, F., Mattia, D., Bianchi, L., Marciani, M. G., Salinari, S., Gaudiano, I., Scarano, G., Soranzo, R., & Babilori, F. (2008) Brain activity during the memorization of visual scenes from TV commercials: An application of high resolution EEG and steady state somatosensory evoked potentials technologies. *Journal of Physiology—Paris,* 103(6), 333–341.

Ballard, J. C., Murty, V. P., Carter, R. M., MacInnes, J. J., Huettel, S. A., & Adcock, R. A. (2011) Dorsolateral prefrontal cortex drives mesolimbic dopaminergic regions to initiate motivated behaviour. *Journal of Neuroscience,* 31, 10340–10346.

Bekelman, J. E., Li, Y., & Gross, C. P. (2003) Scope and impact of financial conflicts of interests in biomedical research. *Journal of American Medical Association,* 277, 1238–1243.

Beldona, S., & Wysong, S. (2007) Putting the "brand" back into store brands: An exploratory examination of store brands and brand personality. *Journal of Product & Brand Management,* 16(4), 226–235.

Bloch, P. H. (1981) An exploration into the scaling of consumers' involvement with a product class. In K. B. Monroe (Ed.) *Advances in Consumer Research 8,* pp. 61–65. Ann Arbor, MI: Association for Consumer Research.

Bond, M. H. (1988) Finding universal dimensions of individual variation in multicultural studies of values: The Rokeach and Chinese value surveys. *Journal of Personality and Social Psychology,* 55, 1009–1015.

Braetigam, S. (2005) Neuroeconomics—from neural systems to economic behaviour. *Brain Research Bulletin,* 67, 355–360.

Butler, M. J. R. (2008) Neuromarketing and the perception of knowledge. *Journal of Consumer Behaviour,* 7, 415–419.

Calvert, G. A., & Brammer, M. J. (2012) Predicting consumer behaviour. *IEEE Pulse Magazine,* 3(3), 38–41.

Camerer, C. F., Lowenstein, G., & Prelec, D. (2004) Neuroeconomics: Why economics needs brains. *Scandinavian Journal of Economics,* 106(3), 555–579.

Celsi, L. R., & Olson, J. C. (1988) The role of involvement in attention and comprehension processes. *Journal of Consumer Research,* 15, 210–224.

Celuch, K., & Evans, R. (1989) An analysis of the convergent and discriminant validity of the personal involvement inventory and the consumer involvement profile. *Psychological Reports,* 65, 1291–1297.

Cesario, J., Grant, H., & Higgins, E. T. (2004) Regulatory fit and persuasion: Transfer from "feeling right". *Journal of Personality and Social Psychology,* 86, 388–404.

Cesario, J., Higgins, E. T., & Scholer, A. A. (2008) Regulatory fit and persuasion: Basic principles and remaining questions. *Social & Personality Psychology Compass,* 2, 444–463.

Chib, V. S., Rangel, A., Shimojo, S., & O'Doherty, J. P. (2009) Evidence for a common representation of decision values for dissimilar goods in human ventromedial prefrontal cortex. *Journal of Neuroscience,* 29(39), 12315–12320.

Costa, T., Rognoni, E., & Galati, D. (2006) EEG phase synchronization during emotional response to positive and negative film stimuli. *Neuroscience Letters,* 406, 159–164.

Crosby, L. A., Bitner, M. J., & Gill, J. D. (1990) Organizational structure of values. *Journal of Business Research*, 20, 123–134.

Dholakia, U. M. (1997) An investigation of the relationship between perceived risk and product involvement. In *Advances in Consumer Research*, Vol. 24, pp. 159–167. Chicago, IL: Association of Consumer Research.

Dholakia, U. M. (2001) A motivational process model of product involvement and consumer risk perception. *European Journal of Marketing*, 35(11/12), 1340–1362.

Dijkstra, A. (2008) The psychology of tailoring-ingredients in computer-tailored persuasion. *Social & Personality Psychology Compass*, 2, 765–784.

Dittmar, H. (2004) Understanding and diagnosing compulsive buying. In R. Coombs (Ed.) *Handbook of Addictive Disorders: A Practical Guide to Diagnosis and Treatment*, pp. 411–450. New York, NY: Wiley, ch. 13.

Dittmar, H. (2005a) A new look at compulsive buying: Self-discrepancies and materialistic values as predictors of compulsive buying tendency. *Journal of Economic Psychology*, 21, 109–142.

Dittmar, H. (2005b) Compulsive buying—a growing concern? An examination of gender, age, and endorsement of materialistic values as predictors. *British Journal of Psychology*, 96, 467–491.

Edwards, E. A. (1993) Development of a new scale for measuring compulsive buying behaviour. *Financial Counseling and Planning*, 4, 67–84.

Edwards, K. (1990) The interplay of affect and cognition in attitude formation and change. *Journal of Personality and Social Psychology*, 59, 202–216.

Faber, R. J., & O'Guinn, T. C. (1992) A clinical screener for compulsive buying. *Journal of Consumer Research*, 19, 459–469.

Farah, M. J. (2005) Neuroethics: The practical and the philosophical. *Trends in Cognitive Science*, 9, 34–40.

Fazio, R. H. (1986) How do attitudes guide behaviour? In R. M. Sorrentino & E. T. Higgins (Eds.) *The Handbook of Motivation and Cognition: Foundations of Social Behaviour*, pp. 204–243. New York, NY: Guilford.

Fazio, R. H. (1989) On the power and functionality of attitudes: The role of attitude accessibility. In A. R. Pratkanis, S. J. Breckler, & A. G. Greenwald. (Eds.) *Attitude Structure and Function*, pp. 153–179. Hillsdale, NJ: Lawrence Erlbaum Associates.

Fenigstein, A., Scheier, M. F., & Buss, A. H. (1975) Public and private self-consciousness: Assessment and theory. *Journal of Consulting and Clinical Psychology*, 43, 522–527.

Fishbein, M., & Ajzen, I. (1974) Attitudes towards objects as predictors of single and multiple behavioural criteria. *Psychological Review*, 81, 59–74.

Fisher, C. E., Chin, L., & Klitzman, R. (2010) Defining neuromarketing: Practices and professional challenges. *Harvard Review of Psychology*, 18(4), 230–237.

Fitzgerald, T. H. B., Seymour, B., & Dolan, R. J. (2009) The role of human orbitofrontal cortex in value comparison for incommensurable objects. *Journal of Neuroscience*, 29, 8388–8395.

Fleming, J. (2006) Is that a neuromarketer in your brain? *The Gallup Management Journal*, pp. 1–4. Available at: http://gmj.gallup.com/content/20785/neuromarketer-your-brain.aspx

Fugate, D. L. (2007) Neuromarketing: A layman's look at neuroscience and its potential application to marketing practice. *Journal of Consumer Marketing*, 24(7), 385–394.

Fugate, D. L. (2008) Marketing services more effectively with neuromarketing research: A look into the future. *Journal of Services Marketing*, 22(2), 170–173.

Fullerton, R. A. (2010) "A virtual social H-bomb": The late 1950s controversy over subliminal advertising. *Journal of Historical Research in Marketing*, 2(2), 166–173.

Garcia, J., & Saad, G. (2008) Evolutionary neuromarketing: Darwinizing the neuroimaging paradigm for consumer behaviour. *Journal of Consumer Behaviour*, 7, 397–414.

Glimcher, P. W., & Rustichini, A. (2004) Neuroeconomics: The consilience of brain and decision. *Science*, 306, 447–452.

Gray, J. A. (1987) The neuropsychology of emotion and personality. In S. M. Stahl, S. D. Iverson, & E. D. Goodman, pp. 171–190. Oxford, UK: Oxford University Press.

Greenwald, A. G., & Leavitt, C. (1984) Audience involvement in advertising: Four levels. *Journal of Consumer Research*, 31, 11–32.

Grube, J. W., Weir, I. L., Getzlaf, S., & Rokeach, M. (1984) Own value system, value images, and cigarette smoking. *Personality and Social Psychology Bulletin*, 10, 306–313.

Hawkins, D. I., Best, R. J., & Coney, K. A. (2001) *Consumer Behaviour*, 9th Ed. New York, NY: McGraw-Hill.

Hirsch, J. B., Kang, S. K., & Bodenhausen, G. V. (2012) Personalized persuasion: Tailoring persuasive appeals to recipients' personality traits. *Psychological Science*, 20(10), 1–4.

Homer, P. M., & Kahle, L. R. (1988) A structural equation test of the value-attitude-behaviour hierarchy. *Journal of Personality and Social Psychology*, 54, 638–646.

Horton, R. L., & Horton, P. J. (1990) Organ donation and values: identifying potential organ donors. In M. P. Gardner (Ed.) *Proceedings of the Society for Consumer Psychology*, pp. 55–59. Washington, DC: American Psychological Association.

Houston, M. J., & Rothschild, M. L. (1978) Conceptual and methodological perspectives on involvement. In H. K. Hunt (Ed.) *Advances in Consumer Research*, Vol. 5, pp. 184–187. Ann Arbor, MI: Association for Consumer Research.

Hubert, M., & Kenning, P. (2008) A current overview of consumer neuroscience. *Journal of Consumer Behaviour*, 7, 272–292.

Hunt, K. (2008) Brand surgery. *The Globe and Mail*. Available at: http://www.theglobeandmail.com/report-on-business/brand-surgery/article718559. Accessed 4th March 2015.

Javor, A., Koller, M., Lee, N., Chamberlain, L., & Ransmayr, G. (2013) Neuromarketing and consumer neuroscience: Contributions to neurology. *MBC Neurology*, 13, 13. Available from: 10.1186/1471-2377-13-13

Jensen, T. D., Carlson, L., & Tripp, C. (1989) The dimensionality of involvement: An empirical test. In T. K. Sroll (Ed.) *Advances in Consumer Research*, Vol. 16, pp. 680–689. Provo, UT: Association for Consumer Research.

Kenning, P., & Plassmann, H. (2005) Neuroeconomics: An overview from an economic perspective. *Brain Research Bulletin*, 67, 343–354.

Kenning, P., Plassmann, H., & Ahlert, D. (2007) Applications of functional magnetic resonance imaging for market research. *Qualitative Market Research: An International Journal*, 10(2), 135–152.

Khushaba, R. N., Wise, C., Kodagoda, S., Louviere, J., Kahn, B. E., & Townsend, C. (2013) Consumer neuroscience: assessing the brain response to marketing stimuli using electroencephalogram (EEG) and eye tracking. *Expert Systems with Applications*, 40, 3803–3812.

Kinley, T. L., Conrad, C. A., & Brown, G. (1999) Internal and external promotional references: An examination of gender and product involvement effects in the retail apparel setting. *Journal of Retailing and Consumer Services*, 6, 39–44.

Knutson, B., Rick, S., Wimmer, G. E., Prelec, D., & Loewenstein, G. (2007) Neural predictors of purchases. *Neuron*, 53, 147–156.

Krugman, H. E. (1967) The measurement of advertising involvement. *Public Opinion Quarterly*, 30, 583–596.

Laaksonen, P. (1994) *Consumer Involvement: Concepts and Research*. London, UK: Routledge.

Lastovicka, J. L., & Gardner, D. M. (1979) Components of involvement. In J. C. Maloney & B. Silverman (Eds.) *Attitude Research Plays for High Stakes*, pp. 53–73.Chicago, IL: American Marketing Association.

Lee, N., Broderick, A. J., & Chamberlain, L. (2007) What is neuromarketing? A discussion and agenda for future research. *International Journal of Psychophysiology*, 63(2), 199–204.

Lindstrom, M. (2009) *Buyology: How Everything We Believe about Why We Buy Is Wrong*. London, UK: Random House.

Lovell, C. (2008, 3rd October). Close-up: Live issue—is neuroscience making a difference? *Campaign*. Available at: http://www.campaignlive.co.uk/news/851185/Close-Up-Live-issue-neuroscience-making-difference/?DCMP=ILC-SEARCH

Madan, C. R. (2010) Neuromarketing: The next step in market research? *Eureka*, 1(1), 34–43.

Manolis, C., & Roberts, J. A. (2008) Compulsive buying: Does it matter how it's measured? *Journal of Economic Psychology*, 29, 555–576.

Markus, H. (1977) Self-schemata and processing information about the self. *Journal of Personality and Social Psychology*, 35, 63–78.

McCarty, J. A., & Shrum, L. J. (1993a) The role of personal valuneuromarketing the next step in market researches and demographics in predicting television viewing behaviour: Implications for theory and application. *Journal of Advertising*, 22(4), 77–101.

McCarty, J. A., & Shrum, L. J. (1993b) A structural equation analysis of the relationships of personal values, attitudes and beliefs about recycling, and the recycling of solid waste products. In L. McAlister & M. Rothschild (Eds.) *Advances in Consumer Research*, Vol. 20, pp. 641–646. Provo, UT: Association for Consumer Research.

McCarty, J. A., & Shrum, L. J. (1994) The recycling of solid wastes: personal and cultural values and attitudes about recycling as antecedents of recycling behaviour. *Journal of Business Research*, 30, 53–62.

McClure, S. M., Li, J., Tomlin, D., Cypert, K. S., Montague, L. M., & Montague, P. R. (2004) Neural correlates of behavioural preference for culturally familiar drinks. *Neuron*, 44, 379–387.

McGregor, S., Klingander, B., & Lown, J. (2001) Comparative analysis of Canadian, American and Swedish bankruptcy policy: Why do governments legislate consumer debt? *International Journal of Consumer Studies*, 25(3), 208–227.

McQuarrie, E. F., & Munson, J. M. (1990) A revised product involvement inventory: Improved usability and validity. In J. F. Sherry & B. Sternthal (Eds.) *Advances in Consumer Research*, Vol. 19, pp. 108–115. Provo, UT: Association for Consumer Research.

Michaelidou, N., & Dibb, S. (2008) Consumer involvement: A new perspective. *Marketing Review*, 8(1), 83–99.

Miller, E. K., & Cohen, J. D. (2001) An integrative theory of prefrontal cortex function. *Annual Review of Neuroscience*, 24, 167–202.

Mittal, B. (1989) Measuring purchase decision involvement. *Psychology and marketing*, 6(2), 147–162.

Mittal, B. (1995) A comparative analysis of four scales of consumer involvement. *Psychology and Marketing*, 12(7), 663–682.

Mittal, B., Holbrook, M. B., Beatty, S., Raghubir, P., & Woodside, A. G. (2008) *Consumer Behaviour: How Humans Think, Feel and Act in the Marketplace*. Cincinnati, OH: Open Mentis Publishing Company.

Mittal, B., & Lee, M. S. (1989) A causal model of consumer involvement. *Journal of Economic Psychology*, 10, 363–389.

Munson, J. M. (1984) Personal values: Considerations in their measurement and application to five areas of research inquiry. In R. E. Pitts & G. A. Woodside (Eds.) *Personal Values and Consumer Psychology*, pp. 13–34. Lexington, MA: Lexington Books.

Noar, S. M., Benac, C. N., & Harris, M. S. (2007) Does tailoring matter? Meta-analytic review of tailored print health behaviour change interventions. *Psychological Bulletin*, 133, 673–693.

Ohme, R., Reykowska, D., Wiener, D., & Choromanska, A. (2010) Application of frontal EEG asymmetry to advertising research. *Journal of Economic Psychology*, 31(5), 785–793.

Park, C. W., & Mittal, B. (1985) A theory of involvement in consumer behaviour: Problems and issues. In J. N. Sheth (Ed.) *Research in Consumer Behaviour*, Vol. 1, pp. 201–231. Greenwich, CT: JAI Press.

Petty, R. E., & Cacioppo, J. T. (1981) Issue involvement as a moderator of the effects on attitude of advertising content and context. In K. B. Monroe (Ed.) *Advances in Consumer Research*, Vol. 8, pp. 20–24. Ann Arbor, MI: Association for Consumer Research

Petty, R. E., & Cacioppo, J. T. (1986) *Communication and Persuasion: Central and Peripheral Routes to Attitude Change*. New York, NY: Springer-Verlag.

Pitts, R. E., & Woodside, A. G. (1983) Personal value influences on consumer product class and brand preferences. *Journal of Social Psychology*, 119, 37–53.

Plassmann, H., O'Doherty, J., & Rangel, A. (2007) Orbitofrontal cortex encodes willingness to pay in everyday economic transactions. *Journal of Neuroscience*, 27(37), 9984–9988.

Plassmann, H., O'Doherty, J., Shiv, B., & Rangel, A. (2008) Marketing actions can modulate neutral representations of experienced pleasantness. *Proceedings of the National Academy of Science*, 105, 1050–1054.

Plassmann, H., Zoega Ramsoy, T., Milosavljevic (2012) Branding the brain—a critical review and outlook. *Journal of Consumer Psychology*, 22, 18–36.

Pratkanis, A. R., & Greenwald, A. G. (1988) Recent perspectives on unconscious processing: Still no marketing applications. *Psychology of Marketing*, 5(4), 339–355.

Randal, K. (2011, 25th February) Rise of neurocinema: How Hollywood studios harness your brainwaves to win Oscars. *Fastcompany*. Available at: http://www.fastcompany.com/1731055/rise-neurocinema-how-hollywood-studios-harness-your-brainwaves-win-oscars

Reimann, M., Schilke, O., Weber, B., Neuhaus, C., & Zaichokwsky, J. (2011) Functional magnetic resonance imaging in consumer research: A review and application. *Psychology of Marketing*, 28(6), 608–637.

Renvoise, P., & Morin, C. (2007) *Neuromarketing: Understanding the "Buy Button" in Your Customer's Brain*. Nashville, TN: Thomas Nelson, Inc.

Richardson, P., Dick, A., & Jain, A. K. (1994) Extrinsic and intrinsic cue effects on perceptions of store brand quality. *Journal of Marketing*, 58(4), 28–36.

Richins, M. L. (2004) The material values scale: Measurement properties and development of a short form. *Journal of Consumer Research*, 31, 209–219.

Richins, M. L., & Bloch P. H. (1986) After the new years off: The temporal context of product involvement. *Journal of Consumer Research*, 3, 280–285.

Riedl, R., Hubert, M., & Kenning, P. (2010) Are there neural gender differences in online trust? An fMRI study on the perceived trustworthiness of eBay offers. *MIS Quarterly*, 34(2), 397–428.

Roberts, J. A., Manolis, C., & Tanner, J. F. (2003) Family structure, materialism, and compulsive buying: A re-inquiry of Rindfleisch et al. *Journal of the Academy of Marketing Science*, 31, 300–311.

Rothschild, M. L. (1979) Advertising strategies for high and low involvement situations. In J. C. Maloney & B. Silverman (Eds.) *Attitude Research Plays for High Stakes*, pp. 74–83. Chicago, IL: American Marketing Association.

Rothschild, M. L. (1984) Perspectives on involvement: Current problems and future definitions. In T. C. Kinnear (Ed.) *Advances in Consume Research*, Vol. 11, pp. 216–217. Provo, UT: Association for Consumer Research.

Schaefer, M., & Rotte, M. (2007) Favourite brands as cultural objects modulate reward circuit. *Neuroreport*, 18(2), 141–145.

Sherif, C. W., Sherif, M., & Nebergall, R. (1965) *Attitude and Attitude Change: The Social Judgement-Involvement Approach*. Philadelphia, PA: Saunders.

Shrum, L. J., & McCarty, J. A. (1992) Individual differences in differentiation in the rating of personal values: The role of private self-consciousness. *Personality and Social Psychology Bulletin*, 18, 223–230.

Shrum, L. J., & McCarty, J. A. (1997) Issues involving the relationship between personal values and consumer behaviour: Theory, methodology and application. In L. R. Kahle & L. Chiagouris (Eds.) *Values, Lifestyles and Psychographics*, pp. 139–160. Mahwah, NJ: Lawrence Erlbaum Associates, Ch. 7.

Shrum, L. J., McCarty, J. A., & Loeffler, T. L. (1990) Individual differences in value stability: Are we really tapping true values? In M. E. Goldberg, G. Gorn, & R. W. Pollay (Eds.) *Advances in Consumer Research*, Vol.17, pp. 609–615. Provo, UT: Association for Consumer Research.

Slama, M. E., & Tashchian, A. (1985) Selected socio-economic and demographic characteristics associated with purchasing involvement. *Journal of Marketing*, 49, 72–82.

Snyder, M., & DeBono, K. G. (1985) Appeals to image and claims about quality: Understanding the psychology of advertising. *Journal of Personality and Social Psychology*, 49, 586–597.

Stone, R. N. (1984) The marketing characteristics of involvement. In T. C. Kinnear (Ed.) *Advances in Consumer Research*, Vol. 11, pp. 210–215. Provo, UT: Association for Consumer Research.

Vecchiato, G., Kong, W., Maglione, A. G., & Wei, D. (2012) Understanding the impact of TV commercials. *IEEE Pulse Magazine*, 3(3), 42–47.

Venkatraman, V., Clithero, J. A., Fitzsimons, G. J., & Huertel, S. A. (2012) New scanner data for brand marketers: How neuroscience can help better understand differences in brand preferences. *Journal of Consumer Psychology*, 22(1), 143–153.

Wheeler, S. C., Petty, R. E., & Bizer, G. Y. (2005) Self-schema matching and attitude change: Situational and dispositional determinants of message elaboration. *Journal of Consumer Research*, 31, 787–797.

Wicker, A. (1971) An examination of the 'other variables' explanation of attitude-behaviour inconsistency. *Journal of Personality and Social Psychology*, 19, 18–20.

Zaichkowsky, J. L. (1994) The personal involvement inventory: Reduction, revision and application to advertising. *Journal of Advertising*, 23(4), 59–70.

9 Practicalities, Pros, and Cons of Psychological Profiling

Early consumer markets were uncomplicated. Most markets operated on a local basis, with local suppliers of specific commodities and services providing a source of supply to local consumers. Often, the idea of competition was completely absent. Consumers turned to a single supplier for a specific type of product. Most commodities for everyday consumption and for home making were not just locally bought, but also locally sourced. With the evolution of technology, industrial development took place that resulted in the migration of mass populations from rural to urban areas. Technology increased productivity and improved transportation and communications systems. Populations grew in size and became more densely concentrated within specific geographic locations. These locations were not self-sufficient as sources of the production of all the day-to-day items people needed. People grew accustomed to making purchases of products that were no longer made locally. Furthermore, product variants expanded giving purchasers of specific product ranges more choices.

These changes meant that consumers needed more information to help them to decide between different sources of supply and product variants. Because most of these supply sources were non-local, it was not possible for consumers to inspect the premises and production infrastructures of suppliers. They therefore needed a different type of information that would nonetheless give them confidence in the authenticity and quality of specific product variants.

Against this backdrop, further changes in consumerism occurred. Consumers developed idiosyncratic tastes and preferences. Product variants were identified and differentiated through their branding. Different brands established their own consumer fan bases. Brands were defined not simply in terms of the functions of the products they described: these labels carried symbolic meanings that attached distinct social status attributes, lifestyle aspirations, and 'personality' profiles to specific product variants that shaped their 'image'. Consumers could therefore use 'brands' to make statements about themselves. Consumption was no longer governed just by base drives, but also by higher-order needs linked to social standing and personal identity.

Manufacturers and service suppliers also recognised that they did not need to try to supply their wares to everyone. Instead, it might be economically more effective to aim at specific consumer categories that had emerged as the heaviest users of whatever they were selling; hence, the notion of "target marketing" emerged (Gunter & Furnham, 1992). As products and services diversified and became defined through brands, they acquired a range of attributes beyond what they were originally developed to provide to consumers. Consumers then came to define themselves through the purchases they made. When everyone needed to go to the same production source for a basic commodity such as food, they were all in the same category as consumers. As food types evolved and specific food items derived from more diverse sources of supply with different packaging and pricing and in turn recognisably different quality levels and accompanying price levels, so consumers faced more choices. The choices they made might initially have reflected their relative affluence, but in time came also to signify their individual taste.

Target marketing meant that producers and suppliers needed to understand these more subtle features of consumers. Consumer populations needed to be divided into different sub-groups and types according to the characteristics important to a broader understanding of the consumption behaviours. Segmentation was initially based on the most visible characteristics of consumers, such as their gender, their age, where they lived, and how much money they had to spend. Later, it became apparent that consumers could be differentiated purely in terms of their purchase patterns. Thus, in addition to geographical and demographic segmentation, consumer behaviour patterns could be adapted to yield 'behavioural segments'.

During the 20th century, consumer marketplaces, marketing techniques, and market research methods all evolved. Consumer research developed more and more elaborate typologies based on geographic, demographic, and life stage factors. These typologies were given eye-catching acronyms such as MOSAIC, SAGACITY, and SuperProfiles. Each attempted to represent normative population segments and they were often linked to census data to yield population-wide segments for which population distributions were known (Gunter & Furnham, 1992). These market segments represented purely descriptive attributes of consumer populations. As markets grew increasingly complex, marketers needed to go beyond simply describing market characteristics. They needed to know why consumers developed brand preferences, reacted favourably or unfavourably to advertising campaigns, and bought specific product variants. They needed to understand consumers' thought processes, emotions, motives, and behavioural choices. This meant turning to the discipline of psychology.

The Application of Psychology

The application of psychological techniques to consumer segmentation has been promoted as helping marketers develop a better understanding of the needs and concerns of consumers as well as of the way they recognise attributes of products and services, define the meanings of brands, and utilise these different elements to guide their purchase decisions. These techniques can also yield measures that can form the basis of the definition of different consumer categories and communities or groups and sub-groups that give a specific product market its form. Such classifications are not simply descriptions, but are grounded in processes that can play an active role in determining consumer choices and behaviour. They can also provide insights into how consumers might respond to marketing campaigns and specific promotional messages.

In practical terms, the use of 'psychographics' can help marketers identify target markets, to describe and explain consumers' choices, and to guide the ways they market their wares. Marketers must think carefully about whether to use psychographics. Do they elect to buy off-the-shelf datasets that have already defined consumer populations? Do they conduct their own research to develop psychographic typologies that are linked to consumers and their behaviour in relation to a specified demographic group or product range or even more closely targeted at a specific brand?

Put simply, marketers should not profile consumers for the sake if it, but should do so with a clear purpose in mind. It is important to consider the psychological dimensions and other segmentation criteria that have the most relevance for each specific business application. One approach is to cast the net wide initially in the way consumers are defined and then narrow down segmentation options following a step-wise process that might begin with a theoretical review of the phenomenon in need of explanation and then follows through with a series of empirical tests of measurement instruments that provide valid and reliable indicators of key variables (Miller, 2009).

Marketers (and researchers) should ask a number of specific questions about segmentation procedures and models. How robust and useful are specific segmentation methods in terms of providing added value to marketing campaigns? How valid and reliable are off-the-shelf consumer profiling typologies? Are established psychological tests, initially developed outside the marketing field, relevant to the prediction of consumer behaviour? Do supposedly normative lifestyle-type systems truly and accurately represent the populations they were built to classify? Do the consumer classifications provided by lifestyle-linked models have validity as predictors of consumer tastes, choices, and behaviour? Do established personality dimensions provide useful predictors or indicators of consumers' attitudes and behaviours? How important is it to develop robust psychographic tools from which population-wide normative data can be obtained? These are important questions for marketers intent on utilising consumer profiling grounded in psychology. This chapter discusses them with reference to relevant empirical evidence from the rest of the book.

Pros and Cons

The idea that psychological measures could be used to classify consumers emerged in the 1930s but took prominence in the 1960s. Professional marketers took their lead from wartime researchers who were interested in the study of how audiences responded to mediated messages, whether these were designed specifically for persuasive purposes or had more general information or entertainment aims. Part of this effort focused on what motivated people to turn their attention to specific mediated content, whether it was presented to them in print form, through sound broadcasts, or on film or video. Another part of this area of study was concerned with the way people subsequently reacted after exposure to mediated, persuasive content. How did they process the information? Did they accept it at face value? Were they likely to make conscious changes to their beliefs, attitudes, and behaviours as a result of that exposure?

There has been much debate about how beliefs, attitudes, and intentions can be developed, changed, and used to shape behaviour. Psychologists have developed numerous models to explain these processes, from attribution theory (Hewstone, Fincham & Jaspars, 1983), balance theory (Heider, 1958), conformity theory (Asch, 1956), congruity theory (Osgood & Tannenbaum 1955), dissonance theory (Festinger, 1957), expectancy value theory (Eccles, 1983), theory of reasoned action (Fishbein & Ajzen, 1975; 2010), and the theory of planned behaviour (Madden, Ellen & Ajzen, 1992; Ajzen, 2011). The latest models, such as the theory of planned behaviour, have been broadly regarded as providing the most comprehensive model for the analysis of these psychological processes. While these models were not devised for consumer profiling purposes, they have indicated that internalised cognitive structures such as attitudes and beliefs, which can differentiate consumers, are in turn linked to behavioural outcomes. The efficacy of this model can also be tempered by other factors including social experience and individual differences between people that can shape their propensities to develop certain kinds of beliefs and attitudes in the first place (Armitage & Conner, 2001; Sutton, 2002).

A further question that emerged was whether certain motivations or reactions were universal or whether people differed in their interests in and reactions to specific marketing or promotional messages. If they did differ, what kinds of differences were most important in the context of how they used or reacted to specific media or commodities? There were, of course, the standard population classifiers—or demographics. However, these variables were descriptive rather than explanatory. If the aim is to understand why specific groups of people react to a promotional campaign in a certain way, why does this happen? Why do other people react to the same messages differently? Why are some campaigns accepted, whereas others are rejected? There must be something going on inside people's heads that relates to the way they process information and make judgements about content that then determines how they subsequently think, feel, or behave. In invoking phenomena such as thoughts and behaviours, we are entering the realm of psychology. In makes perfect sense, therefore, that any consumer classification or segmentation systems that are founded on principles of measurement that are guided by the psychological reactions of people to media or marketing campaigns should adopt psychological variables as people classifiers.

In developing a psychology-based system of consumer classification, marketers sought a system that could identify 'types' that could be measured in a standardised fashion. In some instances, these 'types' were developed in relation to the use of one specific product range. The idea here was principally to understand the motives or reasons consumers had for using a specific commodity and also the expectations they had of it. In addition, there was an interest in developing a consumer typology that could be mapped onto entire consumer populations rather than just on those consumers who purchased a particular product or service. The adoption of a methodology that could generate population-wide data could result in the production of normative distribution data for consumer types based on generic psychological classifiers. Such classifiers would have a similar status to demographics but with an additional explanatory dimension that would enable marketers to understand not just that one consumer type was especially likely to be a user of product class A, but also why. The term '*psycho*graphics' was coined to underline this notion that they were analogous to *demo*graphics, but with this extra dimension.

As we have seen, some psychographic measures were custom-built by marketers for the purpose of defining and segmenting consumer populations. Other measures were adopted from personality profilers that were not originally developed for marketing applications. The former tended to be influenced by the disciplines of anthropology and sociology as well as by psychology and classified consumers according to 'lifestyle' types. These types embraced not simply psychological variables, but also demographic elements (especially ones associated with the definition of the demographic compound classifier of 'life stage') and cultural variables such as values. The latter comprised personality variables such as extraversion, neuroticism, conscientiousness, internal-external locus of control, sensation seeking, masculinity/femininity, and many others.

Research with product-specific psychological typing approaches has yielded evidence that these measures of consumer types can help marketers to understand more about their customers and what the attributes of their product variant (or brand) are that people like or dislike. Research with population-wide psychological classifiers of consumer segments has generated less clear-cut evidence of this sort. The key questions for consideration here therefore are:

(1) How useful are generic consumer segmentation types based on psychological variables?
(2) Does psychology work best when consumer classifications are linked to specific product types?

(3) Do custom-built consumer types work better than the adoption of generic personality types originally developed for non-marketing applications?

Generic Types Versus Product-Specific Types

Most psychographic research has adopted psychological techniques to measure consumer types for specific product or service ranges. These measures have been deployed to understand the reasons why consumers prefer one brand over another or to determine whether some consumers are more demanding or fussy than others in their expectations. Some psychographic research has been more ambitious and has sought to find ways of generating psychology-based maps of entire consumer populations, independent of any product/service types. A further differentiating characteristic of psychographic research is that whether generic or product specific, some researchers have developed consumer typology measures from scratch, whereas others have adapted established measures of human personality that were originally developed for clinical diagnostic or other scientific purposes.

There has been a great deal of debate about psychographic measures in marketing and no consensus point of view has emerged, at least from within the academic world. Commercially, psychographics have been utilised in many product and service marketing research contexts, although demographics remains a staple diet for most marketers and market researchers when they seek to deconstruct datasets by population classifiers.

Generic psychological classifiers have not been as widely used as product/service-specific psychological measures of consumers. Certainly the dearth of population data based on normative psychology-based consumer classifiers has meant that psychographic variables cannot be used in the same way as demographic variables to establish quotas for population sampling. Even though some lifestyle measures, such as the iterations of the VALS system, were tested on large samples designed to establish their population-wide distributions, these normative data were not as robust as equivalent data derived from censuses for demographic category distributions.

Hence, for critics of psychographics, normative psychological types have little value as marketing tools because there is no comprehensive evidence concerning how distinctive and widely distributed these types are. Given the limited evidence on the predictive validity of these generic types in relation to consumer preferences and purchase patterns, it is questionable as to whether they add much more value to demographic classifiers.

Proponents of psychographics have argued that even though psychological classifiers of consumers cannot provide precise predictions of product and service choices, they can narrow down the probable choices that might be made beyond those that might derive from demographics. Moreover, because psychographics use consumer types that are grounded in the psychological reasons why specific product or service choices might be made, they go beyond simple descriptions of consumers and provide explanations for why certain product/service/brand choices are made. This level of understanding about how consumers psychologically engage with products and services and with brands can provide important insights for marketers in how to adjust their promotional campaigns for specific brands to ensure that they provide incentives known to be valued most by potential users.

Acceptance of Psychographics: Changing Times

Psychographics emerged across the 1960s and 1970s, and was critiqued by some marketing scholars almost from the start. Major reviews of early research evidence presented a number of challenges to the proponents of psychographics (see Wells, 1974; Wind, 1978). Many of these criticisms were levelled against custom-built measures. Many custom-built segmentation schemes were regarded as little more than additional descriptors of consumer populations that emerged from statistical analyses of selected attitudinal and belief items. The consumer types were statistical creations, but were often not underpinned by a robust psychological theory from which valid and reliable explanations of human behaviour would usually derive (Pernica, 1974; Wind & Green, 1974; Wells, 1975).

The fact that some psychographic types offer novel, rich, and intriguing descriptions of consumers does not automatically equate to a valid explanation of consumer behaviour or offer high predictive validity in terms of future consumer product/service choices or brand preferences (Wells, 1974).

There was some evidence early on that lifestyles and value measures could provide broad statistical indications of consumers' behaviour patterns that went beyond what would be revealed by demographics alone. However, the predictive performance of generic psychographic types in pinpointing consumer choices was often weak and therefore offered little advantage to marketers who invested in them (Wells & Tigert, 1971; Frank, Massey & Wind, 1972).

Taking the last point further, some critics observed that in its attempt to provide classification variables covering entire consumer populations, psychographics merely provided a further layer of description over demographics that triggered further questions that needed additional exploration before segmentation definitions could be reached that would have direct links to consumer outcomes (Hustad & Pessemeier, 1974; Wind & Green, 1974).

Another important gap in early psychographic research was that it failed to recognise the complexity of consumer decision-making when confronted with a product range comprising a number of competing brands. Consumers weight up products and product variants in terms of a number of attributes. They are often confronted with different promotional messages for competing brands, which they experience in different mediated and non-mediated settings. These messages as well as the brands themselves are evaluated at a number of levels defined by their functionality, novelty and distinctiveness, performance, and outcomes against expectations. Psychological classifiers must be able to explain how consumers might react at these different levels to provide truly accurate and precise predictors of purchase outcomes. Early models of psychographics lacked this sophistication (Wind, 1978).

There was a sense that the initial success of psychographic measures and the enthusiasm with which they were adopted by the business world derived mainly from their novelty value. They provided brand marketers with richer descriptions of their consumers than standard demographics, which, in comparison, are rather dry. Extended descriptions of apparent thought processes and feelings that consumers experienced in relation to commodities and services provided their manufacturers and suppliers with more tangible images of who their consumers really were.

Knowing that your primary customers are women partially narrows down your choices in how to promote and package your brand, but knowing also that they are women who are self-assured, outgoing, sociable, crave personal achievement, and like to wear premium brands as signals of their personal taste to impress others gives a much richer impression of the type of person you need to be thinking about when designing your brand messages. However, if you wished, you could use this information to plot a media-buying campaign that ensured that brand promotions were placed in media locations most likely to deliver that psychographic type.

At the time when psychographics was emergent, there was a sense that many adopters embraced this approach because others were doing likewise. Subjective judgements were swayed by the appeal of rich and almost biographical descriptions of human personalities among brand developers and distributors. Many users perceived that they needed this new methodology, but they could not always give a clear, scientific reason as to why psychographics added significantly to demographics to aiding with key marketing decisions.

As William D. Wells observed:

> From the speed with which psychographics have diffused through the marketing community, it seems obvious that they are perceived as meeting a keenly felt need. The problem now is not so much one of pioneering as it is one of sorting out the techniques that work best. As that process proceeds, it seems extremely likely that psychographic methods will gradually become more familiar and less controversial, and eventually will merge into the mainstream of marketing research.
>
> (Wells, 1975, p. 209)

It is clear that the early application of psychology to consumerism was met with suspicion. Attempts to understand what people think suggested that marketers were interested in trying to manipulate people into buying things they did not necessarily need. It painted a picture of a world in which marketers sought to control people's actions without them necessarily knowing what was happening at the time. Any such conclusions, however, represented gross overreactions to the truth of what was happening. While marketers were acquiring persuasive techniques through which they could influence decisions made by consumers, they never had total control over their targets.

Ultimately, consumers could make up their own minds about products and services, about what they liked and did not like, and even about whether advertising campaigns were credible. The challenge for marketers was not to take total control over consumers, but rather to persuade them to decide for themselves to opt for one brand over another. There was recognition of the truism that no brand could expect to please everyone. Maybe it did not need to be in order to be a viable business proposition. It simply needed to establish a lucrative enough niche market to be sufficiently profitable to sustain itself. To give their brand an edge, marketers needed to get into the minds of target consumers enough to increase the probability that they would like the marketed brand over its rivals.

Evaluating Psychographics

Like any other marketing or social scientific research tool, psychographics can add value or not, depending upon how it is done. Marketers need to know that psychological measures are reliable and valid indicators of the variables they purport to measure. They also need to utilise the knowledge that psychology can provide to know how to construct a brand image and promotional messages around it that resonate with the interests, aspirations, and personalities of the target consumers.

The concept of *reliability* is important in social scientific and market research. It generally refers to the ability of a specific scale to produce consistent results when it purports to measure some permanent psychological aspect of a person. Thus, if an individual is scored high on extraversion on one occasion, and extraversion is conceived to be a relatively unchanging characteristic, then it is expected that that person will score high on that scale if measured again six months or a year later. If a scale that is designed to measure a permanent attribute of a consumer exhibits scoring volatility over time, such that the score a respondent receives at time 1 does not resemble the score received at time 2, then it has low reliability and must be regarded as either a poor indicator of that psychological construct or as showing that the construct itself cannot be regarded as a lasting attribute of a person's psychological makeup.

The failure to achieve high reliability does not necessarily invalidate the usefulness of a psychological scale in a marketing research context. Some psychological measures signal cognitive or emotional responses that are ephemeral or temporary and might be situation specific. Public attitudes and beliefs, for example, represent psychological responses that can and often do change over time.

One reason for this is that these cognitive constructs are dependent on the individual's latest experiences. So, for example, whether or not an individual likes a specific variant of a product (i.e., brand) or whether or not he or she believes it is one of the best-performing and value-for-money product variants of its type can be influenced by their most recent experience with that brand. If they had previously been satisfied by the brand's performance, they would develop positive beliefs about it and like it (i.e., positive attitude). If during their last experience with the brand, it failed to live up to its usual expectations, their beliefs about it and any accompanying attitudes might change.

In the case of psychographics, whether they derive from clinically or empirically developed personality research outside a consumer context or custom-built consumer-related psychological construct research, there is an expectation that the characteristics being measured have a degree of permanence about them. This means that an individual consumer will exhibit similar personality trait/lifestyle type scores and profiles over time. This phenomenon is known as test-retest reliability. This reliability is usually expressed as a coefficient (i.e., a score along a range from zero to 1.0).

Past research has shown that custom-built psychographic measures have exhibited equivocal performance on test-retest reliability tests. In one investigation of 16 psychographic variables, 11 were found to have high test-retest reliability scores (i.e., a reliability coefficient of 0.70 of higher). None had reliability coefficients lower than 0.59 (Tigert, 1969). In this study, the kinds of psychographic dimensions that exhibited high test-retest reliability were fashion-consciousness, propensity to monitor own weight, and propensity to look for premium price offers. A subsequent test of psychographic items found test-retest coefficients similar in magnitude, between 0.60 and 0.69 (Bruno & Pessemeier, 1972).

Elsewhere, similar empirical exercises with psychographic measures yielded poorer reliability scores In one study, these scores varied between 0.40 and 0.60 (Villani & Lehmann, 1975). In another study, only half the psychographic items used demonstrated consistency in the responses they triggered from the same respondents over two tests conducted one year apart. A quarter of the items gave rise to clearly highly changeable responses (Burns & Harrison, 1979). Such findings do not mean that psychographic measures have no value. It does mean that researchers need to take care with the individual scales they use to represent specific psychological constructs to differentiate between scales that provide robust and stable indicators of lasting traits and those that measure temporary mood states of situation-specific responses. These two types of items should not be aggregated into factors that purport to measure permanent characteristics of consumers. Both types of items could have value in consumer research contexts, but they represent different types of psychological measurements that have different meanings in terms of how they might help us understand consumer's tastes, preferences, and choices.

These observations are important and for some researchers, they signal that psychographics could often turn out to be a blunt instrument for measuring and predicting consumers' choices. Brands have meaning for consumers that derive from personal experiences, the shared experiences of other consumers, and marketing promotional messages. The surface, functional, and symbolic characteristics that can define a brand's image are internalised by consumers as memories that might comprise past experiences with the product variant and its performance, positive, negative and neutral recommendations about the brand from other consumers, evaluations of those recommendations and their sources, memories of claims about the brand in brand promotions and comparisons between these claims and personal experience, and other factors. Many of these brand perceptions and memories can change over time as fresh brand-related experiences generate new information about the brand. Such is the complexity and potential volatility of these psychological variables that they can prove elusive in terms of their predictability by psychographic factors alone (Bass, 1974).

A further aspect of reliability in psychographic research is concerned with the consistency of intertrait relationships. Statistical tests can be used to show whether one psychological construct is systematically related to another. Thus, taking two constructs, is a high score on one usually associated with a high score or a low score on the other? Does this positive or negative relationship consistently achieve significance and display the same direction from one consumer sample to another and from one point in time to another with the same sample of consumers? These relationships are important as further indicators of psychological construct stability and reliability (Pessemeier & Bruno, 1971).

Psychological construct *validity* is another important test of its potential marketing value. Validity is a distinct concept from reliability, although the two are linked and test-retest reliability is an indication of whether a specific construct has a lasting structure that might in turn strengthen confidence that it really does measure what it says it does. Hence, a valid construct should behave the same way across many independent samples, unless it is known from the outset to be culture specific. The items that are used to measure the construct should consistently exhibit high levels of intercorrelation across samples and studies, again confirming that what the construct is actually measuring is unwavering. The validity of a psychological construct also derives from its ability consistently to predict, in a significant way, specific outcomes.

Despite what was said above about the relationship between reliability and validity, it is quite possible for a set of measures to demonstrate reliability over time and yet fail to measure in a valid way the construct they purport to measure. Even quite early on in the development of custom-built psychographic systems based on lifestyles and values, evidence emerged that some lifestyle factors could demonstrate consistency in their emergence over different consumer samples, but only some could accurately and significantly predict consumer behaviour outcomes and hence in that respect, they lacked validity (Lastovicka, 1982; Lesser & Hughes, 1986).

The validity of a construct therefore can be demonstrated if it is consistently found to be unrelated to constructs it should not be related to (because it measures something completely different) and if it can effectively predict specific outcomes it purports to explain (Pessemeier & Bruno, 1971; Bruno & Pessemeier, 1972). Thus, if we would normally expect people high in extraversion to be high on sensation-seeking and found that some items purporting to be measures of extraversion exhibited a negative relationship to sensation-seeking, this might lead us to question whether those items truly belonged on an instrument designed to measure extraversion. Equally, if we would expect, from theoretical and past empirical work, that people who score high on extraversion are generally much more likely than introverts to prefer products coloured red, and found that a new set of scales we tested for measurement of extraversion/introversion did not differentiate between consumers who preferred red products, we might be led to ask once again whether this new instrument really did measure that personality dimension.

In marketing research, original sets of attitude and belief scales are frequently constructed by researchers to represent specific psychological responses to products/services and their variants. As heuristic or purely descriptive devices, these types of items can serve relevant purposes for marketing professionals seeking to find out the current status of their brands, particularly if comparisons are made with rivals. These measures provide insights that have relevance in the moment in which or at best, for a temporary period after, they were obtained. They should not be treated as measures of lasting psychological characteristics of consumers even when developed purely as a product-specific typology.

In the psychological literature, personality scales are accompanied by handbooks that instruct users in the proper application, scoring, and interpretation of the scales. Empirical studies will also usually be cited that have pre-tested the scales and established not only the existence of stable psychological constructs, but also validation exercises that confirm that these scales measure specific psychological characteristics.

The Need for Validation: A Case Example

Within commercial market research, market segmentation scales based on measures of attitudes, beliefs, motivations, or intentions have been developed and, in some instances, distributed internationally. One of the best known of these instruments is the Target Group Index (TGI). This survey was originally established in the United Kingdom by British Market

Research Bureau in 1969 but has spread across more than 60 countries worldwide. The survey is currently run by Kantar Media.[1]

The TGI collects data across a range of topics, such as food, diet and health, DIY and home, luxury/status goods, travel/holidays, personal appearance, drink, finance, and others. For each topic, a number of what are called "attitudinal statements" is presented to respondents, who are invited to score their level of agreement usually on a five-point scale (definitely agree, tend to agree, neither agree nor disagree, tend to disagree, definitely disagree). In fact, the items that make up typical TGI item batteries ask people about their attitudes, beliefs, motivations, and activities. The Index is a comparison of a target group against a specific benchmark group. The latter is generally the average score for the entire population. The extent to which specific sub-groups defined by consumer type or product category depart from a pre-defined benchmark is indicated by the Index score. The benchmark (or average) is fixed at 100 and the Index can be a score above or below that mark. A score above the benchmark means that the target being assessed has a stronger tendency than average on that dimension, whereas a score below 100 means it has a weaker tendency than average.

The TGI has been rolled out internationally and used to generate cross-national comparisons on the same measures. One example of this application is Kantar's survey of over 60 countries for its "What Makes the World's Consumers Tick 2014" research (Kantar Media, 2014; available at: http://tgi.kantarmedia.com/international/news-insights/what-makes-worlds-consumers-tick). Consumers' responses to 18 commodity/service sectors covering around 400 product groups and 3,000 brands were obtained. Structure is given to the massive battery of data through the use of statistical techniques such as cluster analysis to produce smaller numbers of response categories often linked to specific product types.

The psychological constructs represented by TGI items, however, vary. Some items comprise attitudes (e.g., 'I enjoy eating foreign food', 'I really enjoy cooking', 'I like taking risks'). Some items represent beliefs (e.g., 'Money is the best measure of success', 'It is important to respect traditional customs and beliefs', 'I look on the work I do as a career rather than just a job'). Other items represent intentions (e.g., 'I want to get to the very top in my career', 'I would be prepared to pay more for environmentally friendly products').

Some items represent broad cultural values or norms (e.g., 'A woman's place is in the home', 'If at first you do not succeed you must keep trying', 'You should seize opportunities in life when they arise'). In models such as the theory of planned behaviour, for instance, 'attitudes', 'beliefs', and 'intentions' are conceived as distinct psychological entities that have specific roles to play in shaping behaviour patterns towards objects (Ajzen, 1985). The distinct psychological implications of these different constructs are not recognised by the TGI survey and could represent a further layering of the data in terms of how specific measures are used in analyses and in turn related to other variables measured by other data sources that might be integrated with TGI measures.

Validity of Personality Measures in Consumer Contexts

The same standards of reliability and validity testing must be applied to psychographic scales that have been developed to classify consumer populations as a whole or communities of consumers known to purchase specific product or service types. Furthermore, if marketing researchers decide to utilise established psychological tests rather than build their own from scratch, they must still conduct pre-tests into the ability of those scales to operate effectively in the consumer domain. Most psychological tests of personality have not been developed in marketing contexts. This means that while they may have 'validity' as classification instruments, for example, in clinical settings, if that is where they were originally developed, it should not be assumed that they will exhibit equal validity in a different applied setting, such as that of measuring consumers.

Marketing decisions based on psychographic data must therefore be preceded by tests that evaluate the ability of specific psychological tests and their constructs to represent valid and reliable measures that measure characteristics of consumers known to predict their consumer-related reactions and responses. These principles apply both to generic lifestyle/personality measure applications and to those applied to markets for specific product/service types.

It is important to recognise that reliability and validity might not be enough to guarantee success with psychographics. It has been noted already that reliability does not equal validity, but it is usually an important precursor. Validity might be demonstrated by a specific psychological construct having been tested against other established constructs or in relation to behavioural responses in non-consumer contexts. Thus, even when a psychological construct or 'psychographic' does have this kind of pre-test history, it is wise to err on the side of caution and conduct further tests if that psychological variable is an unknown quantity in terms of its proven ability to add meaning to specific types of consumerism (Jacoby, 1971a).

Ultimately, the use of psychological measures to predict consumer outcomes cannot be done haphazardly. There must be good theoretical and logical reasons for using a specific personality inventory to understand the market for particular products and services or even to indicate broad consumerist orientations. In the absence of clear theoretical reasons that might indicate in advance the potential relevance of specific personality scales to certain types of consumer behaviour, the only likely outcome is results that lack any statistical or social significance or cannot be interpreted in meaningful ways.

Several early studies that experimented with personality measures as consumer behaviour predictors when those scales had no history of application of this sort and had not originally been developed as market segmentation tools struck blanks precisely because the researchers had given no advance consideration to their possible relevance in this context. One personality inventory called the Edwards Personal Preference Schedule measures traits such as the need for autonomy, dominance, and order. Researchers tried using this instrument to understand the market for toilet tissue choices and found that it was unable to differentiate consumers meaningfully (Advertising Research Foundation, 1964).

In another study, the same Edwards inventory was found to be unable to differentiate between owners of Chevrolet and owners of Ford Motor vehicles (Evans, 1959). Other researchers found that other personality measures developed outside the marketing context were unable to predict propensities to make impulse purchases or try new products (Kollat & Willett, 1960; Robertson & Myers, 1969).

These investigations showed that psychographics cannot be used in a random way to understand consumer markets. It is important that marketers and others who might use these tools in consumer behaviour contexts develop a thorough understanding of different personality scales and what they were originally developed to measure. It is also essential to develop an understanding of the psychological theories that underpin each personality scale and provide explanations of why it might be relevant to the prediction of specific classes of behaviour. This preparatory work is needed even before pilot fieldwork is attempted. It will usually save time and expenses in the development of psychographic toolkits and will increase the likelihood that relevant measures are used that will yield usable data.

New Trends

Various emerging trends can be tracked during the 21st century that have taken the form of evolved and new forms of consumer market segmentation. While some of these trends have grown out of technology developments that have made them necessary or opened up the possibility of their existence, all have tended to be underpinned by consumer psychology, whereas commercial market segmentation has continued to be populated by agency-developed- and-owned consumer research instruments that can yield custom-built psychographic typologies.

One of the most widely used of these is the Target Group Index. As discussed earlier, this service collects and regularly updates data from very large consumer samples from around the world about many product and service categories. Clients can construct their own consumer types if they wish and commission relevant analyses from the supplier agency. The instrument used here tends not to differentiate between psychological constructs such as attitudes, beliefs, intentions, and behaviour, nor are its consumer types underpinned by any theory from which explanations might emerge of the efficacy of specific consumer segments as indicators of consumer brand preferences or purchase behaviour patterns.

The need to use psychological instruments that measure individual differences by enduring psychological (or personality) constructs that offer the potential of explaining why different consumers exhibit distinctive brand likes and dislikes, different reactions to advertising campaigns, and different product purchase patterns has led marketers increasingly to explore established personality tests. These tests provide extensively tested and validated measures of human personality dimensions that are known to underpin enduring behavioural dispositions.

One problem for marketers in using these tests, for a long time, was that there were so many of them that measured many different personality characteristics. A second problem was that no normative data existed for them in terms of the population-wide distribution of specific personality types. During the last decade of the 20th century, a broader consensus was reached among psychologists about the personality dimensions that were conceived to be the most significant in defining the human character. Five factors emerged: Extraversion, Conscientiousness, Agreeableness, Openness, and Neuroticism. Then, initial attempts were made to establish normative data for these personality dimensions.

The absence of normative data akin to demographic profiling for the psychological measures determined by the Big Five Personality Inventory is an issue that has been taken up, with recent inroads being made in establishing nationwide profiles in the United States. As reported in Chapter 2, Rentfrow et al (2013) surveyed 48 American states and collected personality data for nearly 1.6 million people. This exercise was carried out over more than ten years, starting in 1999. Five surveys were deployed and these used different versions of the personality inventory devised to measure the five core personality types: Agreeableness, Conscientiousness, Extraversion, Neuroticism, and Openness to experience. The entire exercise was also enhanced because it collected geographic, demographic, religious, political, health status, and crime data. State personality profiles were created alongside more traditional geo-demographic data. This type of exercise will need to be repeated, as with a population establishment exercise, because consumer populations are in a constant state of flux. The development of validated, shorter, and therefore more manageable personality inventories and the emergence of an online population that now represents most social groups has created more economical methods for the administration of this complex consumer profiling exercise.

How useful the 'Big Five' will prove to be as a generic psychology-based model of consumer segmentation remains to be seen. It is probably asking too much of it that it should be able to explain significant amounts of variance in purchase levels down to specific brands. Evidence has emerged, however, that the five personality factors might be able to explain the effectiveness of marketing promotions. The growing body of research into personalising persuasive messages has revealed that brand promotions that use arguments and presentation styles that resonate well with specific consumer personality types could prove to be more effective with those consumer types. For example, messages devised to make different appeals for the same product according the personality type of targeted consumers (e.g., extraverts versus introverts and consumers high versus low in the need for cognition, which is linked to conscientiousness) proved to be differentially effective, exhibiting strong appeal to the consumer type for which they were written (Kaptein, Markopoulos, de Ruyter & Aarts, 2015).

Unobtrusive Consumer Profiling: Getting the Right Tools

The field of text or data mining has grown massively in a short period of time and has yielded many techniques and methods of data classification and analysis. There are tools established by major commercial players in the online world, especially the dominant search engines such as Google, Yahoo, and Bing. The biggest social media and micro-blogging sites such as Facebook and Twitter have also developed their own user-monitoring metrics. In the context of the measurement of meanings and opinions that are expressed in the online world, however, there are many independently developed toolkits, many produced by researchers working in universities, under the broad heading of computer-assisted qualitative data analysis software. Historically, the earliest versions of these techniques date back to the pre-Internet era and were used to assess unstructured data produced by qualitative social research involving in-depth interviews with participants that yielded verbal transcripts and ethnographic research that produced descriptive field notes of naturally occurring events and settings (Fielding & Lee, 1998).

One of the key developments in computer science that has underpinned much of this work is natural language processing (NLP). This entails the production of algorithms or grammatical rules written into computer software programmes that can then read and make sense of open verbal text. These software tools were equipped with their own internalised dictionaries that comprised an extensive lexicon of words and their definitions, together with further codes that enabled these tools to understand language grammar. In other words, just as with human beings, they were taught rules concerning how words can be sequenced to create sentences that in turn expressed larger units of meaning. These larger units of meaning did not just describe people, objects, or other entities, but also actions and events involving those entities, or feelings that were expressed about them.

Initial text mining tools were restricted to detecting the denotative definitions of words. Later tools, developed under the heading of sentiment analysis, went further and detected expressions of feelings, such as attitudes and opinions, from verbal texts. Thus, NLP tools were created that could 'read' not just objective meanings expressed in texts, but also subjective ones—or 'sentiments' (Pang & Lee, 2004). Sentiments are in effect disclosures of private states that are experienced internally by those who express them (Banfield, 1982).

Different variants of sentiment analysis have been developed. One approach is for human coders to 'teach' computer software how to identify the polarity of feelings being expressed (positive, negative, and neutral) by assigning relevant sentiment codes to words and building up a dictionary over time that enables an algorithm to read other texts and identify the presence of sentiments it has already been 'trained' to recognise (Pak & Paroubek, 2010; Thelwall et al., 2010b; Peng & Park, 2011). This has been called the machine-learning approach.

A second approach has been to create a large thesaurus of words already pre-coded for sentiment polarity. The software can then identify occurrences of words from this lexicon in texts and assign appropriate sentiment ratings to them. Within this framework of analysis, algorithms can be produced that also allow some recognition of context in the form of the linguistic context of a sentence or the descriptive context of the setting in which the target word occurs. Word meanings, especially when voicing feelings, can sometimes vary with the contexts in which they are expressed, and for any NLP system to replicate human language processing, it must be able to detect these subtleties of meaning variation (Thelwall et al., 2010b; Peng & Park, 2011). Early sentiment tools were often unable to deal with contextual features, and thus, when they were validated against opinions generated by human respondents, they failed to generate accurate accounts of the subjective feelings being expressed (O'Connor, Balasubramanyan, Routledge & Smith, 2010).

The use of sentiment analysis tools to measure public opinion has extended across several fields, including politics and elections (Soroka et al., 2009; Tumasjan et al., 2010; Park et al., 2011), expressions of opinion on blogs (Godbole, Srinivasaiah & Skiena, 2007; Balahur et al., 2009), and expressions of happiness and other public mood states (Kim et al., 2009; Bollen, Pepe & Mao, 2010; Mogilner et al., 2011).

The online world is a potentially rich source of public opinion data. Much of this data is unstructured. Nevertheless, if opinions are being genuinely expressed, they could have considerable value to the commercial world when they concern brands. The absence of structure and vast scale of content online initially meant that it was too cumbersome to handle. The emergence of computer software tools capable to rapidly scanning massive amounts of content and then 'reading' it to extract meanings from it meant that a new and potentially useful source of business intelligence opened up. For the first time, marketing professionals might have access to massive amounts of naturally expressed opinions, on a scale previously only achieved by unnatural questionnaire survey responses. Moreover, new analysis tools meant that these huge quantities of qualitative data could be: (1) Structured and combined with other structured data, (2) Analysed in its own right within a manageable time frame, and (3) Generated at less costs than offline research with the same business objectives. Why spend tens of thousands of dollars, euros or pounds sterling on new offline market research when much more data could be produced and analysed at least as quickly and could provide the required information for a fraction of the cost?

Early research on sentiment analysis applications examined how these tools could be used to measure public opinion, predict voting outcomes in elections, and monitor the spread of opinion. Each of these forms of analysis has taken place mostly outside consumer contexts, but has relevance in terms of demonstrating how NLP tools could have value to brand marketers. Having reviewed what has been learned from research in this field so far, we can then consider the relevance it has in the context of consumer profiling.

Three factors have boosted interest in the use of NLP tools as new methods for measuring public opinion: the massive amount of relevant content that exists and is being updated every day, the availability of tools (hardware and software) with the ability to quickly and efficiently handle large quantities of data and convert unstructured data into structured data, and finally, the growing costs of offline market research. Data in which public opinions are openly expressed on a wide range of issues are mostly available on blogs, micro-blogs (e.g., Twitter) and social media sites (e.g., Facebook). Twitter has emerged as a source that has been especially widely and enthusiastically used to track public opinion on political and social issues (Anstead & O'Loughlin, 2011). The texts generated in tweets can provide useful sources of opinions about people, objects, and issues and frequently reflect the authors' moods or feelings. Sentiment analysis has been used also to track news coverage of current issues, blog chatter about financial markets, and public opinion about terrorist acts and threats to public safety, and about the groups associated with those acts (O'Hare et al., 2009; Remus et al., 2009; Cheong & Lee, 2011; Yang et al., 2011).

Offline opinion profiles have been monitored alongside those produced from online sources via sentiment analysis to indicate the degree of consistency between the two. Evidence has emerged from the United States that feelings expressed on Twitter about the status of the economy, about consumer confidence and attitudes towards the president largely reflected those obtained through offline opinion polls (O'Connor et al., 2010).

Further evidence from the US indicated that Twitter posts produced public sentiment profiles that were sensitive to current events. Tweets were analysed using an established mood states profiler along dimensions such as anger, confusion, depression, fatigue, tension, and so on. Mood states fluctuated with positive and negative social, political, and cultural events (Bollen, et al., 2010).

NLP tools have been used to assess emotional meanings expressed on political issues in tests such as news articles, readers' comments on the news, and other general online chatter on news websites (Soroka et al., 2009; Tumasjan et al., 2010; Park et al., 2011). This research was interested in whether the emotional nature of media coverage of specific objects might subsequently influence the way people behave towards those objects. Although this research has largely derived from non-consumer/brand marketing contexts, it is helpful in determining the potential consumer opinion/brand image measurement relevance of this type of analysis.

One study conducted in Canada obtained electronic archives of newspapers to extract news coverage given to federal election campaigns from 1993 to 2008. A sentiment analysis tool was applied to identify emotionally positive and negative verbal references to political parties and candidates. The overall tone towards political contenders in each election was compared with the public tone assessed through regular offline opinion polls and respondents' voting intentions. The researchers found that the public's preference for a specific candidate tended to be consistent with the tone of media coverage he or she received (Soroka et al., 2009).

A German study applied sentiment analysis to tweets about election candidates and measured the volume of tweets and types of sentiments (positive versus negative) being expressed. The findings indicated a significant rank correlation between the volume of tweet chatter about a candidate and the share of votes they received in the election (Tumasjan et al., 2010).

The online world has created a setting for the more dynamic spread of word-of-mouth opinions and recommendations and this phenomenon has important implications to professional marketers. If a brand attracts positive or negative publicity, this could be more easily contained in the offline world. In an online setting, however, opinions can spread like wildfire. One especially critical question for marketers is whether negative opinion is likely to spread faster than positive opinion.

Sentiment analysis has been used to assess the speed with which opinions can go viral online. This research has mostly been conducted with news stories. Can emotional news stories that trigger strong emotional reactions in the public prove to be particularly viral? A body of work has been published to show that public emotion can spread rapidly online and that sentiment analysis can be used to track it (Berger & Milkman, 2009; Hansen et al., 2011; Chmiel et al., 2011a, 2011b; Gruzd et al., 2011; Wu et al., 2011).

The emergent evidence has not always been consistent. Different studies have found positive tweets in the ascendancy over negative tweets in triggering viral comments and negative tweets being more influential in this respect than positive ones (Berger & Milkman, 2009; Hansen et al., 2011). One investigation found that both types of tweets could give rise to increased interest in a topic as evidenced by the propensity of Twitter users to re-tweet particular messages (Naveed et al., 2011).

Much of this sentiment analysis research has been restricted to descriptive analyses of online events. What it does not always reveal are the reasons why online content characterised by specific 'sentiments' is more likely to attract attention, get repeated by others, or have more impact. Some scholars working in this field have called for the introduction of relevant social science theory to inform the design of studies and interpretation of findings (Thelwall et al., 2010a, 2010b, 2011). Although commercial applications are of interest insofar as they can reveal relationships between variables that could produce useful insights into online behaviour practices, they do not always tell why specific behaviours occurred. More fine-grained analysis that might, for instance, be signalled by communication or psychology theory could lead to more thoughtful analyses of data, resulting in fresh insights about consumer segments defined in terms of the descriptive or emotional comments they make online. Evidence has emerged in this vein that women both give and receive more positive comments than do men when expressing their opinions on social media sites (Thelwall et al., 2010a).

The marketing potential of 'big data' research that is restricted to assessing patterns of online behaviour or emotional expression might only be fully realised when combined with consumer segmentation measures. Traditional methods defined in the online world for assessing the psychological attributes of consumers can be cumbersome to implement on a large scale in the online world. New research techniques have begun to emerge as psychologists, linguistics experts, and computer scientists work together to develop software tools that can scan, read, and interpret vast quantities of unstructured online data and yield structured data that can be used to classify people through their online postings. How people use social media sites and, in particular, the linguistic content and style of the texts they post online might be able to reveal clues about their personalities. These new techniques are still being developed and validated. They hold the promise of being able to provide marketers with non-intrusive methods of segmenting consumers and modelling their online activities and feeling states in relation to their psychological characteristics.

Note

1 See: http://www.kantarmedia.com/product/tgi-surveys/.

References

Advertising Research Foundation (1964) *Are There Consumer Types?* New York, NY: Advertising Research Foundation.
Ajzen, I. (1985) From intentions to actions: A theory of planned behaviour. In J. Kuhl & J. Beckman (Eds.) *Action-Control: From Cognition to Behaviour*, pp. 11–39. Heidelberg, Germany: Springer.

Ajzen, I. (2011) The theory of planned behaviour: Reactions and reflections. *Psychology & Health*, 26(9), 1113–1127.

Anstead, N., & O'Loughlin, B. (2011) The emerging viewertariat and BBC question time: Television debate and real-time commenting online. *International Journal of Press/Politics*, 16(4), 440–462.

Armitage, C. J., & Conner, M. (2001) Efficacy of the theory of planned behaviour: A meta-analytic review. *British Journal of Social Psychology*, 40, 471–499.

Asch, S. (1956) Studies of independence and conformity: 1. A minority of one against a unanimous majority. *Psychology Monographs: General and Applied*, 70(9), 1–70.

Balahur, A., Kozareva, Z., & Montoyo, A. (2009) Determining the polarity and source of opinions expressed in political debates. *Lectures Notes in Computer Science*, 5449.

Banfield, A. (1982) *Unspeakable Sentences: Narration and Representation in the Language of Fiction*. London: Routledge & Kegan Paul Ltd.

Bass, F. M. (1974) The theory of stochastic preference and brand switching. *Journal of Marketing Research*, 11, 1–20.

Berger, J. A., & Milkman, K. L. (2009) *Social transmission, emotion, and the virality of online content*. Social Science Research Network (SSRN), December 25, 2009.

Bollen, J. (2011) Computational economic and finance gauges: Polls, search & Twitter. Paper presented at the Behavioural Economics Working Group, Behavioural Finance Meeting, Palo Alto, CA. Available at: www.nber.org/~confer/2011/BEf11.BEf11prg.html. Accessed 3rd March 2013.

Bollen, J., Pepe, A., & Mao, H., (2010) Twitter mood predicts the stock market. *Journal of Computational Science*, 2(1), 108.

Bruno, A. V., Hustad, R., & Pessemeier, E. (1972) *An Integrated Examination of Media Approaches to Market Segmentation*. Lafayette, Ind: Faculty Working paper No.342. Institute for Research in the Behavioural Economic and Management Sciences, Krannert Graduate School of Industrial Administration, Purdue University.

Bruno, A. V., & Pessemeier, E. (1972) An empirical investigation of the validity of selected attitude and activity measures. In *Proceedings of the Third Annual Conference of the Association for Consumer Research*, pp. 456–74. Chicago, IL: Association for Consumer Research.

Burns, A. C., & Harrison, C. (1979) A test of the reliability of psychographics. *Journal of Marketing Research*, 16, 32–38.

Cheong, M., & Lee, V. C. S. (2011) A micro blogging-based approach to terrorism informatics: Exploration and chronicling civilian sentiment and response to terrorism events via Twitter. *Information Systems Frontiers*, 13, 45–59.

Chmiel, A., Sienkiewicz, J., Thelwall, M., Paltoglou, G., Buckley, K., Kappas, A., & Holyst, J. A. (2011a) Collective emotions online and their influence on community life. *PLoS ONE*, 6(7), e22207.

Chmiel, A., Sobkowicz, P., Sienkiewicz, J., Paltoglou, G., Buckley, K., Thelwall, M., & Holyst, J. A. (2011b) Negative emotions boost users activity at BBC Forum. *Physica A: Statistical Mechanics and its Applications*, 390(16), 2936–44.

Eccles J. (1983) Expectancies, values and academic behaviors. In J. T. Spence (Ed.) *Achievement and Achievement Motives*, pp. 75–146. San Francisco, CA: Freeman.

Evans, F. B. (1959) Psychological and objective factors in the prediction of brand choice: Ford versus Chevrolet. *Journal of Business*, 32, 340–369.

Festinger, L. (1957) *A Theory of Cognitive Dissonance*. Stanford, CA: Stanford University Press.

Fielding, N. G., & Lee, R. M. (1998) *Computer Analysis and Qualitative Research: New Technology for Social Research*. London, UK: Sage.

Fishbein, M., & Ajzen, I. (1975) *Belief, Attitude, Intention and Behavior: An Introduction to Theory and Research*. Reading, MA: Addison-Wesley.

Fishbein, M., & Ajzen, I. (2010) *Predicting and Changing Behavior: The Reasoned Action Approach*. New York, NY: Psychology Press.

Frank, R. E., Massey, W. F., & Wind, Y. (1972) *Market Segmentation*. Englewood Cliffs, NJ: Prentice-Hall.

Godbole, N., Srinivasaiah, M., & Skiena, S. (2007) Large-scale sentiment analysis for news and blogs. In *Proceedings of International Conference on Weblogs and Social Media (ICWSM 2007)*. Boulder, Colorado, USA, March 26–28, 2007.

Gruzd, A., Doiron, S., & Mai, P. (2011) Is happiness contagious online? A Case of Twitter and the 2010 Winter Olympics. In *Proceedings of the 44th Hawaii International Conference on System Sciences (HICSS 2011)*, Kauai, HI, USA, January 4–7, 2011.

Gunter, B., & Furnham, A. (1992) *Consumer Profiles: An Introduction to Psychographics*. London, UK: Routledge.

Hansen, L. K., Arvidsson, A., Nielsen, F. A., Colleoni, E., & Etter, M. (2011) Good friends, bad news affect and virality in Twitter. In *Proceedings of the International Workshop on Social Computing, Network, and Services (SocialComNet 2011)*, Crete, Greece, June 28–30, 2011.

Heider, F. (1958) *The Psychology of Interpersonal Relations*. London, UK: John-Wiley & Sons.

Hustad, T. P., & Pessemeier, E. A. (1974) The development and application of psychographic, life style and associated activity and attitude measures. In W. D. Wells (Ed.) *Life Style and Psychographics*, pp. 31–70. Chicago, IL: American Marketing Association.

Jacoby, J. J. (1971a) Personality and innovation proneness. *Journal of Marketing Research*, 8, 244–247.

Jaspars, J. M. R., Fincham, F. D., & Hewstone, M. (Eds.). (1983) *Attribution Theory and Research: Conceptual, Developmental and Social Dimensions*. London, UK: Academic Press.

Kaptein, M., Markopoulos, P., de Ruyter, B., & Aarts, E. (2015) Personalizing persuasive technologies: Explicit and implicit personalization using persuasion profiles. *International Journal of Human-Computer Studies*, 77, 38–51.

Kim, E., Gilbert, S., Edwards, M. J., & Graeff, E. (2009) *Detecting sadness in 140 characters: Sentiment analysis of mourning Michael Jackson on Twitter*. In Web Ecology Project, Pub. 03 (18 August 2009).

Kollat, D. T., & Willett, R. P. (1960) Customer impulse purchasing behaviour. *Journal of Marketing Research*, 1, 6–12.

Lastovicka, J. L. (1982) On the validation of lifestyle traits: A review and illustration. *Journal of Marketing Research*, 19, 126–138.

Lesser, J. A., & Hughes, M. A. (1986) The generalizability of psychographic market segments across geographic locations. *Journal of Marketing*, 50, 18–27.

Madden, T. J., Ellen, P. S., & Ajzen, I. (1992) A comparison of the theory of planned behaviour and the theory of reasoned action. *Personality and Social Psychology Bulletin*, 18(1), 3–9.

Mogilner, C., Aaker, J., & Kamvar, S. D. (2012) How happiness affects choice. *Journal of Consumer Research*, 39, 429–443.

Mogilner, C., Kamvar, S. D., & Aaker, J. (2011) The shifting meaning of happiness. *Social Psychological and Personality Science*, 2(4), 395–402.

Naveed, N., Gottron, T., Kunegis, J., & Alhadi, A. C. (2011) Bad news travels fast: A content-based analysis of interestingness on Twitter. *WebSci 11*, 14–17 June, Koblenz, Germany. Available at: www.tw.rpi.edu/media/latest/WebSciPAPaper50

O'Connor, B., Balasubramanyan, R., Routledge, B. R., & Smith, N. A. (2010) From Tweets to polls: Linking text sentiment to public opinion time series. In *Proceedings of the International AAAI Conference on Weblogs and Social Media (2010)*, Washington, DC, USA, May 23–26, 2010.

O'Guinn, T. C., & Faber, R. J. (1989) Compulsive buying: A phenomonlogical exploration. *Journal of Consumer Research*, 16(2), 147–157.

O'Hare, N., Davy, M., Bermingham, A., Ferguson, P., Sheridan, P., Gurrin, C., & Smeaton, A. F. (2009) Topic-dependent sentiment analysis of financial blogs. In *Proceedings of the TSA'09*, Hong Kong, China, November 6, 2009.

Osgood, C. E., & Tannenbaum, P. H. (1955) The principle of congruity in the prediction of attitude change. *Psychology Review*, 62, 42–55.

Pak, A., & Paroubek, P. (2010) Twitter as a corpus for sentiment analysis and opinion mining. In *Proceedings of the Seventh conference on International Language Resources and Evaluation (LREC'10)*, Valletta, Malta, May 19–21, 2010.

Pang, B., & Lee, L. (2004) A sentimental education: Sentiment analysis using subjectivity summarization based on minimum cuts. *ACL '04 Proceedings of the 42nd Annual meeting of Association for Computational Linguistics*, Article No. 271. Strousberg, PA, USA.

Park, S., Ko, M., Kim, J., Liu, Y., & Song, J. (2011) The politics of comments: Predicting political orientation of news stories with commenters' sentiment patterns. In *Proceedings of the CSCW 2011*, Hangzhou, China, March 19–23, 2011.

Peng, C., & Park, S. I. (2011) A real time system of crowd rendering: Parallel LOD and texture preserving approach on GPU. *The Fourth International Conference on Motion in Games 2011*. Edinburgh, UK, November 2011.

Pernica, J. (1974) The second generation of market segmentation studies: An audit of buying motivations. In W. D. Wells (Ed.) *Lifestyle and Psychographics*, pp. 279–313. Chicago, MI: American Marketing Association.

Pessemeier, E. A., & Bruno, A. (1971) *An empirical investigation of the reliability and stability of activity and attitude measures*. Reprint Series No. 391, Krannert Graduate School of Industrial Administration, Purdue University.

Remus, R., Ahmad, K., & Heyer, G. (2009) Sentiment if German language news and blogs and the DAX. In *Proceedings of the Text Mining Services 2009, Leipzig, Germany*, 23rd March.

Rentfrow, P. J., Gosling, S. D., Jokela, M., Stillwell, D. J., Kosinski, M., & Potter, J. (2013) Divided we stand: Three psychological regions of the United States and their political, economic, social, and health correlates. *Journal of Personality and Social Psychology*, 105(6), 996–1012.

Robertson, T. S., & Myers, J. H. (1969) Personality correlates of opinion leadership and innovative buying behaviour. *Journal of Marketing Research*, 6, 164–168.

Soroka, S., Bodet, M. A., & Young, L. (2009) Campaign news and vote intentions in Canada, 1993–2008. In *Proceedings of the Annual Meeting of the American Political Science Association*, Toronto, ON, Canada, September 3–6, 2009.

Sutton, S. (2002) Testing attitude-behaviour theories using non-experimental data: An examination of some hidden assumptions. *European Review of Social Psychology*, 13, 293–323.

Thelwall, M., Buckley, K., & Paltoglou, G. (2011) Sentiment in Twitter events. *Journal of the American Society for Information Science and Technology*, 62(2), 406–18.

Thelwall, M., Buckley, K., Paltoglou, G., Cai, D., & Kappas, A. (2010a) Sentiment strength detection in short informal text. *Journal of the American Society for Information Science and Technology*, 61 (12), 2544–58.

Thelwall, M., Wilkinson, D., & Uppal, S. (2010b) Data mining emotion in social network communication: Gender differences in MySpace. *Journal of the American Society for Information Science and Technology*, 61(1), 190–199.

Tigert, D. J. (1969) A taxonomy of magazine readership applied to problems in marketing strategy and media selection. *Journal of Business*, 42, 357–363.

Tumasjan, A., Sprenger, T. O., Sandner, P. G., & Welpe, I. M. (2010) Predicting elections with Twitter: What 140 characters reveal about political sentiment. In *Proceedings of the Fourth International AAAI Conference on Weblogs and Social Media*, Washington, DC, May 23–26, 2010.

Villani, K. E., & Lehmann, D. R. (1975) An examination of the stability of AIO measures. In E. M. Mazze (Ed.) *Marketing: The Challenges and the Opportunities*, pp. 484–488. Chicago, IL: American marketing Association.

Wells, W. D. (1974) *Life Style and Psychographics*. Chicago, IL: American Marketing Association.

Wells, W. D. (1975) Psychographics: a critical review. *Journal of Marketing Research*, 12, 209–229.

Wells, W. D., & Tigert, D. (1971) Activities, interests and opinions. *Journal of Advertising Research*, 11, 27–35.

Wind, Y. (1978) Issues and advances in segmentation research. *Journal of Marketing Research*, 15, 317–337.

Wind, Y., & Green, P. E. (1974) Some conceptual measurement and analytical problems in life style research. In W. D. Wells (Ed.) *Life Style and Psychographics*, pp. 99–126. Chicago, IL: American Marketing Association.

Wu, S., Tan, C., Kleinberg, J., & Macy, M. (2011) Does bad news go away faster?. In *Proceedings of the Fifth International AAAI Conference on Weblogs and Social Media*, Barcelona, Spain, July 17–21, 2011.

Yang, M., Kiang, M., Ku, Y., Chiu, C., & Yijun, L. (2011) Social media analytics for radical opinion mining in hate group web forums. *Journal of Homeland Security and Emergency Management*, 8(1), article 38.

Index

financial luxury value dimension 93
Financial Optimist factor 59
financial personality types 91
financial products 90–1
Followers lifestyle type 84
food consumption 131
Food Is Fuel type 110
food preparation types 109–10
food products 85
Ford motor vehicles 86, 234
Ford Pinto 87
4C model 68–9
France 136, 144
frequency-of-use data 59
Freudian psychoanalytic model 31–2
Freud, Sigmund 31
Friendly and Conventional states 40
Fromm, Erich 34
Frustrated type 59
Fulfilleds type 63–6
fun and enjoyment in life value 66–8
functional luxury value dimension 93
functional magnetic resonance imaging
      (fMRI) 203, 205
'The Fun-Loving Routine User' type 88
Furniture Outshopper 82
furniture shopping 14, 45, 56, 69, 78,
      82, 86

gender 1, 106–11
General Foods Corporation 89
Generation X 172–3
Generation Y 172–3
generic classifiers 5
generic consumer segmentation map 5
generic corporate brands 3
generic profiling measures 21
generic psychological types 225–6
Genital Stage 32
geo-demographic groups 8–9
geo-demographic segmentation systems
      10–11, 24
geographic segmentation 7, 8, 10
Germany 41, 42, 136, 239
global consumer profiling: comparisons
      of values models 144–5; cultural
      traits and advertising 145–7;
      cultural values and consumerism
      129–31; high context and low
      context cultures 136; Hofstede's
      classification of cultural values
      137–41; individualism and
      collectivism 147–9; LOV

model 144; persuasion 147–9;
      Schwartz psychological structure
      of human values 141–4;
      universal values versus culture-
      specific values 131–6
Global Leadership and Organisational
      Behaviour Effectiveness
      (GLOBE) 133, 135–6, 150
goodness of fit 24
Google 236
grey market psychographics 106,
      113–17

Haire, Mason 32
hand soap 85
health 40
health care services 58
health-giving products 209
health-related behaviour 201
healthy food consumption 201
hedonic behaviour 44
Hedonism motivational type 143–4
Hedonistic type 92–3
high context cultures 136
highly involved shoppers 84
highly read type 183
high risk-taking personality types 45
high-status people 137–8
'high street shopper' 78
Hofstede's classification of cultural
      values: adoption and limits
      of 135; development of 132;
      dimensions of 137–41, 150–3;
      individualism/collectivism
      dimension 132, 138–40, 144,
      151; long-term versus short-
      term orientation dimension 132,
      141; masculinity-femininity
      dimension 132, 140, 144, 151;
      power distance dimension 132,
      137–8, 144, 150; uncertainty
      avoidance dimension 132,
      140–1, 144, 151; values factors
      144–5, 149
holiday choices 92–3
Homebody factor 58
Home-Centred type 69
Home Entertainment Outshopper 82
Home-Loving type 92
homemakers 79
home purchases 44–5
'in-home shopper' 78
home shoppers 95